"The first task of any Marxist reck  to condemn but to contextualize exemplary in this regard. Rather th acknowledges his genius while reminding his Left admirers that he took sides in the class struggle, with the dominators against the dominated. Downplaying this inconvenient fact, leftist recuperations of Nietzschean politics proceed by displacing social contradiction from politics to culture, proposing aesthetic resolutions to social antagonisms. In exposing this strategy, Tutt's evaluation of the consequences of Nietzschean politics is more lucid than Left Nietzscheans might wish."

RAY BRASSIER, AUTHOR OF *NIHIL UNBOUND*

"Providing a detailed exposition of the political foundations of Nietzsche's philosophy, Tutt performs exceptionally well the task of derailing leftist readings of Nietzsche that have sought to contrive an "elective affinity" with a philosophy fundamentally at odds with their political principles. Written with clarity and force, sensitive to historical context and covering an extensive array of the Nietzsche literature, this book animates a new standard in reading Nietzsche."

DON DOMBOWSKY, AUTHOR OF *NIETZSCHE AND NAPOLEON*

"*How to Read Like a Parasite* is what many of us have long awaited: the first systematic post-Losurdian reading of Nietzsche. Taking very seriously the ultra-reactionary dimensions of Nietzsche's thought, Tutt paints the Anti-Christ as the great opponent and rival of the socialist left. What follows is a careful and considerate revelation of decades of left-Nietzschean thought. Beautifully written and bursting with spirit *How to Read Like a Parasite* is destined to be vital reading."

MATTHEW MCMANUS, AUTHOR OF
NIETZSCHE AND THE POLITICS OF REACTION

"It is fascinating to see that an author can achieve both: to self-analyze the liberative impact Nietzsche had on his life as an adolescent growing up under the conditions of a broken family, alcoholism and drug abuse and to reveal the fundamentally reactionary character of Nietzsche's hierarchical philosophy — and this not only in the late 19th and 20th centuries, but also in our neoliberal society of fragmented singularities. As Daniel Tutt shows convincingly, Nietzsche's super-individualistic cult of authenticity fits seamlessly to a capitalist ideology which calls upon the subjects to live out their subjectivities in a competitive way and to pursue their own "brand". And he paints a compelling picture of the ways that Nietzscheanism hijacks the left where it undercuts the egalitarian perspectives and reduces counter-hegemonic politics to countercultural gestures of revolt."

JAN REHMANN, AUTHOR OF
DECONSTRUCTING POSTMODERNIST NIETZSCHEANISM

"Tutt avoids both traps that haunt leftist readings of Nietzsche: a quick condemnation of Nietzsche as an irrationalist precursor of Fascism, and the elevation of Nietzsche into a philosopher of new authentic life who was falsely appropriated by the extreme right. Tutt doesn't achieve this by way of playing the safe middle ground — on the contrary, he first fully assumes the Nietzschean standpoint, recounting his own experience of its liberating aspect, and then gradually brings out the illusory character of this liberation. In the full sense of the term he knows what he is talking about: in his critique of Nietzsche, he settles the account with his own past illusions. Today, in our age of quick new right or new left dismissals, such a stance is needed more than ever."

SLAVOJ ŽIŽEK

HOW TO READ LIKE
A PARASITE

HOW TO READ LIKE
A PARASITE

Why the Left Got High
on Nietzsche

Daniel Tutt

Published by Repeater Books

An imprint of Watkins Media Ltd

Unit 11 Shepperton House

89-93 Shepperton Road

London

N1 3DF

United Kingdom

www.repeaterbooks.com

A Repeater Books paperback original 2024

1

Distributed in the United States by Random House, Inc., New York.

Copyright © Daniel Tutt 2024

Daniel Tutt asserts the moral right to be identified as the author of this work.

ISBN: 9781914420627

Ebook ISBN: 9781915672261

Printed and bound in the UK by TJ Books Limited

Contents

For Elijah

If the working classes ever discover that they easily could surpass us in matters of education and virtue, then it is all over for us! But if this does not occur, then it is really over for us.

Nietzsche, *Notebooks, Summer-Autumn 1873*[1]

No one can read Nietzsche authentically without being *Nietzsche.*

Georges Bataille, "Nietzsche in the Light of Marxism"[2]

Marxists were coming perilously close to the notion that egalitarian man as such is bourgeois, and that they must join him or become culture snobs.

Allan Bloom, "Leftist Nietzscheanism or Vice Versa"[3]

You must be proud of your enemy: then the successes of your enemy are your successes too.

Nietzsche, *Thus Spoke Zarathustra*[4]

*Indeed, I counsel you to go away from me
Leave me and defend against Zarathustra!
And even better: be ashamed of him!
Perhaps he deceived you.*

Nietzsche, *Thus Spoke Zarathustra*[5]

CHAPTER ONE
We Live in Nietzsche's World.
So What?

What first drew you to read Nietzsche? Perhaps it was an accident. Perhaps you stumbled across him in a used bookstore in your hometown as you strolled by the philosophy and spirituality section. How could the name Nietzsche not stand out. You had heard the name before, of course. So, you bought a Nietzsche book, went home, and opened it up. Like an album you immediately fell in love with, you were hooked rather quickly. All of a sudden you found yourself transported and your journey into Nietzsche's world began.

Any lover of Nietzsche will remember what it was like when they first encountered him, whether the encounter was by surprise or whether you sought him out. Nietzsche is more like a bolt of lightning than a slow burn. In a matter of weeks after reading him, the experience can begin to feel like a rite of passage. He opens something inside us. If we are hooked on him — and not everyone gets hooked — we return to him at different times throughout our life. And each time we return we find something new, something fresh. We must lose him to truly find him again, as he reminds us repeatedly in his late work *Thus Spoke Zarathustra*. Reading Nietzsche can be a life's work. He always finds a way to make his mark on you.

Nietzsche is read by the right and the left — and everyone

in between. As his one-time romantic interest Lou Salomé noted, he writes not to convince or to persuade, but to *convert* passionate followers. But regardless of his broad appeal across the political spectrum, Nietzsche remains a mysterious political thinker. Many scholars of Nietzsche claim that politics is merely *a part* of what his philosophy is about, while others suggest that art and aesthetics, or historical genealogy, are the core to his thought.

What is not disputed among these scholars, however, is the fact that he brings a profound depth of insight and erudition to bear in his writings. His works are full of references to Ancient Greek philosophy, theology, the history of philosophy, literature, the hard sciences, and psychology. He combines an uncanny level of erudition with an idiosyncratic style and method. His books feel as if they are spiritual-political pamphlets. Nietzsche's writing style is untimely and he wrote what he named a "philosophy for the future." In this way, Nietzsche writes to be our contemporary, and when we read him, we feel that he is writing for us even though he has transported us to a different world.

Before we even have our first encounter with Nietzsche, the popular lore about him has likely already shaped how we approach him. Buzzwords about Nietzsche proliferate in popular culture: the "death of God," the "transvaluation of all values," "nihilism," the "godfather of postmodernism." Nietzsche's reputation always precedes him. We ask ourselves when reading him, is this radical? Is this reactionary? Something in between? Or perhaps Nietzsche blurs the boundaries of what we thought was radical. Perhaps there is very little politics in Nietzsche after all. The claim that there is no politics in Nietzsche is in fact a popular position across large swaths of today's Nietzsche industry — especially in academia. And the truth is that Nietzsche's radicality, or possible radicality, is posed to readers as a question they must decide for themselves.

His popularity has resulted in the widescale diffusion of his concepts, ideas, and frameworks for viewing the world into the crevices and deep pockets of our culture. Nietzsche's thought has shaped the way we think about ideas from value, nihilism, resentment, down to how we understand fate, inequality, and envy — Nietzsche has molded these categories in such deep ways that it is not an exaggeration to claim that we live in Nietzsche's world. Of course, Nietzsche is not the sole originator of these concepts, but his thought has significantly shaped the way we think of them. This means that even for those of us who have never read Nietzsche, we are still shaped by him. We are, in many ways, Nietzsche's children. If Nietzsche has shaped our world this also means that if we want to change this world, we must take the time to understand Nietzsche's thought.

This book is an attempt to shine a new light on Nietzsche's philosophy, to understand his profound influence in ways that have largely been ignored and overlooked by scholars for many years. We propose to read Nietzsche as driven, fundamentally, by politics; by a highly sophisticated, reactionary political vision that has attracted the left with its anti-capitalist romanticism and appealed to the right with its unabashed support for rank, order, and hierarchy. Nietzsche's thought has shaped the world we live in precisely because he has influenced so many prominent intellectuals, artists, political thinkers, psychoanalysts, and politicians, as well as entrepreneurs and popular writers. In a recent biography of the entrepreneur Steve Jobs, the founder of Apple, the American civic leader Walter Isaacson wrote that "although

Jobs never read Nietzsche, he had internalized his teachings of the overman."[1] What Isaacson meant is that Nietzsche does not have to be read or interpreted for his resounding influence to be absorbed. This is what we will define as *Nietzscheanism*, the various ways that Nietzsche's thought produces a set of ideologies that continues to interact with and shape our liberal, entrepreneurial, capitalist society, a society that tells us that *only* rare geniuses push culture, innovation, and art forward, while the vast majority exist as a hindrance or as mediocre subalterns. Nietzscheanism is thus defined here as the cultural effect of Nietzsche's philosophy, which makes up a certain type of common sense — or ideology, in a more colloquial sense — regarding how we relate to hierarchy and equality, to the way we understand morals, to art, suffering, and aesthetics.

Any real lover of Nietzsche will likely be aghast at the mere suggestion that Nietzsche's thought has been victorious in this way. For if that proposal were true, that would mean there is nothing new in his thought and that any reading of Nietzsche would have to be on the defensive, for if Nietzsche was truly victorious, then how might we still read him and find something subversive or fresh? The reality is that our world is riddled with massive problems, from a capitalist ruling class that controls wealth among a tiny fraction of elite oligarchs, to a slightly larger creative and managerial class that has blocked the sorts of system changes that the vast majority demand, such as universal health services and the freedom to experience leisure time outside of constant wage labor and debt peonage. These oppressive realities weigh down our world and sap our resolve to change it. We live in a world in which class domination has made it nearly impossible to change the status quo.

How is all this Nietzsche's fault, you might ask? It's not directly his fault. The claim I am making here is different. What I want to stress is that Nietzsche and Nietzscheanism — the industries and important followers and expositors of his doctrines — have played an important role — although not an exclusive role, to be sure — in creating a philosophy that justifies the persistence of an unjust social order. This is the elusive aspect of Nietzsche and Nietzscheanism. It must be read as a philosophy that aims to justify the persistence of the status quo, and that is reactive to any changing of the world. Nietzsche is not particularly unique in this regard, as a rejection of a more egalitarian social order is hardwired into most liberal thinkers throughout the modern period. But Nietzsche stands out in the history of thought as an ingenious and cunning thinker whose concepts must be read as tied back in to this reactionary political intention.

We will define a "reactionary" as someone who concocts a series of strategies to prevent and block any changing of the world. As such, reactionaries should not be thought of only in terms of their extreme varieties, like someone who express blatant racism or hatred of their political opponents. Bob Dylan once encapsulated the elusive basis of the reactionary position when he wrote, "The enemy I see wears a cloak of decency." In this way, the very concept of the reactionary describes the elusive means by which the status quo of capitalist social relations remains intact. To maintain an unjust status quo, it is necessary that the ruling class perfect an ideological rationale for the world as it is, despite all its inequality and exploitation and the cascade of suffering it engenders. The ideology of liberal capitalism is premised on the lie that informs the reproduction of our educational and business institutions, namely that we live in a meritocratic, free, and fair society. We are told that our version of advanced Western liberal democracy is the beacon of freedom in the world and that those who are successful earned that success because they fought and struggled with greater grit and determination than those who did not make it.

In many ways, the basic common sense of our culture is sadomasochistic: we see the world as divided between winners and losers. We are fearful that we may grow to become a loser, that others might see us as a loser. And so we compete in a game that we can't — or that we refuse to — see is rigged. We struggle in a system that is stacked against us. But this is the only world we know, and it is very difficult to protest this common sense, for to protest it would be to protest reality itself. The ideology of our world maintains that what is determined on the site of the market — competition for work, status, recognition, etc. — is to be internalized by us as *natural*.

What makes Nietzsche so important to understand in this regard is that his influence on readers is often subtle and ambidextrous; he creeps into different political perspectives and cannot be pinned to one dominant position, whether liberal meritocratic, libertarian, or even anarchist. Indeed, there are a wide range of anarchist Nietzscheans who deploy his thought in the service of a critique of the market and capitalism. But even these "left-Nietzschean" perspectives must face the fact of his reactionary agenda and the way it infuses into political positions.

Nietzsche's thought must be read as giving ideological support to a social order where both joyful affirmation and anarchic celebration are experienced at the same time as a cruel and brutal defense of rank order. This makes Nietzsche's thought a Janus face which must be understood in its highs and lows. But we will argue that if Nietzsche's reactionary thought is brushed over, ignored, or de-emphasized, then he performs a certain victory over the left that can and often does compromise any socialist or Marxist approach to changing the world.

Moreover, his philosophy must be read as a comprehensive and esoteric strategy of reaction that has at its very center a political agenda. What precisely is this political agenda, and does it infect any attempt to work with his ideas? The answer to this question depends on how you read Nietzsche. Do you read him in a historical context that does justice to the true development of his thought, or do you read him as a timeless philosopher completely decontextualized from modern capitalist life? We propose to read him in a wider historical materialist context, that is, as a thinker who is not timeless and who was directly engaged in the class struggle of his time. A class-struggle perspective on Nietzsche sees his philosophy as primarily concerned with pacifying any attempt to modify the status quo. He intended for his philosophy to be a preventative strategy against what the egalitarian social movement of the French Revolution had brought to the world-historical scene. Nietzsche's concepts are meant to pacify any changing of the status quo to ensure that rank order is maintained and that any unruly plebeian or working class is kept in place, if not eradicated as an agent of social transformation.

It is well known that Nietzsche invented a life philosophy bent on affirming, nay, *loving* one's fate. But to love one's fate is itself a curious suggestion, especially in a world where one's place is one of day-to-day oppression and suffering. Although he was not an advocate of a revolutionary idea of utopia as the socialists and communists envision it, Nietzsche once wrote what his vision of utopia would be:

A social order in which the hard work and misery of life will be allotted to the man who suffers least from it, that is, to the dullest man, and so on step by step upwards to the man who is most sensitive to the highest, most sublimated kind of suffering and therefore suffers even when life is most greatly eased.[2]

This is not a vision of utopia that has overcome capitalist social relations or fundamentally changed the power relations of the social order. Any socialist vision of utopia requires a break from the mode of capitalist production that dominates our world and produces misery for so many people, and is premised on the abolishment of the commodity form, which determines labor and all value under capitalism.

There is a dominant view that socialism is forever cursed by the experience of the Cold War, during which the "socialism in one country" model under Stalin's rule in the USSR is thought to have represented the final blow to the Marxist view of history and society. Many liberals maintain that socialism is a fundamentally flawed political philosophy that represents a danger to human freedom. But the perspective we will take in this book is different; we instead understand socialism as a set of demands within liberal capitalist social life that emerge from below, specifically from the broader working class. Socialism has a diverse ideological spectrum, from democratic socialism to communism, but it emerges from agitations and demands from the working masses for more egalitarian improvements to their quality of life and a refusal of the status quo arrangements of power.

Socialism names a distinct set of class-based social forces that demand a radical change to the status quo of capitalist exploitation and domination. It is this idea of socialism, as a movement of demands for more egalitarian forms of politics that are beyond what the liberal political parties — either right or left — can meet, that makes socialism such a danger to the ruling order. Socialist politics have been present in industrial capitalism since the 1830s, and they continue to this day. They can be identified through agitations and struggle that are borne from the contradictions of the so-called free market. Socialist politics challenge the reigning social order at the level of political epistemology — how we come to know social reality — by contesting the basic and conventional liberal accounts of social suffering in capitalist social life; that is, the socialist and liberal accounts of political truth and what constitutes harm in society tend to clash in serious and irresolvable ways.

Marx is the most important thinker of socialism, as he was the first socialist thinker to develop a version of "socialism from below," as the American historian Hal Draper once put it.[3] For Marx, society must be organized around an entirely different maxim than the law of capitalist accumulation and profit. This motto is summed up as "To each according to their abilities, to each according to their needs," and in many ways it constitutes a dialectical opposition to Nietzsche's vision of utopia — a hyper-capitalist conception of social life. At the core of Nietzsche's idea of utopia is a society where a small coterie of rare geniuses bask in the leisure time they have been given by virtue of their cultivation of a higher form of "aesthetic" suffering. For Nietzsche, there exists an intricate rank order and modes of suffering in which those at the very top, the men of intellect, the "overmen," are those who suffer in their privilege, suffer in their leisure time. And this rank ordering is Nietzsche's formula for how a society can fend off decadence and working-class agitation from below.

But let us be more charitable to Nietzsche's philosophy. You could say that some of Nietzsche's intentions are noble. For example, he wants to further the project of great art-making to achieve the highest possible form of aesthetics and living. Isn't his philosophy meant to inspire the creation of a new man and a new philosophy for the future to bring this exceptional culture into existence, after all? It's true that Nietzsche's philosophy is about the invention of a new myth for our culture, and he wants his readers to accept their fate as the leaders of this new vision. But the problem with this vision is that it's all upside down. Nietzsche is wrong in his analysis and diagnosis of what is driving decadence, resentment, and nihilism — all extremely important Nietzschean concepts that we will encounter throughout this book — and he is even more wrong about how to correct the very problems that he diagnoses.

It is in Nietzsche's prescriptions for remedying the social situation of socialist and democratic demands that we find the core of his politics. And we find his reactionary politics hardwired into each of the concepts he invented to achieve this objective — the will to power, perspectivism, the eternal return of the same, the pathos of distance. Nietzsche argues that the cause of great art and culture requires that most of the population, namely the broader working class, toil in conditions that are akin to slavery. Nietzsche wrote at the time of the dissolution of slavery in Europe and America, which took the form of the brutal and cruel transatlantic slave trade, forcefully displacing millions of black Africans and committing a slow genocide in the process over the course of several centuries. He was not in favor of most liberal and socialist arguments of the time that slavery must be fundamentally abolished for good, but rather argued that slavery must be *re-thought* and retained in the culture. He invited his readers to take the bold and courageous initiative to permit a new social order to emerge in which Europe's industrial factory-working proletariat are to be thought of as homologous to a slave class. One of Nietzsche's most well-known concepts is the idea of "herd mentality," which stems not only from a more archaic historical idea of the masses stretching back to Ancient Greek society, but also from the danger that the modern masses, whom Nietzsche knew firsthand in his own time, posed to his wider vision.

Now, if Nietzsche's utopian vision is already realized by the contemporary liberal bourgeois social order, that is, if Nietzsche's concepts function to describe and reinforce the ideology of the ruling class today, then this goes unacknowledged or is even directly challenged by many of his followers. Specifically, it is Nietzsche's left-oriented followers — primarily socialists and anarchists — who contest this argument. But importantly, we are not claiming that Nietzscheanism is completely successful or that it is always reactionary. To the contrary, there are some aspects of his thought and ideas that must be worked with, but only on the condition that we have acquainted ourselves with his reactionary worldview and the ways that reactionary politics inform his thought. After we have given this reading proper airing time and consideration, each reader will have to decide for themselves. Thus, this book asks you to consider a new perspective on Nietzsche, one you have likely never before encountered.

This book proposes to open a new reading of Nietzsche, one that acknowledges his thought as extraordinarily influential and therefore as a great antagonist to the prospect of changing this world. This reading is informed by a Marxist perspective that goes against the grain of predominant leftist readings of Nietzsche since the end of World War II that sought an "elective affinity" with Nietzsche. This is a particular type of incorporation of Nietzsche that neglects his Janus-faced reactionary intentions and refuses to learn from him on that level.

The elective-affinity approach to incorporating Nietzsche as the primary philosopher of the left poses many dangers and promotes several common tendencies that distort socialist and egalitarian politics. The list of problems with embracing Nietzsche through a model of elective affinity includes: the tendency to develop a conception of leadership that is elitist, the removal of a rational understanding of class-based social forces and struggle, the adoption of an irrationalist outlook in understanding political and social conflict, and the politicization of the sphere of culture in a way that de-emphasizes the field of political economy.

We propose to read Nietzsche with the understanding that he has a *center* to his thought, that he is coherent and consistent, and that this center is knowable because it repeats across the entirety of his work. Moreover, we can decipher this center as a guiding logic in each of his different concepts. It is only by honoring Nietzsche's victory and taking him at his word — even when his word and intentions are shrouded in esotericism — that we can begin to overcome him.

Finding Nietzsche, Finding Ourselves

Now I bid you lose me and find yourselves; and only when you have all denied me will I return to you.

Nietzsche, *Thus Spoke Zarathustra*[4]

Readers and lovers of Nietzsche should not be afraid of this book. The French philosopher Alain Badiou has referred to Nietzsche as an "anti-philosopher," or an antagonist to the philosopher who insists on keeping their personal experience out of their philosophy. Nietzsche is constantly confessing and drawing from the range of his personal experiences in his work. As Lou Salomé once wrote about Nietzsche's vision of philosophy, "One should always test their systems against their personal actions." And Nietzsche himself wrote in *Beyond Good and Evil* that "every great philosophy has been the personal confession of its author and a form of involuntary and unperceived memoir."[5] To get at the heart of Nietzsche, we too must feel at liberty to draw from our own personal experience.

When I first read Nietzsche, in my early twenties, I was immediately seized. At first it was the sense of rhythm in his style and prose, the signature poetic style expressed in short aphorisms, which immediately drew me in. Nietzsche's aphorisms get you up and out of your seat. Nietzsche himself was always in motion and went on daily three-hour walks. It's no surprise that his philosophy inspired a youth movement that inaugurated the by-now widely popular fad of backpacking. German youth, struck and mesmerized by Nietzsche's prophecies, took to the wilderness by the thousands, searching for the mysteries that he laid out.[6]

The effect of reading Nietzsche, even for someone who

knows very little about his motives and intentions, is often profoundly inspirational. As a young student in college, it was *Beyond Good and Evil* that first drew me in. It was through reading this book that I first really connected my two intellectual loves at that time: poetry and spirituality on the one hand, and history and philosophy on the other. Admittedly, I knew very little of what I was reading. I had no idea what this obscure German philosopher, the so-called inspiration for postmodern philosophy, was on about. And in a way it didn't really matter. What seized my interest was the rhythm and movement of the writing. I had encountered for the first time a new type of thinking that forced me to ponder my existence and question everything.

When we say that we live in Nietzsche's world, this should not be read as total hyperbole or exaggeration. According to the German philosopher Peter Sloterdijk, Nietzsche gave birth to the "era of narcissism." His philosophy gave rise to the personal injunction that shapes our culture, namely the demand that we must invent a singular and unique "way of life." According to Sloterdijk, Nietzsche revealed the truth that "all the various tribes and peoples are self-praising entities that avail themselves of their own inimitable idiom as part of a psychosocial contest played to gain advantage for themselves."[7] In Sloterdijk's view, Nietzsche broke the chains of metaphysical and moral traditions that were weighed down with resentment. This is the resounding event of Nietzsche in the history of thought that he opened, a transvaluation of all values. Nietzsche ushers in a "fifth gospel" which heightened the intensity and drama involved in the ancient Socratic demand that kicked philosophy off, the injunction to "know thyself."

Nietzsche's "fifth gospel" identifies the demand for

continual self-examination as the key to self-discovery, adding a twist: the disciple is invited to take a more active perspective on life and reality that seeks nothing less than a continual "illusion-destruction." Sloterdijk says that he has made "the task of leading life out of its raw material likeness" take on the "quality of a life-and-death struggle."[8] Nietzsche's philosophy gives the reader a new way to view the world by shifting the terrain of self-discovery toward a pursuit that only a few can truly master. And importantly, he sets a very high bar for his readers. "I write only for those whose lives have turned out well." This statement contains the core of a sadomasochist worldview that Nietzsche aimed to naturalize: a brutal, quasi-dualistic, and Manichean vision whereby an ascending and descending line of humans compete on a field composed of impersonal forces. The reader is invented and brought to life on an imaginary social battlefield composed of impersonal forces with their will to power.

Part of the reason Nietzsche attracted me as a young person was due to the repressive conditions of my broken family and my working-class background. My life was full of restless antagonism and struggle, but my emotions and restlessness had no real outlet. Nietzsche channeled my antagonistic energy by rerouting my restlessness toward something that felt more authentic and even radical. At the time I first encountered him, I was caught in the highs and lows of my life, wanting to find a way to reinvent my life and eager not to be defined by the pains of a broken family. I was hungry for movement, and Nietzsche provided it.

Nietzsche once wrote that all great ideas come from free movement of thought: "Sit as little as possible; do not believe any idea that was not born in the open air and of free movement — in which the muscles do not also revel. All prejudices emanate from the bowels."[9] This statement reveals the community-building and religious-like appeal in his thought; he calls for a radical uprooting of tradition, family, class, and religion. Nietzsche invites his readers to detach themselves, to become nomadic. To think with Nietzsche is to be thrown into a tailspin, to embrace the chaos that comes with pursuing a higher level of independence than you ever thought imaginable. He leads you to question all your attachments and allegiances in thought and practice, and in so doing, to form a new community.

Nietzsche calls forth a division within humanity, his "philosophy of the future" is an invitation to become someone new in distinction to the herd majority and its pitiful mentality. In this sense, we should understand Nietzsche as both a secular prophet calling forth a new community and, in a way very similar to the socialist philosophers he despised, as having created his own "praxis," or an engaged and practical theory of action for this community he aimed to usher into existence. But what sort of community does Nietzsche call forth? Who are the enemies to his community? And what are the terms of initiation into this community? We must read Nietzsche as a community-builder to truly understand the political vision at the core of his thought. And to truly appreciate how Nietzsche's calls for community have been answered and fulfilled in the last 120 years since his death, we must grasp both the historical situation in which he wrote and the various Nietzschean communities and thinkers that emerged shortly after he died, as his name became enshrined in the pantheon of philosophical greats.

When I first encountered Nietzsche, I was not concerned with gaining a truer understanding of his thought and legacy. I just wanted to find a way to move away from the cycles of alcoholism and drug addiction that much of my family and surrogate family had experienced. Nietzsche's radical doctrine of independence offered what felt like an exit from these dynamics. In reading him, I encountered an authoritative voice that gave me permission to move beyond these restless feelings and experience. He allowed me to see the world with a certain elevated clarity, to challenge conventions.

His resounding clarity was like a bolt of lightning that opened a path of self-discovery and singularity. Nietzsche gave me a bibliography for the Ancient Greek world, and he shaped the philosophical prejudices of my early intellectual life: Hegel was a bad systematizer, Socrates the pinnacle of mob philosophy, Rousseau a wicked moral spider, and Christ a brilliant moral teacher who founded a religious community that betrayed everything he stood for, as Christianity only valorized the weak and its followers obeyed a slave morality, even *ressentiment*. In a pretentious way, I imitated Nietzsche's preferences. But I also became more comfortable with the world of ideas and philosophy through reading him. With Nietzsche as your guide, a young person can feel quite bombastic and confident in assessing other philosophers. Nietzsche shaped not only my worldview as I absorbed more of his thinking, but also how I saw the world of philosophy itself.

If Nietzsche's ideas have truly triumphed in our world, if Nietzscheanism is the common sense of liberal capitalism, what is the real testament to his resounding influence on our culture? A concept from the German sociologist Andreas Reckwitz, the "society of singularities," helps to explain Nietzsche's influence. For Reckwitz, our society is defined by the logic of singularity, which refers to the common demand to live out our most authentic selves at all costs. In the society of singularities, everyone must be unique and creative; no longer are we content to merely find a career in which we clock in and clock out day to day. Rather, the society of singularities is marked by a desire to imbue one's career and life with a sense of purpose and uniqueness in all endeavors.

This demand to singularize yourself, to perfect your "brand," is adopted as a criterion for all sectors of professional life, from the NGO sector to the governmental and corporate sectors. We are judged based on this rubric, and we seek out recognition based on the degree to which our singular and uniquely cultivated individual brands stand out. This means that self-realization, in what Sloterdijk calls our "age of narcissism," has merged with a middle-class ethic of workplace advancement. No longer is self-realization separable from what you do. The new ethic for the middle class, or those who aspire to move from the working class to the middle class — as was the case with me — involves self-realization through building a commodified brand that is singular and unique.

In Reckwitz's analysis, our society is no longer one in which the normative or instrumentalized modes of living that modernity has imposed on us are the regulating principle of social power and authority. In other words, power and authority in our contemporary society are no longer structured around a repressive norm that we struggle to overcome. The society of singularities is structured in a way very much akin to what the German-Korean philosopher Byung-Chul Han calls the "achievement society," a social order of enforced affirmation and positivity. Our culture forces each of us to internalize an "empowerment" model of authority in which we delegate the law to ourselves. We are our own best censors. He argues that we no longer adhere to a discipline-based form of social authority that enforces a normative code of behavior on us whereby we follow repressive authority injunctions such as "you must" or "you will." We now govern and enforce obedience on ourselves. What both Han and Reckwitz reveal is that our society has not merely absorbed these demands as ideologies, for that would imply that we voluntary comply with them. These demands indicate that to derive obedience we must become "willing slaves of capital," as the French Spinozist thinker Frédéric Lordon puts it.

There has thus occurred an important historical shift in power and discipline away from the more repressive form of power that the May '68 generation and the New Left of student and youth protesters fought against. At that time, the capitalist social order and the wider liberal institutions of the family, the school, and the corporation were repressive at their very core. Liberation from these repressive institutions called for a philosophy that could thoroughly decode and liberate the subject from these binds of authority. Nietzsche's philosophy of joyous rebellion, with all its seemingly subversive aesthetic-community-building ethos, was one of the primary philosophical inspirations for the '68 generation.

The American philosopher Alan Bloom, reflecting on teaching philosophy during the '60s and '70s, said that his college students would frequently come to his office hours complaining of experiencing madness and schizophrenic episodes. There was one common association these students would raise, and it was the name "Nietzsche." It is not surprising that Nietzsche evoked feelings of madness in the context of a social order undergoing a revolutionary upsurge. When we read Nietzsche by centering the logic of his reactionary politics, we discover a new way to understand how his philosophy interacts with movements for equality and radical social change.

For Nietzsche, the radical advancements in demands for democratic and socialistic equality in his time were a problem as they empowered the masses and promoted a leveling of social relations. These movements posed a significant danger to the very foundation of the individual subject in Western social life and therefore required the creation of a comprehensive philosophy designed to prepare a community to face and overcome these forces in society. As a testament to the effectiveness of Nietzsche's concepts, it seems that when he emerges as a philosophical muse of a social movement toward greater equality — from the French '68 generation of philosophers and student protestors to the American students wrestling with rampant social injustice through the Civil Rights movement and the New Left — he functions as a deterrent to the success of these movements.

At face value, the society of singularities seems quite compelling. What could be wrong with a society in which everyone is free to pursue their own brand? The reality is far different than it may seem, and Reckwitz points out how the society of singularities — our own society — is in a fundamental crisis. The first basis of this crisis is political, and it has to do with the fact that culture is now conceived as the very foundation of collective social life. The society of singularities cannot think, let alone *work through*, the contradictions of capitalism, from massive wealth inequality to new forms of racialized politics, popular rebellions, strikes, and populism. These destabilizing features of the social order have thrown our society into a tailspin. The second crisis of the society of singularities is one of equality and class — the fact that our social order does not permit everyone to fully realize their potential. What happens to those whose lives do not turn out well in the society of singularities? What about the so-called losers whose singular brand never got off the ground?

Nietzsche experienced class struggle and a social order in a similar form of disarray to our own. He lived and wrote in Germany under Otto von Bismarck's reign during the Second Reich from 1871 (the same year as the dawn of the Paris Commune) to 1890. Socialist parties were constantly vying for power, but Bismarck, a reactionary liberal Bonapartist leader, successfully stifled the socialist threat. Testifying to the striking similarity between Nietzsche's world and our own, the United States Congress recently passed a resolution that "denounces the horrors of socialism," which is strikingly similar to the anti-socialist laws that Bismarck passed during his rule.[10] Nietzsche's political thought, starting with his first major work, *The Birth of Tragedy and the Genealogy of Morals* in 1872, was in part inspired by politics, and specifically by the Paris Commune, the first major seizing of state power by anarchists and communists. Nietzsche lived in a world that was not very different to our own, in which inequality, worker unrest, war, and imperialism were all common features of the social order. But in the historical context of his time, Nietzsche's concepts and ideas, to borrow a phrase from the Marxist philosopher György Lukács, "remained only a form of 'self-criticism' of the ruling and falling classes, or criticism of capitalist society from the positions of its most reactionary groups."[11]

It is crucial that we put forward the following clarification: Nietzscheanism is a mediated phenomenon, not a pure, undiluted philosophy that somehow magically becomes a cultural common sense due to his genius. To move from Nietzsche's philosophy to Nietzscheanism, there is invariably a domestication of his aristocratic radicalism at play. In other words, the reactionary Janus face of Nietzsche is often overlooked in the movement from Nietzsche's philosophy itself to the cultural influence that it has on our world. Moreover, there is no pure or completely correct form of Nietzscheanism. For a philosopher who prides himself on a lack of a coherent center and an undecipherable style, we must affirm that there is indeed a center to Nietzsche. Nietzsche is a community-building philosopher. He actively builds a tradition and a following, but he does so in such a way that his members are so radically untethered from conventions and norms that they don't acknowledge themselves as part of a coherent community. Perhaps Nietzscheans, while they may not realize it yet, need a former member of the tribe to help point out some more hidden aspects of the community and the tradition they are taking part in and reproducing.

As a mediated ideology, Nietzscheanism describes the predominant neoliberal capitalist ideology of our time. The philosopher Slavoj Žižek is fond of remarking that if we were to identify a core philosophy of late capitalism, it would best be described as Spinozist, given that Spinozism stands for an immanent philosophy whereby contradictions and ruptures are integrated back into the stability of the system. With this claim, Žižek means to suggest that neoliberal capitalism has effectively solved the proper management of its own contradictions.

The French philosopher Jean-Claude Michéa takes this insight even further by arguing that Spinoza's philosophy was the most formative in enacting the ideology of liberalism from the nineteenth century through to today's more hyper-neoliberal variant. Michéa argues that in terms of the class struggle, the Spinozist philosophy foreclosed a form of subject that would be an exception, that would exceed the unitary substance of liberalism. We must point out an important qualification distinguishing Spinoza's philosophy and Spinozism — the latter represents a composite effect of how Spinoza's thought has been applied toward liberalist ideological ends. Michéa argues that the bourgeoisie, especially its most progressive wing, developed a conception of the liberal subject that is unitary and total, a "process without subject," which means that in the class struggle, Spinozism functions to prevent any working-class exception to the liberal subject. The ideology of progressive liberalism has one core objective: the achievement of civil peace and equilibrium so that competing individual pursuits of liberties can persist. But what liberalism denies in this unitary conception of the subject of the modern citizen are any contesting, universalizable virtues that come from below; that is, from a Marxist point of view, liberal Spinozism finds the proletariat a hostile threat that must be suppressed.

We will argue that today's predominant neoliberal ideology is better defined as Nietzschean than Spinozist at its core. With its emphasis on entrepreneurial, affirmative singularity combined with its Janus-faced understanding of how to exert austerity and punish the working class with brutality and discipline, Nietzscheanism describes the core of the reigning ideology today better than Spinozism. Nietzscheanism possesses its own logic for the management of the contradictions of capitalism that is far more effective, precisely in the way that Nietzsche is adopted by the entire political spectrum. Nietzsche's concepts perform this function even when his reactionary intentions are ignored. Nietzscheanism provides a more apt description of philosophical complicity with today's power than Spinozism precisely for the way that Nietzsche can be deployed both in moments of acute crisis, when the very alteration of the status quo is on the table, as well as during moments of liberal stability — when the ruling elect need a theory of meritocratic legitimacy, Nietzsche provides one.

A Janus-Faced Philosophy

Nietzsche is our contemporary in two ways: first, his philosophy helped play a significant role in ushering in the era in which we live, when individual self-exploration and the society of singularities are our highest aims. Second, he offers a repertoire of concepts that helps the bourgeoisie, especially the creative class and entrepreneurs, find justification for the status quo and thus fend off the different crises of a society overwhelmed by inequality and class struggle. Nietzsche's political thought centered the importance of pacifying the masses and their demands, and he was deeply concerned with creating a comprehensive philosophy meant to mitigate the emergence of socialist challenges to the social order from below.

As capitalism has grown more rapacious and produced greater wealth and class inequalities — especially following the global economic depression of 2008 — and as the social order struggles with embedded forms of racism, the more common ideological justifications for the status quo have fallen by the wayside. We have entered a stage of capitalism in which the "bootstrap" mythology and social mobility are increasingly seen as a phony, sham ideology. Since the economic crash of 2008, our social order has been in a stage of crisis after crisis. Indeed, crisis is the new norm, and this condition has led to massive apathy and distrust of elites and leaders of major institutions at record levels.[12] The good news is that socialist and Marxist ideas have re-emerged in today's political discourse as new generations of young people are turning to the "big ideas" to think through what it means to forge alternatives to capitalism. The political perspective of this book should thus be made clear — we intend to interrogate Nietzsche as a philosopher whose reactionary political thought can offer the socialist and egalitarian tradition a great deal of insight, but only after facing him head-on, without any apologetics for his own political intentions.

Nietzsche is among the three great thinkers of modernity — the other two being Marx and Freud — whom the French philosopher Paul Ricœur once called the "masters of suspicion," thinkers whose thought is hidden and indeterminate. Among these three, it is arguably Nietzsche's philosophy that has eluded and seduced readers the most. Every generation must wrestle with Nietzsche, and his philosophy has emerged as a central reference in major moments of political and social crisis, from the German World War I soldiers who read *Thus Spoke Zarathustra* in the trenches for spiritual uplift, to the student rebels that aimed to overthrow society in May '68. Today is no different.

We must read and re-read Nietzsche in our time. We must do this in order to better understand the shortfalls that beset any left-wing incorporation of his thought; that is, when the left adopts Nietzsche as its main philosophical muse, it runs a risk of betraying its very principles. But this does not mean that we must hysterically abandon Nietzsche, because in fact he helps us see the situation of our world with fresh eyes. Nietzsche helps us to understand the ways that power and ideology work, how resentment and social suffering function, and how these things block our efforts to truly change the world.

It is important that we address an ambiguity in Nietzsche's presence on and attraction for the left, which is that Nietzsche professes a romantic anti-capitalism. Romantic anti-capitalism is a form of critique of the capitalist system that proposes the return to a better version of capitalism, or to a more harmonious management of capitalism, in distinction to transformation or total revolution. Romantic anti-capitalism is thus an ingenious form of ideological operation that has proven attractive to the bourgeois class, especially the creative class, because the capitalist ruling class requires a philosophy and an ideology that can make the degradations and injustices that are produced by its system of exploitation and division of labor seem natural and "par for the course." Nietzsche's philosophy is a Janus-faced dialectical philosophy that aims to enact a new social order and bring about a society in which artistic and aesthetic greatness is relegated to the vocation of a small elite capable of bringing it about. Nietzsche's philosophy is unabashedly elitist, and this is why it has remained attractive to elites, precisely because the joyful, rebellious aspects mesh with his obsession with rank order and blunt its more vulgar side. Nietzscheanism remains elusive because it appears edgy and critical.

In fact, Nietzsche fundamentally redefines elitism because his philosophy offers a way for elites to detach themselves from their involvement in a class project. A common motif in Nietzsche's political thought is the idea that the *Übermensch* is marked by their detachment from class relations entirely. As the scholar Ishay Landa notes, the Nietzschean "great man" is he who breaks from communal limits, declaring himself radically independent and self-sufficient, and it is this destructive breaking off that Nietzsche converts into the very goal of society.[13] In Landa's analysis of Nietzsche's influence on popular culture, he shows that what really concerned Nietzsche was the modern masses becoming a sovereign political power. Nietzsche's "superman" and *Übermensch* were elevated as figures of heroism, and his philosophy is an invitation to the individual to radically separate themselves from the decadent, degenerate, and vulgar masses.

In a way, whether one is seized by reading Nietzsche, as I was, or has never read him doesn't matter. The imprint of Nietzschean super-individualism is already deeply embedded in our culture, for example in characters such as "Tarzan, Howard Roark, James Bond, and Hannibal Lecter."[14] As Landa comments regarding Nietzsche's influence on popular culture:

> The Nietzschean hero of 20th-century popular culture is a social metaphor against democratic values denounced as herd-mentality, upholding the grandeur of the competitive individual, glorying in struggle and conquest. In that respect, he signifies a refutation of the bourgeois heritage of realism and mediocrity and a harking back to distinctly pre-bourgeois heroism; yet, as I try to show, this is not a merely nostalgic move, a last, die-hard, almost suicidal battle for the revival of past glories, as in Carlyle. Rather, the Nietzschean heroic model dovetails nicely with the new needs of the bourgeoisie, that has become the dominant class in modern, Western societies.[15]

This is the core of Nietzsche's Janus-faced philosophy, a philosophy which remains one of the main inspirations of the society of singularities, a joyful and trans-value-based affirmative philosophy, while simultaneously containing a concealed agenda for how to keep an unjust social order intact. The joyful and affirmative face of his philosophy is what we might call the overt aspect of his thought, while the second, "political Nietzsche" is its covert face. Crucially, this Janus face is concealed by Nietzsche through the motif of what he calls the "mask" and a highly sophisticated political praxis that places a major emphasis on deception. Nietzsche does not want his readers to fully know all his secrets, his agenda is meant to be elusive. The psychoanalyst Carl Jung once said that Nietzsche's "*Zarathustra* should be reserved for people who have undergone a very careful training in the psychology of the unconscious. Only then, having given evidence of not being overthrown by what the unconscious occasionally says, should people have access to the book."[16]

As a young reader of Nietzsche, I didn't have the tools to fully understand the deeper significance of the Janus-faced and reactionary nature of his thought. I did not heed Jung's advice to approach Nietzsche with caution because the translations available to me were all watered down and the academic authorities on Nietzsche that I consulted mentioned nothing about any political core to his thought. And this is part of the problem with the Nietzsche industry today — it is full of apologetics and omissions of Nietzsche's political agenda. Nietzschean studies practices what the late Italian Marxist historian Domenico Losurdo called the "hermeneutics of innocence" — a concerted effort on behalf of Nietzschean scholars and philosophers to brush over and minimize the significance of his reactionary agenda.

This interpretation of Nietzsche has been shared by several generations of readers, and we now encounter his thought predominately through the lens of the hermeneutics of innocence. This reading of Nietzsche — it also appears in translations where radically reactionary ideas are removed or glossed over — first really took off with Walter Kaufmann, an influential German translator and interpreter of Nietzsche who came to prominence for his well-known existentialist work *Nietzsche: Philosopher, Psychologist, Antichrist*, published in 1950. Kaufmann rose to prominence for an interpretation of Nietzsche that sought to change the "cultural" understanding of Nietzsche as a reactionary thinker. That the English philosopher Bertrand Russell referred to World War II as "Nietzsche's war," and that there was general agreement on the fact that Nietzsche's concepts contained a political agenda that deeply influenced the Third Reich, as well as Mussolini and Italian fascism, was all decentered in Kaufmann's Nietzsche. Indeed, Kaufmann ushered in a new sort of Nietzschean interpretation that was hostile to the mere suggestion that Nietzsche contains a political core. Although it looks at Nietzsche on the left primarily, the connection between Nietzsche and fascism will come up throughout this book.

As we will see in Chapter Five, "Nietzsche within the Left," even though Kaufmann described Nietzsche as practicing an "anti-politics" that refused any of the politics of his time, there is a great irony that emerges in Kaufmann's apolitical Nietzsche, which is that even Kaufmann's apolitical and defanged Nietzsche still inspired political movements such as the Black Panthers. Even when Nietzsche is read apolitically or as having no clear political position or agenda, a politics is still derived from his thought. This points to the fact that Nietzsche is such a thoroughly political thinker — even when you seek to skirt around his politics, they still manage to emerge.

In my own journey with Nietzsche, it became evident that he had deeply influenced the intellectual life of my early twenties, and that his life philosophy had given me my own sense of singularity. He invited me to go out and discover a calling in philosophy, a calling that was not in the direction of the stuffier, more academic thought that I found in analytic philosophy, which was concerned with logic, math, and language games. Nietzsche opened a more vitalist life philosophy, and he gave me an ethics to both live and to love life to its fullest — *amor fati*. However, there were some moments when reading Nietzsche that hinted there was a political core to his work. I began to detect a manic-depressive mood in his writing. While some of his aphorisms exhibited a softness and admiration for beauty, they would suddenly turn on a dime and he would switch up his emphasis and begin to demand that the reader be prepared to enact cruelty and brutality toward the degenerate and the weak. This is the Janus-faced quality of Nietzsche. As an example, let's consider Nietzsche's later notebook fragments from 1885, where he writes:

My need for new philosophers. Where will they come from? Only where a noble way of thinking reigns, one that believes in slavery and in many degrees of bondage as the prerequisite of any higher culture; where a creative way of thinking reigns, which does not set the world's goal as the happiness of repose — this lie is called "equality of human beings."[17]

Later I would learn, in the very translations of Nietzsche I was reading by Walter Kaufmann, that this dark side was watered down: words and emphasis regarding his support for slavery were removed; his hatred for socialism and the working class and his embrace of a society based on aristocratic rank order were all toned down and de-emphasized. Why did Kaufmann and the wider "Nietzsche industry" hide the dark side of Nietzsche's face, the covert side of his thought, from us? Perhaps if I had known about the political agenda that so deeply informs his concepts, I would not have been so resolutely turned on to him as a young reader. But as I began to see the dark side of him, I reasoned that these brutal and cruel sentiments were merely odd mood swings, attributable to Nietzsche's much-discussed chronic illnesses and severe mental breakdown.

But we now have good reason to infer why Kaufmann, the most widely read English translator of Nietzsche, de-emphasized Nietzsche's darker, more aristocratic side. In addition to the reasons we cited above regarding the effort to "de-Nazify" Nietzsche, Kaufmann did not have access to the entire standard edition of Nietzsche's complete works, including the unpublished notebooks, which were not released in their German original until 1977.[18] An additional reason is that Kaufmann adopts the widely held view that Nietzsche's political motives and reactionary intentions — to the extent Kaufmann even thinks Nietzsche is driven by reactionary politics! — are ultimately not of central importance for truly understanding his philosophy. This line of thought is emblematic of what we identified as Losurdo's hermeneutics of innocence.

Hermeneutics is a branch of philosophy that analyzes the ways that different methods of interpretation are applied to a given thinker's work. The hermeneutics of innocence is a play on the important motif of the "innocence of becoming" in Nietzsche's moral thought, which refers to the state of being Nietzsche invites his readers, the "Free Spirits," to learn to inhabit. Far from an apolitical, ethical-aesthetic idea, Losurdo shows that the innocence of becoming was tied into a political program whereby a "Dionysian theodicy of happiness" would reinforce it, to help it to challenge the Christian-socialist theodicy of suffering Nietzsche encountered in the Germany of his time.[19]

From a philosophical perspective, the concept of innocence is a major motif in Nietzsche's thought — it is at the core of his critique of Christianity as a guilt-inducing system that must be rejected and overcome. In the concept of the innocence of becoming, Nietzsche develops an entirely novel conception of the innocence of nature. As we develop in chapter three, the innocence of becoming is an idea that Nietzsche develops for his community of readers, whom he often refers to as free spirits. The free spirits inhabit a position of innocence in distinction to the socialists and "levelers" of his time. Although Nietzsche was a solitary and private writer, he wrote manuals that were spiritual, philosophical, and political, and which are meant to form a reader and to build a community.

The hermeneutics of innocence refers to the way that Nietzsche seduces his readers into his community of overmen, and it also refers to the scholarly method that aims to whitewash Nietzsche's reactionary intentions, to render them marginal and insist that his politics is not determinative of his concepts and ideas. This scholarly approach began in earnest in the post-World War II period, and it remains dominant today. Importantly, this whitewashing does not make left-Nietzscheans guilty; that is, the objective in using this concept of the hermeneutics of innocence is not to shame left-Nietzscheans by suggesting that they should not read Nietzsche or that he should be canceled. Nietzsche's politics do not conform to any one conventional political position in our political constellation, his thought rather latches onto existing political and ideological tendencies and shapes them in distinct ways, which we will explore throughout this book with a particular focus on Nietzsche within the left.

The hermeneutics of innocence fosters two overlapping interpretative approaches to Nietzsche: first, the insistence that there is no real politics in Nietzsche; and second, it refers to the motif of innocence that appears in his metaphysical and moral thought. We will argue that Nietzschean innocence is harmful to any leftist and socialist politics as it sets the philosopher in a position of romantic anti-capitalism as a free-floating rebel. Nietzschean innocence is a radicalization of the private bourgeois subject in a world of crisis and turmoil. These two registers interact and mutually build on one another by glossing over and marginalizing the reactionary substance of Nietzsche's thought, and as a result the reader enters the Nietzschean community-building project in a state of innocence and is thus more prone to being duped by Nietzsche. Unless we read Nietzsche as *parasites* — that is, with careful attention both to the existential philosophical system meant to retain a particular form of hyper individualism bound up with a particular conception of aesthetic or artistic suffering and as a refined political thinker who sought to offer up a praxis for intellectuals to fend off egalitarian and socialist politics from below — Nietzsche performs his perverse victory over us.

We propose to read Nietzsche as parasites, to enter his community with a new set of tools and knowledge that have been neglected for too long, especially on the left. The hermeneutics of innocence tends to read Nietzsche as driven by profound existential suffering, and individualizes the thrust of Nietzsche's genius, thereby missing the touchstone point of social and political concern that drives his thought. Nowhere are the errors of the hermeneutics of innocence more apparent than in the tendency to treat Nietzsche's views on Christianity as a timeless metaphysical and moral critique rather than an immanently political one.

In lieu of the hermeneutics of innocence, a historical-materialist reading is capable of seeing how Nietzsche in fact praised core aspects of bourgeois Christianity, specifically its capacity to discipline the weak, and that he associated a political critique of Christianity with the "sickness" of egalitarianism, socialism, and the workers' movement — all highly modern and political tendencies. But through the lens of a hermeneutics of innocence, his critique of Christianity is understood simply as a timeless philosophical assault on religion, when in fact Nietzsche's critique of religion has to be understood as both a critique of ideology and as situated in a concrete social and political context — a society wracked by many of the same problems we face today, including intensified class conflict, rampant inequality, imperialist wars, and a Bonapartist liberal ruling order that is designed to discipline and placate agitation from below. And most importantly, we must emphasize that Nietzsche sought to develop strategies for intellectuals — on the right and the left — to quell socialist consciousness in political life.

Losurdo's monumental work *Nietzsche, Aristocratic Rebel: Intellectual Biography and Critical Balance Sheet*, translated by Gregor Benton and with an introduction by Harrison Fluss, has fundamentally transformed our understanding of Nietzsche and the origination of his thought. Losurdo brings a wide contextual analysis to Nietzsche's life and times. The outcome of this thousand-page unearthing of the entirety of Nietzsche's work reshapes our understanding of his thought and opens new directions for understanding the generation of Nietzsche's concepts in relation to the politics of his time. Losurdo does not describe Nietzsche's reactionary politics by way of a personal idiosyncrasy or a psychobiographical account, instead he offers a comprehensive biographical portrait — or what I have elsewhere named a "wide-context" approach to understanding the social and political dynamics of Nietzsche's time.

Another crucial work on Nietzsche that shapes my thinking is *The Destruction of Reason*, published in 1953 by the godfather of modern critical theory, György Lukács, an important — albeit highly ignored and criminally marginalized — work on the history of German philosophy's complicity with the rise of European fascism in the early twentieth century. Lukács is one of the intellectual forebears of the tradition known as "Western Marxism," a movement within Marxist thought that is known for its embrace of philosophy, its eschatological view of revolution, and its emphasis on analysis of cultural trends in capitalism. In *The Destruction of Reason*, Lukács opens one of the most important critiques of Nietzsche from a Marxist point of view, a critique which is significant because Lukács himself was an early Nietzschean. In fact, Lukács maintained an ironic Nietzschean, romantic anti-capitalist affinity in his early work *Soul and Form*, an important book of literary criticism, but he later renounced this early embrace of Nietzsche once he became a Marxist. Lukács's *The Destruction of Reason* was so thorough and perspicacious in its critique of Nietzsche that it led the Frankfurt School thinker Theodor Adorno, a former mentee of Lukács, to write a frustrated, scathing, and perfunctory review of the book, declaring in only a few pages that it constituted the destruction of Lukács's own reason.[20] As a result, the perspective that Lukács develops in this work remains overlooked and ignored, but it must be considered as one of the most important Marxist perspectives on Nietzsche ever written.

Nietzsche's reactionary thought is extreme — there are incitements to genocide and support for slavery in his work — but this extremity should not be read as an aberration or a significant divergence from many of the mainstream liberal intellectuals of his time. Nietzsche's reactionary thought connected him to his contemporary liberal philosophical establishment, and he shared many common political objectives with liberal thinkers, which revolved first and foremost around anti-socialist agendas. It is important that we expose and reveal Nietzsche's liberal affinities and how they dovetail with his reactionary political goals, because this affects any possible synthesis of Nietzsche with Marx or the left more broadly. Before we address any possible synthesis of the two thinkers, we must start with a new emphasis on Nietzsche himself, on the development and especially on the *function* of his concepts. After we have understood the heart of Nietzsche's thought and the intended function of his concepts, we will forever see the innocent elective affinity of Nietzsche with the left in a fundamentally new light.

Our intention is to bring Nietzsche's thought down to earth, to take him out of the trans-historical pantheon of great philosophers from Plato to Descartes to Kant, to put him under a microscope in the historical context in which he worked and thought. Nietzsche is a thinker who took politics incredibly seriously, so seriously that he offers insights even to the left. But these insights must be understood in the context in which he lived and wrote if they are to be of any use to us today. Thinkers such as Plato or Machiavelli offer timeless insights into politics for both the right and the left, and to an extent Nietzsche can offer similar insights. Such arguments are often made by liberal Nietzscheans, such as in Hugo Drochon's recent work *Nietzsche's Great Politics*, but what they miss is the fact that Nietzsche wrote in a time which resembles our own, and that his thought has a direct connection to our modern political and cultural context.

To seek timeless political insight from Nietzsche is to miss the incredible prescience of his thought in understanding the class struggle. Nietzsche is a thinker of modern capitalism, and the fact that he is considered the godfather of postmodernism by so many philosophers even further connects his thought to our present, including and especially his politics. Nietzsche's concepts are elusive precisely for their trans-historical basis, such as the herd mentality — a concept that speaks of the working class across Europe during Nietzsche's time, as well as a trans-historical tendency that links the modern working class back to class dynamics present in ancient Greece.

The hermeneutics of innocence is a method of reading Nietzsche which has many limitations, which we intend to explore throughout this work. It may be surprising to some readers to learn that this method of reading Nietzsche has only become popular since the end of World War II. As we will discover in our reading of pre-war left-Nietzscheans — especially the Bolshevik Nietzscheans — the left used to read Nietzsche with a tacit understanding that his reactionary politics is not marginal to any assessment of his thought. Left readers of Nietzsche used to approach him as an antagonist, with no illusions and without any agenda to conceal the way his politics determine his concepts. At the minimum, such a method of reading represents a far more ethical approach, especially for readers of Nietzsche on the left, than the hermeneutics of innocence.

For a philosopher such as Nietzsche, for whom courage is placed in such a central position of truth, it should be no problem for any Nietzschean to process the political core of his thought with a full embrace and sober assessment of the centrality of his reactionary politics. But even though the Nietzschean scholars who deploy a hermeneutics of innocence insist on omitting and distorting his thought to remove politics from it, we must also recognize that post-war readers of Nietzsche, including Kaufmann himself, and especially the French Nietzscheans such as Pierre Klossowski, Georges Bataille, Gilles Deleuze, and Jacques Derrida, each produced insightful work on the philosopher. What we aim for is a new interrogation and appraisal of these works with an eye toward centering Nietzsche's reactionary political radicalism within his thought, not as a merely incidental part of it.

Nietzsche is a dangerous thinker, and the motif of danger obsessed the philosopher throughout his career. As the psychoanalyst Carl Jung wrote in his multi-year seminar on *Thus Spoke Zarathustra* in 1935, four years prior to the start of World War II:

> If a man reads Zarathustra unprepared, with all the naïve presuppositions of our actual civilization, he must necessarily draw wrong conclusions as to the meaning of the "Superman," "the Blond Beast," "the Pale Criminal," and so on.[21]

Throughout his seminars on Nietzsche, Jung expresses an awareness of the very radical political danger that Kaufmann and so many other existentialist and left-Nietzscheans sought to ignore. It was Nietzsche's idea of the Superman which drew Jung's attention and which he saw as the spiritual core of Nietzsche's thought: "If they develop further as Protestants they will necessarily come to the tremendous problem to which Nietzsche came, namely, to the idea of the Superman, to the idea of the thing in man that takes the place of the God that has been hitherto valid."[22] Although he had an awareness of Nietzsche's aristocratic ideas and how they could be abused by uninitiated readers, Jung would take this very danger and use it as a major inspiration for the basis of his own esoteric concepts and pedagogy in his psychoanalytic school, creating what Lukács calls an "aristocratic epistemology."

Aristocratic epistemology is when a philosopher distorts a universal category of truth, such as the absolute or the universal, and transforms it into a category to which only a select few are granted access. Lukács provides a historical genealogy of aristocratic epistemology within German idealism, starting with Friedrich Heinrich Jacobi, one of the first philosophers to create a comprehensive philosophy that embraced this form of irrationalism. To rely on a conception of truth that is only determined by the strong few is an irrationalist philosophy grounded in an aristocratic epistemology. Such forms of philosophy are alive and well today, and irrationalism is a category of thought which Nietzsche refines and develops in his thought. We will explore Nietzsche's place within the irrationalist lineage of philosophers that Lukács brings out when we deconstruct Nietzsche's important concept of perspectivism.

But how can Nietzsche's reactionary politics be missed by an entire scholarly industry that is dedicated to propagating Nietzschean thought? Why would they choose to paint him as an apolitical thinker? The answer is that there have been generations of interpreters and admirers of Nietzsche who read him as being without a political center because they claim Nietzsche has no center. As the philosopher Kurt Rudolf Fischer comments:

We undercut Nietzsche if we wish to determine what the "*Übermensch*" is. Because I think it is part of the determination of the "*Übermensch*" not to be determined — that we shall have to experiment, that we shall have to create. Nietzsche puts emphasis on the creativity of man and therefore we should accentuate that the conception of the "*Übermensch*" is necessarily not determined. We cannot ask whether an author has confused the issue or has presented us with a dangerous alternative.[23]

In his important study *The Nietzsche Legacy in Germany*, Steven Aschheim has shown that Nietzsche's wild popularity in Germany shortly after his death created a series of political shockwaves. Within less than a decade of his death in 1900, an entire scholarly industry of Nietzscheanism arose. One of the hallmarks of these various Nietzschean scholars was that they refused the explicit aristocratic agenda at work in his thought. Thus, like Kaufmann after World War II, the early German Nietzscheans often insisted on sidelining his aristocratic radicalism, even though Nietzsche himself confessed that "aristocratic radicalism" does indeed accurately describe his politics. Socialist critic Kurt Eisner called this refusal "the Nietzsche problem," which was rampant throughout the fin de siècle period. These Nietzsche scholars concluded that ultimately Nietzsche's politics is "indeterminate," and thus his philosophy came to center on the importance of individual "inner experience." Almost resembling a religious text, Nietzsche's liberationist philosophy, despite its explicit aristocratic commitments, which Nietzsche celebrated openly, was instead taken up by the entire political spectrum, from anarchists and socialists to nationalists and the literary avant garde.

From the turn of the twentieth century to the present, Nietzsche has meant something different in situations where political upheaval and social change is afoot. Losurdo's careful study of Nietzsche's politics reveals — with countless examples — the fact that they were meant to be missed and overlooked by his readers. Nietzsche wrote for times of class struggle. As Eisner, the first real leftist critic of Nietzsche, stated in his work on Nietzsche written in the 1890s: "[He] is a real reactionary because his forward is backward. And because he is a reactionary, the future will despise him. The future is not Nietzsche's!"[24] Eisner's optimism was proven wrong. Nietzsche was far from dead and the political struggles of the future, from the rise of fascism to the catastrophic world wars, pitted Nietzsche as the central intellectual figure across the political spectrum.

The merit of Eisner's text is found in the fact that he conveys a sober understanding of Nietzsche's philosophy as a threat to the legacy of the Enlightenment and the rationalist tradition which he saw as embodied in the workers' struggle and socialism. Although Nietzsche was a great antagonist to the romantic Rousseau, whom he derogatively named "the moral spider," Eisner argues that Nietzsche effectively became a Rousseau in his own time. For Eisner, Nietzsche is a threat to the rationalist socialist tradition due to these romantic commitments, and to follow Nietzsche in politics is to fall prey to the seas of romantic nostalgia for an imagined Hellenic culture that embraces cruelty and slavery. Nietzsche's esoteric doctrines provide "clothing for many monsters," in Eisner's reading.

Indeed, the very monstrous basis of Nietzsche's thought is easy to miss in reading him, and he played with the motif of the mask, a highly calibrated concept in his work, meant to throw off readers from his true political intentions. Nietzsche has proven most catalytic and transformative to bourgeois and petit-bourgeois readers, likely because they are drawn to his insights for their seeming radicality and militant style. Yet, as we aim to elaborate, the appearance of militancy in Nietzsche can only be understood on the basis that he aimed to initiate a confrontation with the socialist and egalitarian elements within socialism in his time. He invites his readers to fight the socialist menace, whether directly or indirectly, and this is the Machiavellian nature of Nietzsche's thought, a political philosophy designed to disarm and neutralize egalitarian and radical socialistic movements, whether from within the left or the right. And while there have been socialist and communist Nietzscheans, we will come to discover that the vast majority of them end up facing internal contradictions and rifts that are often intractable.

What we claim is the following, a warning: if Nietzsche's philosophy is truly a comprehensive reaction through the refinement of a series of concepts — what Nietzsche once called "weapons for the ruling class" — this means that the adoption of his concepts without a careful understanding of their intended function will risk repeating his very agenda that is hardwired into them. This is the danger of Nietzscheanism, whether this is expressed in the liberal academic caste of his scholarly experts or by the student rebels of May '68 who took his philosophy as their primary inspiration. Nietzsche's thought contains a logic — his concepts have specific functions that are too often misunderstood and then repeated and enacted by his main expositors.

Losing Nietzsche, Finding Marx

Over the course of my intellectual journey, Nietzsche remained my philosophical muse even as I began to be drawn more to Marxism, socialism, and political philosophy. But I nevertheless always had a feeling that Nietzsche could not speak to these newfound political interests. I found Nietzsche to be an intellectual self-help guru, offering both political and spiritual counsel. But I had no clue as to what his political wisdom entailed. I only turned to him when I needed inspiration, and with my new interest in politics, and as I began to see my life through the lens of class conflict and struggle, I began to forget him. For the first time, I began to lose Nietzsche.

It was the recession of 2008 that finally cut my ties with Nietzsche. This was a generation-defining event. Something changed in our social relations. New social patterns became irreversible, a new stagnation in our social lives began to set in. People could not leave jobs even if they wanted to. All the promises of the society of singularity and the even more fundamental American Dream promises of homeownership and the prospect of starting a family felt more distant, if not impossible to achieve. Gradually, I began to understand my situation in the world as a working-class person, not as a free-floating entrepreneur. 2008 exposed the class constraints that make up our everyday life. I went to a state university in Southern Oregon on a Pell Grant and some college loans, and by the time I was thrown into the economy to seek employment, I found myself back working construction. There was no compelling work that would pay enough to allow me to pursue my chosen course, which was to continue my studies in philosophy, to research, and write.

The economy had turned punitive and disciplinary; governing through debt servitude, surveillance, and a status quo of radical economic inequality had all become the new norm. Liberal institutions, from college departments and nonprofits to businesses, adopted lean fiscal plans to keep their budgets tight in what is known as "austerity." This austerity would prove disastrous for workplace morale, setting people against one another, fomenting interpersonal tension and a sense of near permanent social conflict. These austerity policies were also the deeper background condition and precursor to what would become the more weaponized trend we now know as "cancel culture." 2008 reset our institutional cultures by molding them as punitive in their structures. This post-2008 punitive turn combined with the new society of singularities; specifically, our society insists that it is only individuals who are required to take responsibility for their actions and their consequences.

Who is culpable for these crises? The ruling class has seemingly evaded accountability time and again, and so we turn on each other. The punitive turn in post-2008 austerity enforcement did not necessarily clash with the new structure of authority, which no longer needs a repressive boss to enforce adherence. Even though we internalize these new punitive norms, it's nearly impossible to identify the culprits or the enemy. Austerity policies in institutions create a paradox whereby everyone is forced to accept conditions of cutthroat competition among their peers and those vying for similar jobs, promotions, and positions, while at the same time it fortifies those managers and the capitalist class which impose these policies as effectively untouchables. The ideology of this situation — and ideology can be defined here as a system of beliefs that works even when we don't believe in it — is sadomasochistic. Most of us don't *really* believe that society is made up of winners and losers, but from the ideological point of view of the institutions that govern our world, this sadomasochistic myth is enshrined as sacrosanct.

While the punitive turn intensified after 2008, labor conditions had been undergoing strains for decades prior. We live in the era that economists call "the long downturn," which refers to the general decline in the real wages of the working class, accelerated by a sweeping set of central bank and government fiscal policies that have become enshrined in macro-economic policy since the 1970s. These policies enforce the culture of austerity, forcing workers to sacrifice pay raises and to work in conditions that are precarious, and stripping away social protections from healthcare to retirement savings. Most American workers experience this profound strain, with over 60 percent of those who work full time living paycheck to paycheck.[25] And amid this punitive turn, the society of singularities still demands that everyone cultivate their own unique, commodified brand in order to have any chance of success.

We see here the clash between two contradictory heads of our system, and it is this contradiction, and the misery that this system produces, that explains the new forms of protest and revolt that have marked the post-2008 period. For the working class to liberate itself, massive solidarity is required, involving organizing at workplaces, forming unions, education in socialist politics, and the development of new modes of class consciousness. But the pressures of austerity and stagnation tend to ignite a cascade of personal and individually driven aggressions and protests instead of mass-level solidarity. We live in a society that is wracked by the contradictory demands of independent, singular individuals seeking to maximize their brand and gain some property, mixed with the daily grind of so many who are barred from such self-realization. Nietzsche encountered a Janus-faced capitalist system much like our own, and his philosophical insights into politics, as well as the invention of his core concepts, are traceable back to this split logic of a ludic individualism and a disciplinary brutality.

Politics is the art of managing social antagonisms and the intractable contradictions of liberal capitalism; the brutal misery it foments clashes with the radically individualist and singular qualities embedded in its promises of independent entrepreneurship. Nietzsche's thought takes place on a similar terrain of social contradictions to our own, and from the site of this battlefield he offered up concepts for ways to "culturalize" and to mitigate political and social antagonisms. Nietzsche understood that politics is the art of displacing and re-directing social and political contradictions onto the site of culture, where a more ludic and expressive resolution can be found. But at the same time, he was deeply aware of the importance of mitigating political contradictions and keeping them from even appearing to begin with. This is a core of Nietzsche's anti-socialist philosophy and what is often called his "anti-politics," which has many resonances with the neoliberal era in which the culturalization of politics has become highly sophisticated and where "culture wars" are the daily distraction from the class-war machinations that lie underneath.

Liberal thought, in all its variety, from the progressive left to the neoconservative right, aims for a culturalizing and what we will call a "nominalizing" of political contradictions, and this can take many forms. Liberals on both the right and the left nominalize the social contradictions inherent to both the market and its tyranny over the working class and the contradictions that are borne from the working class itself. The raison d'être of liberal politics is built on the need to displace antagonisms of capitalism back onto the individual worker; that is, liberals must find ways to stamp down working-class discontent, and the result is that working-class experience and demands are taken to be a scandal affecting the very semblance of social order. The desired end of mitigating these agitations is to foster anti-solidarity and especially hyper-racial animus among workers so that cross-racial solidarity is off the table.

The post-2008 social order has witnessed popular revolts and social movements that have brought out the contradictions inherent to the system. Political movements that span the ideological spectrum have popped up, from the libertarian Tea Party and the anti-capitalist Occupy Wall Street to the global "Movement of the Squares," which was ushered in by the massive protest wave against autocratic regimes across the Arab world and then caught fire in the West. Although its material success was mixed, the Occupy Wall Street movement in the United States put a new face on anti-capitalist struggle. These new protest movements represented a political experiment in enacting a collective solidarity that had been foreclosed. Harnessing the power of digital and social media, people met in local city squares in the places they lived, encampments were set up, and a sustained protest movement took off. Occupy Wall Street framed the struggle with a clear-eyed sense of the enemy: "1 percent vs. the 99 percent" was the rallying cry from the streets.

I was drawn to these movements because they represented the first real sign of a collective break from the imposed regimen of austerity that we had all been subjected to. I was engaged in reading groups on Marx and participated in

Occupy encampments. I began to feel the pull to study with great Marxist philosophers, and even attempted to apply some skills I gained in film production to making a documentary on philosophy and the new uprisings. Reading Marx helped me see the real stakes of these movements at a more systemic level. I also participated in Black Lives Matter, a movement which in its early days in Ferguson, Missouri, incorporated a potent blend of anti-austerity and anti-racist popular rebellion. By forging solidarity with these movements, I made an entirely new network of friends and comrades around the world who also saw the conflicts of our world from a similar point of view.

Finding Nietzsche Anew

It was the COVID-19 pandemic in 2020 that brought me back to Nietzsche. "You have to first lose me before you find me again." Alas, I had made a grand return to Nietzsche, but this time as a *parasite*. I rediscovered Nietzsche with some immunity-boosting methods of analysis, which I didn't have when I first encountered him. I found some antibodies to the existentialist and apolitical Nietzsche I had read earlier in a long-neglected set of Marxist studies of his work, including Lukács's *The Destruction of Reason*, Geoff Waite's *Nietzsche's Corps/e*, and Losurdo's *Aristocratic Rebel*. I re-read Nietzsche's major works, his fragments, and his journals, but this time with a new perspective on the actual historical basis of his thought. After gaining this new orientation, everything he wrote hit differently, and everything that prominent Nietzscheans wrote about him, from Deleuze and Foucault to the American philosopher Brian Leiter and the school of analytic Nietzscheans, seemed as if it were missing the real Nietzsche.

The left has an important, and often neglected tradition of critics of Nietzsche, ranging from Lukács, the founder of critical theory, to the famous American socialist and novelist Jack London, the historian Eric Hobsbawm, the American philosopher Geoff Waite, and the Italian Marxist Antonio Gramsci. It was my engagement with these perspectives, along with returning to the writing of Nietzsche himself, that woke me from my slumber. But would my rediscovery of Nietzsche result in what he predicted? Specifically, would I truly find him again? The answer to that question is left to the reader of this book.

What these authors helped me to discover is a figure who I now consider one of the most important, if not the greatest, antagonists to collective, egalitarian socialist politics in philosophy. Politics is not a pragmatic activity that is separate from thinking. As socialists, philosophizing is not separable from actual politics. This is not to say that everyone is a philosopher, but at the same time, the idea that philosophizing and speculating on problems of the human condition, political epistemology, the problem of suffering, and political consciousness — all areas of thought where Nietzsche's influence is paramount — is to be the reserve of a small cadre of elite academics is a premise that haunts the left to this day. In order for philosophy to serve as a weapon for the proletariat in the class struggle, as Marx once advocated, we must change our idea of how we pair theory and practice; that is, we must come to adopt a different idea of how we philosophize in relation to doing politics in the world.

Nietzsche calls forth a particular understanding of the philosopher that teaches us the vocation of the philosopher is ultimately only for an elect few. This anti-egalitarian conception of the philosopher is a motivation for us to engage with Nietzsche, and given his massive influence on our conception of philosophy, it is only by engaging with Nietzsche's thought that we can truly learn from Marx's provocative suggestion that philosophy be inducted into the class struggle as a weapon. The task of changing the world invites us to think of politics not merely as a pragmatic activity of organizing for change; we must also approach the struggles ahead as thinkers, indeed as philosophers. We have much to learn from Nietzsche, a thinker who wrote, "My philosophy will be read for the next 2,0000 years!" He must be wrestled with by the left, but wrestled with only on condition that he is read in a proper political and historical context. Immersing ourselves in Nietzsche's thought helps us to understand how our society works in its Janus-faced punitive forms of capitalist labor hierarchy and austerity-driven stagnation, as well as in its limited promises of ludic and Dionysian cosmopolitan flexibility.

The chapters that follow will seek to demonstrate how Nietzsche's thought speaks to the limitations of our world, and the ways that his philosophy is designed to ensure that any prospect of egalitarian change is removed entirely. To discover how Nietzsche performs this function for those he seduces, we must master his political and philosophical project to get a better grasp on how to contest the victory his ideas have had in our world. We live in Nietzsche's world; the point is we must change it.

After gaining a better sense of Nietzsche's concepts and the historical context in which he developed them, we will analyze how his concepts function on the left and how "Nietzscheanism" reproduces many of his intended objectives. Our argument is not that Nietzsche is a garden-variety liberal reactionary thinker who happened to share many of the same bourgeois and aristocratic agendas as other intellectuals of his time — support for eugenics and slavery chief among them. Our argument is that Nietzsche must be read as a reactionary thinker whose politics is not separable from the development of his moral, political, and metaphysical thought. The left has taken an approach to Nietzsche that is grounded in a model of elective affinity, which insists that Nietzsche can be an exception and that his political commitments have little to no bearing on understanding his thought, and therefore Nietzschean ideas and concepts are incorporated with little care about their original intention and design. This has led to a Nietzschean takeover on the left and to a method of reading Nietzsche that has compromised the left in ways that are detrimental to how we understand equality and social suffering and the role of the working class in socialist struggle, to how we understand our political enemies and adversaries. Nietzsche has a great deal to teach us, but we have been reading him poorly. We must learn to read him as parasites.

By analyzing how Nietzsche is brought into the left, how his concepts latch onto and transform socialist ideas, we develop a clearer sense of the pitfalls that often come with adopting a left-Nietzschean philosophy. There is no neutral incorporation of Nietzschean ideas, because ideas always have consequences in struggle. This is especially true in the case of Nietzsche precisely because his ideas were forged in and meant to be applied to political struggle. However, not every Nietzschean idea or concept when applied on the left inevitably betrays a commitment to egalitarian and working-class objectives. Our aim is to become better at deciphering and seeing when Nietzscheanism begins to reproduce the very aristocratic philosophy it was meant to, but in ways unbeknownst to those who deploy it. When the function of Nietzsche is put on autopilot and we *innocently* neglect the political function of his ideas, our political stance will tend toward defending the capitalist status quo.

Our argument can be understood in two ways: first, Nietzsche's politics must be understood as the core to his thought; and second, when we understand politics as his core, we unlock invaluable secrets about the way our social order justifies its existing status quo and class relations. We discover the shortcomings in any attempt to rebel against the social order that adopts the romantic anti-capitalist approach that left-Nietzscheans tend to embrace. To unlock the political core of Nietzsche requires that we study his thought by taking him at his word when he tells us about his notions of "great politics" in his philosophy. When Nietzsche states that he "smelled politics where it had never been smelled before," this signals an important insight that suggests his genealogical method offers up micro-level analyses of politics in areas where we had never seen politics before, such as in the family, in music, and in culture.

Nietzsche opens up what Losurdo refers to as a "theoretical surplus" of political insights into historical and political situations and dynamics. The concept of *ressentiment* is an excellent example of theoretical surplus: it identifies something useful to any thinking of political solidarity and the way that resentments can often overwhelm specific groups and classes. But it is the way that Nietzsche theorizes *ressentiment*, namely as the primary affect involved with any revolutionary uprising from below, that concerns us from a socialistic and left perspective. Nietzsche identifies *ressentiment* as an important concept that can often shut down political emancipation on both the left and the right, but it is the way that he couches the concept as an intrinsic part of the species-being level of the herd — or the working masses — which must be isolated and overturned. As a concept, *ressentiment* has a political function that poses a problem for the prospect of revolutionary social change. Perhaps the boldest claim of this book is that *ressentiment* is a completely problematic concept that must be abandoned entirely because its function is to harden political difference, shut down possible solidarities, and make the status quo more rigid.

Why have general readers and the Nietzschean scholarly community tended to neglect the political core of Nietzsche when his work was treated in unabashed political terms for several decades after he died in 1900? To get at the heart of this obfuscation of Nietzsche's politics we need to understand the efforts to water down his reactionary and aristocratic core as a project furthered by an entire Nietzschean industry of existentialists such as Walter Kaufmann and later postmodern Nietzscheans like Gilles Deleuze and Jacques Derrida. Firstly, it is important to understand that Nietzsche himself aimed to obscure the centrality of his political agenda by esoterically imbuing his thought with layers of ambiguity, indeterminacy, and all sorts of fictionalism. As the American philosopher and scholar of Nietzsche Geoff Waite once wrote, Nietzsche's use of esoteric strategies aims to enact a particular political and social arrangement by creating and re-creating a "corps" of readers. The new Marxist critique throws into question this community-building gesture of Nietzscheanism, recognizing in it one of the most effective strategies whereby the political core of Nietzsche is missed, glossed over, or ignored.

We must understand the empirical facts of Nietzsche's agenda and the historical context that drove his thought if we really want to read Nietzsche differently and to make his thought truly ripe for our world. He aimed to invent a cadre of readers who will lead the turbulent anti-democratic and anti-socialist movement for the next two thousand years to come. This cadre must be prepared to embody the Janus face of liberal capitalism in its lows of sadomasochist cruelty and its highs of joyful affirmation and individualist celebration.

Another important question emerges in this study; namely, does attention to a more serious, historically contextualized Nietzsche help us see how his thought gives rise to an actual politics? Indeed, we will argue that we can best understand and decipher Nietzsche's esotericism by centering his politics, because when we center Nietzsche and Nietzscheanism with a concealed politics, that is, when we identify the political Nietzsche as the key to unlocking his thought, we discover how his thought furthers an *anti-politics*. This anti-politics functions in a peculiar relay system: it becomes an effect that is hardwired into the original design of its creator.

Thus, Nietzsche is political, but for his cadre of readers he advocates an anti-politics which has the function of reducing politics to a *countercultural* mode of revolt. This is an ingenious form of transposing the social antagonisms that are borne from class-based forces onto an entirely different scene that helps further the goal of enacting a justification for the preservation of the status quo. Nietzscheanism thus achieves an ideological function when it interacts with politics, whether that politics be revolutionary, reactionary, or centrist, precisely in its counterculture rerouting. Nietzsche's countercultural anti-politics has been one of the main draws to his philosophy on the left, stretching from the early twentieth century up to the present. Now, this is not to say that the left should abandon culture or even counterculture; it is rather to draw attention to the way that Nietzsche sought to politicize culture in particular ways that draw the left away from large-scale, class-based politics.

But with that said, Nietzscheanism is not reducible to one sort of politics, whether that be fascist, liberal, or socialist. Rather, Nietzscheanism lives *within* the political spectrum, and when deployed, it functions to shut down egalitarian and emancipatory politics. When Nietzsche's ideas attach their tentacles to a political community or an ideology, they produce their desired effect. It is important to note here that there have been several works that have tracked Nietzsche's influence on the far right and back to the emergence of European fascism.[26] In this book, we are more interested in the ways that Nietzsche functions when he is brought into the left, especially the radical and Marxist left.

We propose to read Nietzsche as one of the most important antagonists of the modern emancipatory political movements that were opened by the French Revolution. Such an engagement with Nietzsche reopens the very prospect of history and revolution in our time. It is only by renewing the Marxist and socialist perspective on Nietzsche, which has been alive and pertinent since Nietzsche himself was still living and just becoming known as an intellectual, that we can unlock his cryptic, esoteric, and proleptic style and see how it functions to divert collective revolutionary energy on the left. In his later work *Thus Spoke Zarathustra*, Nietzsche wrote, "You must be proud of your enemies; then, the successes of your enemies are also your successes."[27] Nietzsche invites his readers to come to see him as an enemy. It is likely the case that Nietzsche might very well have admired the effort of this book, precisely in that it aims to recenter him as an enemy to the very causes he so truly despised.

This book is written from the perspective of a socialist thinker who is interested in bringing philosophy to the class struggle in our time; it is not written with purely academic concerns regarding Nietzsche in mind. For example, entire books have been written about Nietzsche's views on music, or Nietzsche's views on gender, or Nietzsche's middle period, and so forth. Our objective is to capture something about Nietzsche's thought at its very core and to show how his thought has had such a massive cultural and political influence, especially on the left. We do not rely on only one translation of Nietzsche into English, but rather reference several translations of his work and assess the merits of some translations over others.[28]

Our aim is to read Nietzsche as a symptom of modern politics, which requires, as does any symptom, a full and comprehensive analysis and diagnosis. We will incorporate biographical, theoretical, historical, and comparative analysis. By bringing these methods to bear, my aim is to shed new light on the "Nietzsche symptom" so that we can begin to understand why he moves us so deeply. Why are we drawn to an aristocratic, aesthetic concept after all? Is Nietzsche right about equality? Must society be based on rank order? If yes, then what sort of rank is tolerable or acceptable from a socialist perspective? Are Nietzsche's community-building objectives at all compatible with a Marxist analysis?

It is one thing to reject the reactionary claims of Nietzsche because they don't sound right in an abstract appeal to a moral worldview, or because they promote an anti-democratic or elitist view of the world. But it is another thing to reject Nietzsche by exposing his reactionary intentions which aim to neutralize and pacify the class struggle, that is, to see Nietzsche as a particular antagonist to socialism and the class struggle. The latter point touches more directly on the objectives of the left than does the former, which is more vaguely liberal.

As Geoff Waite once commented, "Nietzscheanism aims to eradicate one specific form of consciousness in capitalist society, namely proletarian consciousness."[29] But at the same time, it is not enough to say that, simply because one has accepted the Marxist and socialist worldview and approach to philosophy and analysis of capitalism, one can by extension reject Nietzsche. His influence has grown too far, he has burrowed too deeply into the left. But before we burrow into Nietzsche as parasites, we must learn how his thought functions and how it has distorted and perverted Marxist, socialist, and left-wing agendas.

CHAPTER TWO
Understanding Nietzsche's Style

It was Nietzsche's style of writing that first drew me in as a young reader. Although I understood very little, I wanted to be among the ranks of his readers that might eventually grasp it all, even the mysterious and more esoteric parts. Perhaps the most remarkable aspect of Nietzsche's style is that he combines a fervent drive to convert the reader to his system of thought with an obscuring of his true intention or point of view. For a young person, the experience of not fully understanding a philosophy text is of course a very common experience. Reading difficult philosophy is a bit like diving into the deep end when learning to swim — how else will you learn? Nietzsche's difficulty is different than that of other philosophers, however, because he makes clear that a fuller understanding of what he is saying will not be for everyone:

> One does not only wish to be understood when one writes, one wishes just as surely not to be understood... All the nobler spirits and tastes select their audience when they wish to communicate; and choosing that, one at the same time erects barriers against "the others." All the more subtle laws of style have their origin at this point.[1]

The Pathos of Distance: A Community-Building Concept

Nietzsche's style is best grasped by understanding how it connects with what we will call his community-building project, that is, with the ways that Nietzsche seeks to split his reader off from the rest of society and point them toward a new form of becoming. At the core of this community-building effort is the important concept of the "pathos of distance," which concerns a Manichean gap that divides humanity between the noble and the plebeian. If Nietzsche, as he tells us, only "writes only for those whose lives have turned out well," what this means is that he proleptically calls forth a division between winners and losers, and this starts with you, the reader.

The pathos of distance, in practice, supports the wider goal of his project, which is the enactment of a social order ripe for higher cultural production where social distinctions across classes are made more resolute. Nietzsche writes, "The rift between people, between classes, the myriad number of types, the will to be yourself, to stand out, what I call the pathos of distance, is characteristic of every strong age."[2] The pathos of distance was thus waning in Nietzsche's time, because his was an era which experienced worker agitations from below and other democratic movements for greater equality and "leveling."

But it is important to note, and we will explore this in the next chapter, that Nietzsche's time was not *always* marked by political movements from below that threatened the social order and the ruling class. Much like our own time, the Second Reich in Germany under Bismarck's Bonapartist rule, during which Nietzsche lived and wrote, experienced long periods of political pacification of the working class. The introduction of austerity discipline over workers and anti-socialist policies suppressed the egalitarian movements. These changes in the class struggle and oscillations in the crisis of capitalism during Nietzsche's time led him to respond to the politics of mass movements and socialism with an adaptive political strategy. Nietzsche faced capitalist politics head on, and the class struggle forced him to constantly recalibrate his concepts toward defeating and overcoming mass movements.

The pathos of distance is central to understanding Nietzsche's style because it concerns the way that his philosophy creates a new community capable of legislating and inventing new values. Importantly, this *must* be done at a distance from modernity and its conditions of massification. The socialist demands for equality and democratic expansions taking place across Europe following the 1848 worker uprising, which occurred when Nietzsche was just a young boy, brought about a political climate in which the working class became an unruly presence in European political life. The workers' movement was a scandal in Nietzsche's eyes, one that had to be rectified in a comprehensive fashion.

We can think of the workers' movement as letting an egalitarian genie out of the bottle that threatened to spread throughout Europe and the world. Unleashed by the most left-wing element of the French Revolution, the Jacobins, this set of leveling forces had to be put back in the bottle, for these impulses of massification threatened the very preservation of higher philosophy, art, and indeed, higher living. The masses were not to be included in the community of the *Übermensch*, and this necessary, exclusionary logic is encapsulated in the pathos of distance. Importantly, the pathos of distance maintains a commitment to preserving the aristocratic *type* of human being, a type that was steadily dissipating due to massification and working-class movements.

Where does aristocratic nobility emerge from in Nietzsche's view? And what, for Nietzsche, determines nobility? This opens up a debate between what Nietzsche argues regarding nobility and what later Nietzscheans have adapted and *interpreted* into the type of the noble. For Nietzsche, it is nobility by blood lineage that explains the true origin of the very category of the noble. As he says in 1888:

> One becomes a respectable [*anständig*] human being because one is a respectable human being, i.e., because one is born a capitalist of good instincts and prosperous conditions [*Capitalist guter Instinkte und gedeihlicher Verhältnisse*]… If one comes poor into the world, of parents that have squandered everything and saved nothing, then one is "incorrigible," ripe for the penitentiary or the madhouse.[3]

Nietzsche formulates his vision of the pathos of distance and the creation of a new nobility based on this more fundamental affirmation of the nobility of blood. It was specifically the nobility of the ancien régime that he saw as undergoing a decline in its power and influence, and it was this class and its relationship to the capitalist class that had to be rethought and preserved. We will explore the various ways that Nietzschean interpreters revise what constitutes the noble and the aristocratic, but what is clear is that Nietzscheans on both the left and the right tend to retain the importance of Nietzsche's distinction between the noble and the mob, or the noble and the masses, but they abstract this crucial, more explicitly aristocratic distinction from what Nietzsche thought about aristocratic distinction.

The pathos of distance is to be understood as a political praxis that is bound up with Nietzsche's goal to create a new nobility which would be capable of preserving rank order, distinction, and "nobility of the spirit." The pathos of distance is thought as a necessary physical distance — and distance here is thought physically, as well as morally and intellectually — the noble individual must differentiate themselves from what is lower, weaker, and of the mob. Thus, Nietzsche's figures of political praxis, the free spirits and the *Übermensch*, were different names for the rare and exceptional individuals he called forth. At the very heart of Nietzsche's style is an invitation to enter this community of readers, to enter into the "innocence of becoming," to take up opposition to the herd mentality of the working masses. When Nietzsche asks us to divide ourselves from the mob or the masses, he is not necessarily thinking of this distinction between noble and mob in an archaic register rooted in ancient pre-civilization. To the contrary, as we will explore in more detail in the next chapter, we should read Nietzsche's theory of community, and the style he used to seduce us into it, as an effort to differentiate us from the working class and its mob, inducing affects of pity and weakness. As we've mentioned, Nietzsche wrote during Bismarck's Bonapartist regime during the Second Reich period in Germany — he did not write from the perch of an ahistorical position.

To enter the new community, the reader must learn to practice a distancing and separation from the herd mentality. In an unpublished fragment from the spring of 1885, Nietzsche writes that "the most powerful human beings feel themselves to be evil," to be "harmful and forbidden," but the contemporary social order suppresses the noble individual's capacity to "exert evil and harm on the world." He continues:

"Goal: the sanctification of the most powerful terrible and best-discredited forces, or to say it old-fashionedly: the deification of the devil."[4] The pathos of distance necessitated a radical reversal of values from the decadent and nihilistic forces in the culture, and the primary movement he encourages is to move away from the pity of the masses. The very word "pathos" refers to the affect of pity, or feelings of sadness, and Nietzsche defines the problem of pity in *Beyond Good and Evil* in the following way:

> What is pity? It is this tolerance for states of life close to zero. Pity is the love of life, but of the weak, sick, reactive life. It is militant and announces the final victory of the poor, the suffering, the powerless and the small. It is divine and gives them this victory.[5]

What's more, the affect of pity is so central in Nietzsche's view that his infamous declaration "God is dead" can only be fully appreciated with reference to the way that pity plays into this world historical act. In *Zarathustra*, Nietzsche writes, "God one day suffocated through his excessive pity,"[6] and "The reactive man puts god to death."[7] Pity is the primary affect of the mob and thus it is the affect of pity that is placed at the core of any reversal of values.

Although Nietzsche locates the affect of envy as the primary driver of *ressentiment*, pity is the affect that is most indicative of the mob and the plebeian class, and Nietzsche goes so far as to associate pity with the dirt and uncleanliness of the lower class. "What separates two people most profoundly is a different sense and degree of cleanliness."[8] Nietzsche's sense of pity is understood on a class basis — the lower classes are not only mired in *ressentiment*, of which the primary affect is envy, they are also mired in pity. But Nietzsche takes this further and argues — through the pathos of distance — that our culture must insist on distinctions that are physical and spatial upon which we can separate people. As he once pointed out in a note on Napoleon, "What does a jumpy and sweaty plebeian like Michelet have to do with Napoleon! It makes no difference whether he hates him or loves him: because he sweats, he does not belong in his vicinity."[9]

The pathos of distance is important because it is only at a distance from the affect of pity that a new form of suffering can be enacted, that a new form of artistic suffering that will not fall into the weak and resentful suffering of the mob might be realized by the new community. Nietzsche encourages his readership to find "all kinds of disguises necessary to protect itself against contact with obtrusive and *pitying* hands and altogether against everything that is not its equal in suffering."[10] The pity of the mob indicates a qualitatively different form of suffering to that of the noble, and this is why "profound suffering makes noble; it *separates*."[11] The pathos of distance is thus bound up with the question of suffering and the centrality of theodicy in Nietzsche's thought, a topic we explore as we turn to Nietzsche's comprehensive critique of Christianity and socialism in the next chapter. Nietzsche aimed to invent a new sort of thinker who can preserve a level of cultural elitism, the model for which he finds in aristocratic blood inheritance. But as Nietzsche matured, the pathos of distance was to be hardwired into the very ethics of the readers and followers he sought to bring about.

But is Nietzsche's call for a new community, what in *Thus Spoke Zarathustra* is referred to as the call for a "new nobility," an explicitly political one? Are the philosophers of the future and the *Übermensch* to be understood in political terms? In his lectures on *Thus Spoke Zarathustra*, the philosopher Leo Strauss argues that Nietzsche's call for a new community is meant to function as a rival community to suppress the movement of leveling and egalitarianism. Consider this fragment from Nietzsche's *Nachlass*:

> The one movement is unconditional: the leveling of humanity, structures of ants… the other movement: my movement: is on the contrary the sharpening of all opposition[s]… removal of equality, the creation of super powerful men. The other movement creates the last man; my movement creates the superman. It is altogether not the goal to regard the superman as the masters of the last men: but: two kinds should coexist, side by side — separated as much as possible; the ones, like the Epicurean gods, not caring for the others.[12]

That the supermen are not to be the "masters of the last men" but should live side by side and be "separated as much as possible" is a crucial distinction. For Strauss, what this indicates is that there is an ambiguity that Nietzsche leaves to his readers which can lead them to associate his community with either the right or of the left. In fact, Strauss goes so far as to argue that Nietzsche's politics, and indeed the very meaning of nobility, are left in question.

Although Strauss begins his lecture series on *Zarathustra* with a clear sense that Nietzsche has never been for the left, pointing to the profound irony that the left has been attracted to Nietzsche's teachings, he now pauses to recognize an important feature of Nietzsche's community-building strategy: the pathos of distance is to be enacted across any social or political situation. In this way, the pathos of distance has a function to divide and separate based on the more abstract categories of "nobility" and the "strong" in distinction to the "mob" and the "weak." The determination of who is of the mob and who is noble is left to the Nietzschean community to enact, to decide.

Prolepsis as a Device of Community-Building

What makes Nietzsche's call to his readers so seductive? What makes us want to heed his call to participate in the community of new nobility? Nietzsche puts his readers to work to set out to establish and to enact his vision, a vision in which, as Strauss points out, the political dimension is left open and esoteric enough to appeal to both the right and to the left. To get on the inside of how Nietzsche calls forth a community, we must examine the writing style known as prolepsis, a primary device he wields. Prolepsis is a form of writing addressed in the future tense, to what will be or to what will become. Prolepsis is the key stylistic device Nietzsche uses to shroud his aristocratic agenda and to invent as well as to invite a new community of readers to participate.

One of the reasons Nietzsche adopts the proleptic style is so that his more overt political intentions can be perceived as *decentered*. As a reader, a proleptic statement has the effect of disrupting the very temporality at play. Through prolepsis, Nietzsche make us feel as if he is speaking to us in our present. For example, in *Zarathustra*, he writes, "But thou, profound one, thou sufferest too profoundly even from small wounds" — and he then juxtaposes you, the reader, to your supposed enemy, the plebeian weaker ones whose "narrow souls think: All great existence is guilty."[13] In this passage, we see Nietzsche's sophisticated form of prolepsis, inventing and inviting the reader in, and then proceeding to place them into his Manichean vision of the world, a world that is divided between the weak and the strong, between winners and losers.

The proleptic style explains why, as a young reader of Nietzsche myself, I did not immediately sense that his voice was of the nineteenth century. Writing in the form of prolepsis can make one come off as untimely, as from another world. And as a stylist, Nietzsche is no doubt a master of uncanny timelessness. Through the proleptic style, Nietzscheanism is made transhistorical, into a philosophy that is "neither historical, nor eternal, but existing across space and time 'nomadically.'"[14] As Strauss indicates, in Nietzsche's call for a new nobility the political agenda by which the new nobility is called forth is itself shrouded and indeterminate. Even though there is a conservative romanticism at play in this idea of nobility, a nostalgia for the ancien régime and an embrace of nobility by blood, the condition of the class struggle had taken any blissful return to such a social order off the table. It would be up to Nietzsche's readers to retain the pathos of distance, to enact it on their own. This is the heart of the political community that Nietzsche aims to invent and call forth.

This means that what Nietzsche's style performs, what its function is about, is the creation of Nietzscheanism, which we will define as a common adherence to the Nietzschean project. Nietzscheanism is an invitation to the reader to continue the suppression of the class struggle and to further the eradication of plebeian and proletarian consciousness. Nietzscheanism is reproduced by the community of readers who both imbue Nietzsche's mission and do so in ways that are unacknowledged. Geoff Waite once remarked that Nietzsche's community is built "under the cover of the production of apparently maximum difference of opinion; it works on a largely unacknowledged consensus."[15] Nietzscheanism is the adoption of a perspective on the world that implicates the follower in the eternal class struggle *between the masses and the elite* and encourages them to defuse the very basis of this struggle.

How does this self-referential and proleptic style function within his philosophy proper? That is, how does Nietzsche's philosophical method link up with his political and community-building objective? The philosopher Alenka Zupančič argues that Nietzsche makes philosophy into a self-referential web such that

> philosophical truths are inextricably bound up with declarations that are 'precipitated statements.' Nietzsche's mode of address aims to create the conditions of their own enunciation, the conditions of the very 'real that they declare.' We see this in Nietzsche's very reflections on being and becoming... it is not recognizing oneself in the other thing but 'becoming it'... yet for Nietzsche, 'there is no true becoming.'[16]

Nietzsche's proleptic style is at the heart of what Zupančič calls the "philosophy of the two" — a strategy whereby Nietzsche makes philosophy illocutionary unto itself; that is, Nietzsche makes philosophy into a self-referential web. This web works on the premise that philosophical truths are inextricably bound up with declarations which are "precipitated statements" or claims that create the conditions of their own enunciation, and with them the "conditions of the very real that they declare."[17] This web functions in a proleptic style, that is, as a mode of address to a thing that does yet exist. This is the heart of the paradox and allure of Nietzschean prolepsis: it is in *not* recognizing oneself in the other thing, but in *becoming* it. "To break a promise is to become the thing one declares"; "Be careful fighting monsters that you don't become the thing you fight": these are examples of Nietzsche's style of prolepsis.

Zupančič's reading of Nietzsche's philosophy is influenced by the year-long seminar that Alain Badiou dedicated to Nietzsche's "anti-philosophy" in 1992–93.[18] In Badiou's vision of philosophy, ever since its very inception with Socrates, philosophers have been haunted by a great antagonist in the form of what he names the "anti-philosopher." The anti-philosopher practices a form of sophistry whereby they tend to deny the universal dimension of the Platonic forms by relativizing truth to a pragmatic scenario in which whoever can best convince those around them through their rhetoric and language that they have the truth effectively does possess the truth. The anti-philosopher is a great pest to the philosopher, shutting down the philosopher's obsession with eternity, the absolute, and the Platonic realm of forms.

Nietzsche is a sophisticated and complex anti-philosopher in Badiou's reading. For Badiou, Nietzsche's philosophy can be understood from the following claim: to evaluate any historically existing statement, you can only do so by identifying the kind of power that is exempted from the statement. Moreover, any statement can only be evaluated from the power of the perspective of the one who uttered it. Nietzsche's philosophical method is thus based on the premise that "there are only relations of power!" Importantly, this means that there is no protocol for an intrinsic evaluation of statements whatsoever; that is, any evaluation of a statement implies the identification of the type of statement that supports it, and therefore of the kind of uttering power engaged with therein.

DANIEL TUTT

A statement is always the summarizing of an investment of power, and the type of investment of power in any truth claim in question can be evaluated based on the statement. Anti-philosophy in a Nietzschean mode is thus understood through perspectivism and the "will to power."

Philosophers from Plato to Kant posit an entity and a subject behind being, and there is thus a *meaning* in philosophical claims on being. The anti-philosopher responds with a profound skepticism or rejection of such a proposal. Nietzsche the anti-philosopher declares that the "there is" of being is always fictional and unprovable, and he takes this even further, arguing that any statement on meaning itself is bound up with an illusion. For Nietzsche, there is no value in being, just as there is no meaning in meaning, and thus what philosophy is about is affirming a principle that is outside of this eternal return. In essence, the eternal return is an affirmation of the static basis of the world itself, a declaration that must be made by the philosopher who has realized becoming does not become. What is affirmed beyond this horizon of the eternal return Nietzsche called the principle of "life," and *amor fati* is the highest affirmation of this principle that the world is subject to the eternal return. The subject is thus an outcome of this performance, an outcome of what Badiou calls Nietzsche's "arch-political act" of the affirmation of the eternal return. Importantly, Badiou recognizes that Nietzsche's anti-philosophy is *political* because it is bent on the political subjectivity of the Superman or the *Übermensch*, which is the outcome of this process of affirmation. Badiou recognizes a hyper-individualism that is reproduced in this process of Nietzschean anti-philosophy. Nietzsche famously declares that he is "not a man, he is dynamite," and by this he breaks the history of philosophy in two.

Nietzsche may be the most important anti-philosopher of all time, according to Badiou. In Badiou's reading, Nietzsche makes an event out of his very name — when Nietzsche says "I am all of the names of history," this means that he has transformed philosophy into an anti-philosophical wager of a subjective performance. The anti-philosopher is also defined by their subjectivism, which means that they place the philosopher's own subjective capacity to realize the truth as the main vehicle of philosophical speculation. Concepts such as Pascal's wager and Kierkegaard's leap of faith are subjectivist affirmations of truth. But unlike Pascal and Kierkegaard, Badiou reads Nietzsche's subjectivist philosophy as what he calls an arch-political event; that is, Badiou reads Nietzsche's proleptic style as producing a politics that is bound up with and inseparable from his metaphysics.

Thus far, we have argued that Nietzsche's style produces Nietzscheanism, a participation in a political movement which is not clearly situated on either of the traditional political poles, but which furthers an aristocratic agenda bent on eradicating the universal and egalitarian basis of mass movements. Nietzsche has politics at his core, but a politics which is open for interpretation by his readers, and the reader is enlisted to join a movement for the suppression of the weak and the eradication of egalitarianism. For this movement to take place, Nietzsche's politics must be interpreted as having no *core* agenda. This is the key way to understand Nietzsche's esotericism, as a tacit suppression of the overt political agenda at work in his thought.

It is important to keep in mind that there are also conceptual and metaphysical commitments that decenter politics in his thought. For example, the priority Nietzsche grants to the drives and emotion over intellect and reason produces a decentered sense of the human subject. Nietzsche's perspectivism is premised on a radical overturning of all the "atavistic" residues in philosophical thought, and he performs an all-out assault on Cartesian rationalism and Hegelian dialectics. The proleptic style aims to cultivate and convert the "well turned-out person" into a subject who does not believe in guilt or in bad luck and who will be capable of exerting cruelty toward the weak.[19]

Nietzsche's philosophical and metaphysical enemies — including Hegel, Kant, and Rousseau — were associated with a tradition of rationalism that was deemed suspect because it suppressed an essential truth — in Nietzsche's eyes, that we are *not* masters of the thoughts that arise in us. This insight is a significant precursor to Freud's notion of the unconscious, and Nietzsche provides ample overlap with what would become psychoanalytic drive theory following Freud's groundbreaking work *Beyond the Pleasure Principle*, published in 1920. In Losurdo's treatment of Nietzsche, we are alerted to the often overlooked political agenda that undergirded Nietzsche's decentered idea of the subject of the drives. For Nietzsche, intelligence and the drives are *reactions* in which old physiological dispositions are transmitted. The dissolution of the rationalist Cartesian subject that Nietzsche aimed to usher in allowed for heredity to re-emerge as a determining basis of subjective difference.

To the extent that there is a unifying interpretation of Nietzsche among his followers, it would be that there is no unifying theme in his thought. Nietzsche has no center, according to his closest acolytes. As Steven Aschheim observes, Nietzscheanism was built off Nietzsche's intentionally obscurantist style: "Nietzsche was hopelessly ambiguous, lacked a coherent philosophy, and was subject to divergent interpretations. The makers of this legend — important Nietzscheans such as Elisabeth Forster-Nietzsche, Stefan George and his circle, Ernst Bertram, and Karl Jaspers."[20] It is not that Nietzsche lied about his political intentions to his readers, it is rather that his agenda is bound up with an esoteric strategy that conceals his motives and calls the very question of his agenda — or any agenda — into question. It is thus crucial that we understand the ways that Nietzscheanism, as an esoteric and proleptic style, is read differently on the left and the right.

The right tends to understand Nietzsche's political agenda far better and more honestly than the left does. Although Strauss acknowledges Nietzsche's political ambiguity, he also makes an important qualification:

> There is some relation between Nietzsche and fascism, whereas there is *no relation* between Nietzsche and communism and hardly a relation between Nietzsche and democracy. To that extent, the crude statement that Nietzsche is the father of fascism contains an element of truth.[21]

The right tends to read Nietzsche exoterically, that is, they read him as he intended. The right is not duped by the political agenda at work; they tend to be content to put that agenda *to* work. The left, however, reads Nietzsche esoterically, that is, they either disregard his reactionary political intentions or they build a philosophy from the foundations of Nietzsche's irrational thought that *thinks* it has gone far astray from his radical aristocratic agenda but remains tethered to it. We will now turn to an example of the former in the case of the French philosopher Jacques Derrida.

Derrida and the Limits of Psychobiography

There is no better example of a left-wing reader of Nietzsche who reads him as utterly devoid of any political core or agenda than Jacques Derrida. Derrida took his cue from Heidegger when it came to reading Nietzsche's style — as he notes, "[I] had already foregrounded the idea that reading for definite meaning in Nietzsche was a nonstarter."[22] While Derrida wrote on Nietzsche widely, including a trilogy of works specifically dedicated to the question of Nietzsche's style, we will consider a seminar which was later turned into a book on the topic of Nietzsche and biography entitled *Otobiographies*. This text offers a psychoanalytic reading of Nietzsche's autobiography, *Ecce Homo*, combined with commentary on an early, highly political text called *On the Future of Our Educational Institutions*, which is based on a series of lectures Nietzsche delivered from 1872 to 1874. We have chosen to focus on this text by Derrida because it exemplifies the tacit avoidance and denial of Nietzsche's political agenda in Derrida's wider assessment of the philosopher.

While Derrida recognizes the darker and even esoteric basis of Nietzsche's thought — what we have named Nietzsche's Janus face — he refuses to unearth what this esoteric side of Nietzsche might imply. Derrida subtitles his work "The Teaching of Nietzsche and the Politics of the Proper Name," and he stresses that Nietzsche's teaching concerns themes of identity. But Derrida does not situate Nietzsche's politics in the context in which Nietzsche wrote; for example, the lectures on education were given immediately following the Paris Commune of 1871, an event that — as we will learn in the next chapter — fundamentally shaped Nietzsche's political and philosophical outlook. In considering Nietzsche's autobiography, Derrida interprets Nietzsche's "wanderings in forbidden realms" as having "taught him to consider the causes of idealization and moralization in an entirely different light."

According to Derrida, Nietzsche is important to philosophers because he has seen the dawning of a "hidden history" and located a "psychology of their great names."[23] Nietzsche's autobiography was written at the "noontide" of his life when he turned forty-five years old. To give an idea of the precise "esoteric" dimension of *Ecce Homo*, consider this passage, which Derrida also quotes in his text:

> I have a subtler sense of smell for the signs of ascent and decline [literally of rising and setting, as one says of the sun: *für die Zeichen von Aufgang und Niedergang*: of that which climbs and declines, of the high and the low] than any other human being before. I am the master par excellence for this — I know both. I am both [*ich kenne beides, ich bin beides*].[24]

From a historical-materialist perspective, the most plausible interpretation of this passage is to understand it in relation to Nietzsche's wider critique of decadence and of the herd mentality overtaking Europe during his time. However, Derrida interprets the "high" and the "low" to refer to Nietzsche's relation to the masculine and the feminine, to his father and mother, and to life and death. Nietzsche is thus extracted from the very political context in which he wrote and is brought into a more eternal and timeless philosophical register. Once in this decontextualized space of philosophical speculation, Nietzsche then becomes a great teacher of what Derrida calls the "politics of the proper name."

Derrida takes the category of decadence, to which the passage cited above alludes, to refer to Nietzsche's depression after he left his teaching post at the relatively young age of thirty-six. Derrida completely *depoliticizes* and personalizes Nietzsche's notion of decadence, a move that conceals Nietzsche's politics entirely and converts the concept of decadence into one stemming from mental illness, not social and political forces. We will explore the more historical-materialist basis of decadence for Nietzsche in the following chapters.

Derrida works with a "psychobiographical" reading of Nietzsche, which the intellectual historian Élisabeth Roudinesco defines as a method of analysis that "restricts itself to the study of the classics and treats writers' lives as though they were case histories, making writing the expression of a neurosis or mental illness."[25] Derrida suggests that Nietzsche finally knew and experienced what decadence is — primarily referring to the decadence of Socrates, the philosopher with whom Nietzsche locates the origin of plebeian values in philosophy — during his depressive illness that started after he retreated from teaching. For Derrida, Nietzsche is a superior philosopher because of what he has endured and overcome in his personal mental depressions of the highs and the lows of his life. Nietzsche created a life philosophy from the vagaries of this position "beyond life."

Derrida refuses the political core of Nietzsche, and this is evident when he remarks, "One may wonder why the only teaching institution or the only beginning of a teaching institution that ever succeeded in taking as its model the teaching of Nietzsche on teaching will have been a Nazi one."[26] But Derrida does not pursue this crucial question any further. The lectures that make up *On the Future of Our Educational Institutions* were delivered in Basel in 1872, and they were part of a far more ambitious effort to encourage Bismarck to fundamentally remold Germany's cultural institutions. Contra Derrida's comment that he never intended for these lectures to be published, Nietzsche says he wrote them for a public audience.

In fact, it was *The Birth of Tragedy* that was written in a more esoteric style and the lectures in *On the Future of Our Educational Institutions* that were meant to be exoteric,[27] the great esoteric moralist pivoting to the more exoteric aristocratic radical. The lectures should thus be considered as an explicit political manifesto that lays out in clear terms a political vision for education in Germany. In the lectures, Nietzsche brings out a full-scale critique of Germany's Second Reich, specifically of the rise of "social democracy," and calls for a new political party that would not be "servants of a mass, especially servants of a party."[28]

Derrida's refusal to acknowledge Nietzsche's actual political agenda leads him to read Nietzsche's call for "destruction of the secondary school" with zero attention to what such a call implies either for Nietzsche or anyone interested in applying such a demand. This then permits Derrida to uncritically take Nietzsche's advice to "destroy the text" instead of the school. Derrida further extends the speculation over what this destruction entails by returning to the theme of "degeneration" in Nietzsche. This denial of politics allows Derrida to sidestep the aristocratic agenda in Nietzsche; he claims that "degenerate is not a lesser vitality: it is a life principle hostile to life."[29] Derrida recognizes no political qualification to the "degenerate" as a social class, but only as a decontextualized principle of life. At one point in the lectures, Nietzsche says that a "*Führer*" is called for as the chief pedagogue holding the school together, Derrida turns to dissociate Nietzsche from Nazism. "Nietzsche died as always before his name and therefore it is not a question of knowing what he would have thought, wanted, or done."[30]

Where Derrida's analysis in *Otobiographies* becomes most original is in its psychobiographical and psychoanalytic analysis of Nietzsche. In this vein, Derrida points out that even the very name of Nietzsche's middle period work *The Wanderer and His Shadow* contains an Oedipal dynamic, a mommy-daddy-me structure. In *Ecce Homo*, Nietzsche says that his father lived a shadow of his life and Nietzsche wanders over the "womb of the world." Derrida points out that Nietzsche's analysis of language, of the "mother tongue," must be preserved and obeyed, and how the mother embodies the living to the dead father — the mother is the metaphoric site of Nietzsche's wandering, of life itself. While Derrida's psychobiography may help us to understand Nietzsche's defense of grammar school and disciplinary adherence to the German mother tongue, against the journalistic leveling of mass democratic education, his refusal to situate Nietzsche's lectures on education within any political or social, or even empirical context in which he delivered them leaves the reader wanting.

Derrida rightly draws attention to the absence of any place for women in Nietzsche's remarks on university education: "She gives rise to all the figures by losing herself in the background of the scene like an anonymous persona. Everything comes back to her, beginning with life; everything addresses and destines itself to her. She survives on the condition of remaining at the bottom."[31] But Derrida concludes his remarks in *Otobiographies* by citing the famous passage from *Ecce Homo* where Nietzsche writes:

I know my fate [*Ich kenne mein Loos*]. One day my name will be associated with the memory of something monstrous

[*Ungeheures*] — a crisis without equal on earth, the most profound collision of conscience [*Gewissens-Kollision*], a decision [*Entscheidung*] that was conjured up against everything that had been believed, demanded, hallowed so far. I am no man, I am dynamite.[32]

We now discover why Derrida places such a central emphasis on the proper name of F. Nietzsche, the name with which Nietzsche signs his autobiography. This signature is emblematic in Derrida's reading of the operation of distancing that Nietzsche enacts from his own proper name through the motif of the eternal return. This distancing from one's own name, from one's own Oedipal dynamics, and this wandering "beyond life," opens a liberatory horizon for any philosopher after Nietzsche. In his exchange with students over this lecture, Derrida received pushback for ignoring the empirical facts of Nietzsche's life in his discussion of *Ecce Homo*. Derrida argued that the proper name of Nietzsche and the empirical basis of Nietzsche's intentions are displaced and rendered indecipherable by the "internal border" that the motif of the eternal return evokes. "As soon as it crosses with the motif of the eternal return, then the individual signature, or, if you like, the signature of a proper name, is no longer simply an empirical fact grounded in something other than itself."[33]

There are merits to Derrida's psychobiography; it is creative and psychoanalytically interesting, but ultimately it is irresponsible in its refusal to properly situate the empirical facts of Nietzsche's agenda at the time of these explicitly political lectures. Derrida's interpretation purports to be about Nietzsche's politics, but nowhere is there a discussion of the ways that Nietzsche argued for German nationalism, declaring in the fifth lecture that the student movement, "after fighting for the 'freedom of the homeland,' once back at university, aimed to free the university also from the 'non-German barbarism, covered artificially under any form of erudition.'"[34] Derrida's refusal to extend his analysis of Nietzsche's early lectures on education to a broader historical context, beyond a psychobiography, results in a partial and ultimately apologetic reading of the political core of Nietzsche's thought. A wider historical contextualization of these lectures, one that pays attention to empirical concerns that drove the development of his early philosophy and worldview, is essential to understanding Nietzsche.

The lectures in *On the Future of Our Educational Institutions* were delivered at the same time that Nietzsche began to refine his genealogical method with *The Birth of Tragedy*. The political concerns that drove these texts were a projection of the crisis of Hellenic culture during the time of Socrates onto the great movements of democratic leveling and mass politics of Nietzsche's era, especially the socialist movements, which represented the "cancer of all high culture."[35] The tendency to project Hellenic culture onto the present social conditions of a philosopher's own time is common in German romantic thought and German idealism, but Nietzsche's projection took a more overt political concern. For Nietzsche, the crisis of classical Hellenism was made homologous with the post-French Revolutionary fallout in European culture and the rise of what Nietzsche called the "optimistic worldview."

In this sense, there is a political double for Nietzsche, beyond the psychoanalytic, Oedipal mother-father dyad that Derrida draws attention to, that is more productively seen as marked by the double that defined the arena of political battle for Nietzsche. This split or double political worldview for the early Nietzsche, facing the immediate aftermath of the Paris Commune, was a struggle between the tragic and the optimistic worldview marked by Socratic culture and socialism with "its optimism, its belief in the originary goodness of the human being (virtue can be taught to anybody and everyone can learn it), with its faithful expectation of a happy world."[36] The movements of the working masses were too optimistic; they promised a world where selfishness would be removed. The socialists called for a world without misery, and this flew in the face of Nietzsche's vision of the tragic worldview, which formed the early basis of his idea of political community.

Derrida's ahistorical reading of Nietzsche's theory of education begs for a deeper analysis of the historical, the social, and the political basis of Nietzsche's thought. We now turn to such an analysis to understand Nietzsche's important concept of perspectivism.

CHAPTER THREE
The Political Context of Perspectivism

How do we understand perspectivism, the concept that might be Nietzsche's most important and which makes him the godfather of postmodernism? Perspectivism is rarely, if ever, understood as a concept that was invented as a response to political concerns and dynamics in Nietzsche's time. In its most general sense, perspectivism refers to the idea that truth claims are fundamentally bound up with one's own perspective. At the heart of perspectivism is a rejection of the Enlightenment subject as an agent eligible for universal rights, which represents a view on subjectivity that stresses the rational basis of the subject as a universal citizen. The French Revolution brought this political subject onto the political stage, however the promises of full democratic representation that undergird this vision would not be fully realizable. In other words, the bourgeoisie undermines any commitment it has to universalism — to the extent they even express support for it — due to its embracing of capitalism.

The philosopher Howard Caygill has argued that Nietzsche's thought must be understood in the broader context of a critique of "the Kantian autonomous, legislative subject of modernity," a subject that would "give itself its own laws, the subject for whom the claims of traditional values have been stripped of their legitimacy by the 'critical tribunal,' who is free but nevertheless subjected, one who is dissatisfied and locked into oppressive and exploitative relations of its own making."[1] Caygill's analysis of what drives Nietzsche's thought is important for our framing of the doctrine of perspectivism, as he shows that this concept has more to do with Nietzsche's theory of the subject — a political and social basis of the individual — than it does with a theory of knowledge or epistemology. But we will argue that Nietzsche's perspectivism must be read in the political context in which he was engaged in order to fully understand why it has been and still is adopted and championed.

What Caygill does not emphasize in Nietzsche's wider idea of the subject, however, is the way that he sought to enact an annihilation of the universal form of the subject: "The task is not 'who is man,' but who overcomes man,"[2] as Nietzsche writes. The *Übermensch* has nothing in common, at the level of perspective, with "the species being of the dialecticians," as Deleuze puts it in his study of Nietzsche. For the philosopher Gilles Deleuze, Nietzsche's perspectivism is a break that sidesteps every iteration or tradition from which a universal basis of the subject has emerged, including Christianity, socialism, humanism, egoism, nihilism, and all theories of history reliant on the dialectic itself.[3] Perspectivism is adopted by Deleuze in his own philosophy, and it's essential to any understanding of the theory of "schizoanalysis" that he and Felix Guattari developed. Perspectivism opens the way for a new way of thinking, feeling, evaluating, and legislating values. French Nietzscheans, such as Deleuze in his experimental text *Logic of Sense*, take up this idea of the destructive Nietzschean subject rooted in a radical notion of perspectivism toward very creative ends, proposing an "ethics of living up to one's wound," or an ethics premised on the erasure of one's proper name. Nietzsche provides the tools for thinking the subject as radically singular, split apart, and set adrift from representation entirely.

But what is the historical context for Nietzsche that made him interested in a theory of the subject based on annihilation and splitting? As a doctrine, perspectivism is known as a theory that posits the importance of subjective interpretation over objective reality as the criterion or basis of truth. Without getting into an exhaustive comparison and analysis of how academic philosophers have interpreted the concept of perspectivism, we can note two general orientations. The first is that analytic philosophers tend to analyze the concept as primarily an epistemological discovery, and they read Nietzsche's philosophical treatment of perspectivism in relation to neo-Kantian theories of cognition, and continental philosophers tend to read the concept as a genealogical and moral theory of affects.[4] But neither of these orientations approach the concept through the *political* context in which Nietzsche wrote, and they fail to see how the concept is best understood as a form of political epistemology.

Our argument is as follows: Nietzschean perspectivism was an attempt to tame and limit the masses' demands that the promises of the French Revolution be fulfilled. After all, what is the epistemological basis — the *truth* — of the people's or the collective's demands for full equality, liberty, and fraternity? Perspectivism was developed as a political epistemology in reaction to the egalitarian demands that emerged out of the French Revolution and which were accelerating in Nietzsche's time, from the worker uprisings of 1848 to the Paris Commune of 1871. Nietzsche developed perspectivism in the maelstrom of these political upheavals, and these events shaped its direction.

To understand what political epistemology is, let us consider the three popular demands that emerged out of the French Revolution: fraternity, liberty, and equality. These demands form three buckets of political representation, guiding values over three domains of social and political life: "fraternity" refers to the question of solidarity and communal and national belonging; "liberty" refers to the individual demands for freedom, which in a bourgeois social order are relegated to the sphere of the market; and "equality" refers to the sphere of the state and its commitments to egalitarian distribution of wealth and resources.

The revolutionary tradition views these popular demands as *unmet*, and therefore as *real* dimensions of political truth. In other words, there is a collective subject within capitalist social life which pushes the unmet demands of the French Revolution, what Marx named the "proletariat," or the excluded, alienated working masses. In this way, the proletariat is the universal class assemblage that represents the truth of these domains of social life due to their experience in relation to the truth of the unmet, *real* dimension of these universal promises. The proletariat is not merely the empirical working class, but is thought of by Marx and Engels in *The Communist Manifesto* as a social relation, not merely a static class position — they use the term "ensemble" to describe the proletariat. An ensemble involves a multiplicity of voices and positions that must seek to create a harmony together. In the practical overcoming of the system of politics that blocks and prevents the unmet universal dimension of political life, the struggle of the proletariat must be read as provoking this real dimension in political life.

We have to relate the concept of a "real dimension of political life" to a debate within the field of political philosophy that concerned Nietzsche in his time, namely the realist/nominalist debate. The terms of this split are significant, and they continue to shape our understanding of political thought in the present. This realist/nominalist debate splits the liberal and socialist or communist perspectives on political truths: the liberal position insists that the universal ideals of the French Revolution must reach certain limits in capitalist society, and most specifically those limits revolve around the persistence of the unjust system of wage labor and the labor market. A nominalist relation to the universal demands established in the Revolution faces the contradictions of bourgeois society that prevent the extension of universal demands in the market sphere, specifically that the wage-labor system cannot be transcended. This is at the heart of why liberals must adopt a nominalist orientation to political truths, because they face inherent limits in what they are able to advocate based on the fact they have accepted capitalist market relations as the guiding force of social and political life. We can understand the socialist position as orienting political struggle toward a fuller, actual fulfillment of the unmet universal demands established in the Revolution. In this way, the socialist position can be thought as a realist conception of political epistemology, one in which politics is about arriving at a universal basis of truth without insisting on distortions or nominalist compromises.

Capitalism is built upon wage slavery, and this poses a stumbling block to the full equality of all citizens. The proletarian position is not to be understood as that of one inert class that poses a realist demand to the liberal bourgeois order which the bourgeoisie and the ruling class cannot fulfill. It is rather that the proletariat — in its ensemble of contradictory class relations, not positions — poses a threat to the liberal nominalist commitment to covering over the brutalities borne of capitalist wage slavery and the class conflict it foments. For example, the persistence of wage slavery also produces a *lumpenproletariat* that is barred from the promises of wage labor entirely. It produces a petit-bourgeois class which is in between a more leisurely and working-class experience, and which also relies on surplus labor from imperial wars. Our argument is that in the face of these contradictions stoked by capitalist class conflict, bourgeois intellectuals nominalize the social antagonisms that compose these contradictory social relations and conflicts. This nominalizing of social antagonisms should be understood as a built-in blind spot of the liberal bourgeois position that is driven not by one's static class position, but by one's engaged and practical standpoint in the class struggle. It is in the following way that Nietzsche must be read as a liberal-adjacent thinker; precisely in that his thought is meant to support the bourgeois standpoint, but by radicalizing it.

Before we get a clearer sense of how Nietzsche's politics supports these tendencies of nominalism, we must broaden our reading of political epistemology. In studying the French Revolution and its aftermath, Nietzsche turned to the budding tradition of historiography as developed by the liberal historians Alexis de Tocqueville and Hippolyte Taine. Both held close to nominalist views of social and political life, and they were acutely aware of the importance of distinguishing between the liberal orientation to political truths on a nominalist basis and the socialist and Jacobin-centered real universalism. This liberal-nominalist and socialist-realist distinction is important for our wider understanding of the politics of Nietzsche, because we see in the nominalist position the key role that the mob and the masses play in social life.

What makes a philosopher a nominalist regarding political or social truths? As we mentioned, a nominalist in political epistemology can be understood as one who refuses the fuller achievement of universal values that undergird democratic demands. This is not to say that liberals are all nominalists full stop. Rather, liberals are nominalists over a particular set of contradictions in capitalist social life, specifically the refusal to extend universal democratic rights and freedoms to the domain of the market and the failure to redress the problems of wage labor and class oppression. The liberal tradition holds close to realist commitments in many spheres of social and political life; for example, they are willing to grant full national citizenship rights to the working class, such as the right to vote. But there are limits to their extension of this universalism, which means there are limits to the implicit promises of the French Revolution and its universalist commitments. The proletariat stands as the hard kernel of the universal in capitalism, but this universal is the unacknowledged underbelly that liberalism disavows and refuses to extend its framework of universalism to.

The wider framework of political epistemology and the realist/nominalist tension we are developing here helps us to situate Nietzsche's relation to the problem of perspectivism, because if liberalism is defined by the necessity of its denying the universal to the proletariat, Nietzsche aimed to radicalize this anti-universalist tendency which was shared by the mainstream of liberal thought. Thus, although we think of liberal thought today as preferring the particular to the universal, supporting a vision of society in which no one community, whether ethnic, racial, or religious possess the universal, the demands that opened modern political life were in fact universal. It is the persistence of capitalist social relations and their intense inequalities, brutalities, and oppressions that stand in fundamental tension with liberalism's more radical and revolutionary history. Capitalism makes liberals nominalists in matters of political truth.

Socialism and the workers' movement keep liberalism in check by insisting that these domains of political and social life continually be expanded. The tension between the realist and nominalist debate drives liberalism and socialism in a dialectical process, which is centered, most crucially, on the class struggle. We can only understand this distinction of liberal nominalism and socialist realism by reference to Marx's class analysis, in which there are two primary classes: the bourgeoisie and the proletariat. As the philosopher Étienne Balibar has noted, "Properly speaking, the bourgeoisie is the only class in history; before it there were only castes, orders, and estates (*Stände*), which were not yet real classes. As for the proletariat, once it matches its definition, it is no longer simply a class but the masses."[5] The bourgeoisie is the class which controls the parliamentary system, property, surplus from capital, the labor process, and the state.

Nietzsche developed the concept of perspectivism as directly linked to the problem of the proletariat in modern capitalist social life, which is prominent in the work of his early period. Both Lukács and Losurdo have shown how the Paris Commune of 1871 stands as the fundamental political upheaval that shaped Nietzsche's early thought. But is this just a Marxist suspicion that is not borne out of Nietzsche's own writings? Does Nietzsche discuss the Paris Commune directly? From a Marxist perspective, we must read Nietzsche as developing a philosophy which took a stance on the class struggle in ways that are comprehensive and thorough. In other words, the class struggle is at the center of Nietzsche's thought. Losurdo goes so far as to suggest an alternative subtitle to Nietzsche's major work *The Genealogy of Morals*, "The Crisis of Civilization from Socrates to the Paris Commune." This suggested subtitle is not to be taken as tongue-in-cheek, given that Nietzsche himself wrote that the communists and anarchists were like "a Saturnalia of barbarism... a haunting spectre embodied in a class of barbaric slaves who have learned to regard their existence as an injustice, and now prepare to avenge, not only themselves, but all generations."[6]

Relying on letters, lectures, notes, and published texts of Nietzsche's early years, Losurdo identifies the two competing political perspectives that Nietzsche marked in the Europe of his time. The first was what Nietzsche named the optimistic worldview, which philosophically had its basis in Ancient Greece and the plebian philosophy of Socrates. The modern socialists were seen as optimists by Nietzsche, and importantly it was not socialism or Christianity that posed the problem, it was rather the socialistic elements within Christianity. This distinction is crucial given that countless readers of Nietzsche have portrayed his critique of Christianity as separate from his fundamental critique of the egalitarian and plebeian elements within it. Bourgeois Christianity is celebrated and lauded by Nietzsche on countless occasions in his writings, most notably in his support for the role of Christianity in the imperial Opium Wars in China.[7]

Although Nietzsche's politics align with the material aims of liberalism — that is, he expresses solidarity with maintaining liberal bourgeois class rule and hegemony — he did not rely on the same conventional tactics and strategies that liberalism deploys to combat the egalitarian, or realist, forces that generate from the class struggle. What were the core political issues that drove this split in political perspectives at the time and generated the optimist threat of egalitarian demands? The primary issues include universal male suffrage and the advancement of democratic rights across Europe, including and especially general advancement and the rights of the working class under wage slavery. This was also during the immediate aftermath of the end of chattel slavery, the early makings of the women's rights and suffrage movement, and the taking-off of the imperialist age of European powers' rapid conquest across the globe. There are crucial similarities that Nietzsche's age shares with our own, the persistence of Bonapartist-style liberal bourgeois class rule over the state being chief among them.

Bonapartism, Then and Now

Although Nietzsche's aristocratic politics abjured many of the conventional methods of liberal politics of his time, and he often strongly critiqued liberal establishment politicians throughout his career, one way to understand his politics is by reference to his support for Bonapartism. Bonapartism is a very important theory for understanding Nietzsche's politics as it accounts for the way that liberal bourgeois political parties on both the right and the left perpetuate reactionary and anti-democratic politics. Bonapartism is a theory of how reactionary elements persist even in an ostensibly progressive or liberal political regime.

The Nietzsche specialist Don Dombowsky has gone so far as to argue that Nietzsche's political philosophy, "his Aristocratic Radicalism, is neither fascist nor liberal democratic but is rather a type or species of Bonapartism."[8] The theory of

Bonapartism has been hailed by the Trinidadian Marxist C.L.R. James as one of the most essential theoretical contributions to Marxist thought. In James's view, Marx's text on Bonapartism, *The Eighteenth Brumaire of Louis Bonaparte*, stands next to Marx's *Capital* and Trotsky's *History of the Russian Revolution* as the primary and most necessary reading material for any Marxist.[9]

The Eighteenth Brumaire of Louis Bonaparte analyzes the political dynamics that led to the rise of Louis Bonaparte III (known as Napoleon III), who came to power in France following the seismic event of the 1848 worker uprisings. Bonaparte came to power by appealing to the highs and lows in the social classes, and his appeal united the lumpenproletariat, or those barred from wage labor, and the finance aristocracy. He fashioned himself as a man of the people, even appearing sympathetic to socialism. Ideologically, Bonaparte was a political figure of pure decadence and irrationalism in the sense that he abandoned any coherent agenda or practical set of interests other than maintaining status-quo, bourgeois class power. His popularity was tied into the mythical status of his name and to the fact that he was a distant relative of the first Napoleon Bonaparte, which is why Marx developed his famous Hegelian notion of "first as tragedy, then as farce" upon his election victory in France.

Nietzsche's support for Bonapartism centered around his admiration for the figure of Napoleon Bonaparte, whom he associated with a rare Renaissance-era level of virtue that had been lost in the contemporary age. According to the most important French intellectual of the time, Gustave Le Bon, what Napoleon and later Napoleon III's rise to power achieved was a re-establishment of the ancien régime.[10] Napoleon III "presented himself as a conservative at heart who in practice was a Saint-Simonist. In other words, he emerged as a figure that promised to erase or mediate this serious opposition."[11] The Bonapartist thus forms a lasting political type that emerges with Napoleon III, but which re-emerges in bourgeois politics following his ascension to power. In fact, this is why Bismarck, who rose to power in Germany the same year as the Paris Commune, is known as a Bonapartist figure himself.

There are specific functions that a Bonapartist leader plays. They enter a situation of crisis in bourgeois political rule and resolve it by restoring balance to maintain the status quo. In this way, we must understand the Bonapartist as a figure of repetition in capitalist social life. We can expect and predict with reasonable accuracy when the bourgeois social order will require a Bonapartist figure to step in. The Bonapartist figure, in the reading of Kojin Karatani, emerges from outside of the two ruling-class parties and offers a separate solution to the crisis of bourgeois democracy. Thus, a figure such as Donald Trump is a Bonapartist leader par excellence in the way that he emerged seemingly from outside the two-party system. Trump rose to power on a highly incoherent ideological platform, but despite the seeming chaos and ideological nonsense that Trump represented — a right populist who was also anti-war, anti-elitist, and an anti-liberal globalist who himself owned and operated a multinational corporation fully embedded in the same system he ridiculed — he, like Bonaparte in Nietzsche's time, united key elements of a disgruntled and disempowered petit-bourgeois class and the lumpenproletariat with the interests of the financial aristocracy. The Bonapartist appears as a chaotic political mess, a clown show. But at a material level, they work to reinforce the status quo.

We must understand Bonapartism as a theory of how the persistent *undemocratic* basis of liberal bourgeois class rule continues unabated in a capitalist society. A Bonapartist regime is one which neutralizes the very sphere of democratic rights and liberties that liberals on both the right and the left allegedly champion and support. From a Marxist point of view, liberal bourgeois capitalism refuses to extend democratic rights over the sphere of the market. For capital to reproduce itself, massively undemocratic measures must be taken to ensure the persistence of unjust and exploitative wage labor and bourgeois class dominance. What links a theory of Bonapartism to our own time is the fact that democracy is not extended to the working class under capitalism. If democratic promises were truly extended then the quality of life of the working class would greatly improve, the promise of healthcare would be fulfilled, the scarcity that makes people go hungry would be eliminated, and so on. A Bonapartist leader is required to step in when liberal bourgeois parliamentary politics reaches a crisis point in the legitimacy of its rule. Bonapartism describes the function of reactionary politics within liberal parliamentary politics; it offers a way to understand how the aristocratic and ossified old elements of bourgeois class rule persist within the supposedly progressive parliamentary and congressional system of liberal democracy. Liberal democracy is a paradoxical system: it produces the Bonapartist figure, who is often reviled by large swaths of the bourgeois ruling class, but at the material level of capitalist social relations, the Bonapartist is quietly welcomed because they stabilize the capitalist system.

In his *Prison Notebooks*, Gramsci refined and developed the concept of Bonapartism by distinguishing the Bonapartist leader from the fascist leader. Gramsci offers a spectrum of Bonapartist rulers, from a "softer" variant to a harder form, which he calls "Caesarism." Both figures enter the liberal parliamentary system amid its crisis of legitimacy and restore order. A "soft" Bonapartist is a figure who sides with the more progressive social forces, such as Franklin Delano Roosevelt in the United States, who consolidated the crisis of bourgeois class rule in solidarity with the progressive bloc but in opposition to socialists. The hard Bonapartist aligns with the more reactionary conservative social forces, and thus figures like Mussolini in Italy qualify as such. Contemporary figures such as Trump or Jair Bolsonaro in Brazil are somewhere between soft and hard, but they do not rise to become clear fascists or hard Bonapartists because the democratic liberal norms of bourgeois parliamentary politics stand in the way of any truly Caesarist ambitions they may possess.

The Caesarist figure and the fascist leader — the two are synonymous for Gramsci — break from the function of stabilizing the social order and move to a more strictly authoritarian form of rule, which Gramsci characterizes as a police state.[12] Today's right-wing populist figures seize on the discontent of the working class, and then harness and re-route the contradictions of liberal capitalist rule toward culture-war politics that distracts their base from any promise of a change in the economic order. These are hard Bonapartists, but they do not qualify as fascists. They are successful because they harness the *irrationalism* that is kicked up by the undemocratic takeover of the public domain by capital. Capital perpetuates irrationalism, and the bourgeoisie must seek out ideological justifications for its rule amid this very irrationalism. The workers' movement in today's time does not possess the same force in numbers and organizational or cultural power as it did during Nietzsche's time in the late nineteenth century, but there is ample reason to believe that the post-2008 period continues to witness popular worker agitation and uprisings at unprecedented levels.[13] We still live in Nietzsche's world.

As a strategy of class rule, Bonapartism fit well with Nietzsche's politics, which were bent on preventing the successful advancement of working-class demands for rights and equality. The base of a Bonapartist leader is composed of overlapping classes who share no material interest other than cultural signifiers: allegiance to nationalist, racialist, identarian or other parochial fetishes. Nietzsche's political thought, as Don Dombowsky argues in his work *Nietzsche and Napoleon: The Dionysian Conspiracy*, was meant to offer cover and implicit support to Bonapartist political rule in Europe.[14] Nietzsche admired Napoleon Bonaparte's effort to overturn the egalitarian development of the French Revolution, and he also admired his more mediocre and farcical relative, Louis Bonaparte III.

What drew Nietzsche to Bonapartism is the way that the Bonapartist leader retains aristocratic elements within the liberal bourgeois order. For all of Nietzsche's insistence on joyful affirmation and creative acceleration, the other side of his Janus face reflects the more sober realization that rank order remains a staple of any social structure. At a political level, Nietzscheanism is a Bonapartist philosophy, and Nietzsche himself can be understood as an aristocratic, bourgeois, layabout intellectual who fostered a political workshop for future intellectuals to utilize. Let us consider one crucial biographical fact of Nietzsche's material situation: he retired from teaching in his late thirties and was able to lead a life of exceptional leisure. Although he dealt with periodic physical and later mental illness, Nietzsche formed a politics that privileged personal leisure time, which he argued large classes of people must also be denied. He saw any form of labor that was not desirable, any form of wage labor, as equivalent to slavery.

In Nietzsche's time, the political force of the socialist parties under the banner of Social Democracy in the Second Reich at times posed a serious and dangerous threat to his own class. As a young man, Nietzsche willingly signed up to fight in the Franco-Prussian War of 1870, just a few years prior to his famous lectures on education in Basel. This was not a neutral or obligatory form of state duty he fulfilled by participating in the war. The brilliant professor of classical philology abandoned a coveted university post to fight in the war, a decision driven by his explicit political ideology, namely his support for the restoration of a lost German national pride following several generations of the Napoleonic incursion and occupation of Germany.

The political orientation of the young Nietzsche was aligned with German National Liberalism, and he saw in the Napoleonic conquests of Germany a form of cultural colonialism, imprinting French egalitarian influences across Germany. The lingering influence of this French Rousseauist influence on Germany had created what the young Nietzsche referred to as an optimistic worldview which was spreading throughout Europe, finding its most egregious presence in the socialist and budding communist movements. Writing in the wake of the seismic worker revolts of 1848 that led Marx and Engels to pen *The Communist Manifesto*, Nietzsche diagnosed this egalitarian philosophy thus: "The pretension of terrestrial happiness for everyone, which more and more characterized the modern world, was thus revealed as madness."[15]

To cure Europe of the madness of egalitarianism, Nietzsche turned to Greek culture, where a similar crisis of egalitarianism was brought about by the figure of Socrates.

The young philologist wrote, "We need to see in Socrates the vortex and turning-point of so-called world history."[16] In a major contribution to Nietzsche studies, Losurdo draws attention to a much-neglected work by the young Nietzsche entitled *The Problem of Socrates*. This represents the first attempt by Nietzsche, prior to his more mature work *On the Genealogy of Morals*, to really project the Greece of the sixth to the fifth century BC onto Europe in the eighteenth and nineteenth centuries. Socratic culture, with its optimism, its belief in the originary goodness of the human being and its faithful expectation of a happy world, was re-emerging in Nietzsche's time.[17]

But Socratism was not isolated to the post-French Revolution scene of Nietzsche's time; the same leveling and originary-goodness doctrines were promoted in Judaism, Christianity, and more recently in the thought of Rousseau. Socratism presented a genealogical line of continuity: each system of thought that took inspiration from Socrates promoted the same idea that "virtue can be taught to anybody and everyone can learn it, with its faithful expectation of a happy world."[18] One year after Nietzsche eagerly joined the Franco-Prussian War, rumors broke out that the Paris Communards had burned down the Louvre in Paris in a riotous orgy, an event that he commented on in a letter to a friend: "I was for some days completely destroyed and drenched in tears and doubts: all scholarly and aesthetic experience seemed to me an absurdity. Never a deeper pain."[19]

The Paris Commune of 1871 sparked a profound melancholy in the young Nietzsche, heightening his need to develop a political alternative to the rise of socialist and radical egalitarian movements. The socialists and other revolutionaries presented a real philosophical problem for

Nietzsche, a problem that Socrates had brought to life in Ancient Greece — namely, they proposed that existence was capable of being modified by thought and reason. But the problem was far deeper than mere epistemology. The socialist movements, like their Socratic and Rousseauist forefathers, were a philosophical problem because they proposed the birth of an entirely new species of humans, what Nietzsche called the "theoretical human being." This concept refers to a form of individual for whom thought and reason are primary and access to the truth is universal and accessible to each.

In *The Genealogy of Morals*, Socrates is cited as the figure who birthed nihilism and developed an entire morality based on pity and resentment. This is a well-established line of Nietzschean critique. However, Lukács and Losurdo both reveal the missing historical context to this line of inquiry by showing how Socratism was a terrifying, egalitarian, trans-historical specter that was re-appearing in Nietzsche's own social and political present. Moreover, this re-appearance of egalitarian philosophy was understood by Nietzsche in the form of a quasi-racial composite of a distinct *type* of human being, one that attracted only the plebeians and those unhappy about their lot in life. Socratism, in Nietzsche's sadomasochist vision of the world, is a philosophy for losers. The theoretical human being includes the intellectuals who continue this Socratic flame and demand plebeian equality, which in Nietzsche's time undoubtedly found expression in the socialist demands for worker equality. Why were such demands for equality such a problem? This links us back directly to Nietzsche's fundamental Bonapartist politics, which always requires the continuity of an anti-revolutionary position.

For Nietzsche, the problem with socialists is that they tell the working class that they should not be happy in their toil, and they thus introduce new instincts and pleasures that must be reserved for those whose lives have turned out well and those born well. For Nietzsche, the problem of socialism is tied to the problem of political affects; that is, if the social order democratizes leisure time and pleasure for the plebian classes, such new rights of pleasure will risk fundamentally destabilizing the social order and disturbing "the feelings of modesty about their little existences."[20] The socialists and revolutionary philosophers were, as Losurdo writes, "inflicted by madness or an even worse sickness mainly because, in fleeing in horror from reality and their dreams of social regeneration, they invented non-existent guilts and responsibilities."[21]

What we are drawing attention to here is the often overlooked fact that Nietzsche's early aristocratic radicalism was stoked by the trans-historical return of Socratism in the Europe of his time, a crisis that inspired him to develop his own praxis and community-building solution. The primary antagonist to the creeping specter of Socratic optimism would be what Nietzsche called the tragic worldview, a concept and a call that Nietzsche would place at the center of his early community-building vision. The tragic worldview would be forged by the development of a comprehensive political alternative to the spread of the Socratic theoretical human being. The early Nietzsche began to consciously write for a new audience: the *Übermensch* and the free spirits. This new audience was meant to identify a "metaphysics of genius" capable of becoming the center of a political program in radical opposition to modernity and the subversive tendencies of massification associated with it. Like the famous *Übermensch*, "free spirit" — composing a hypothetical readership Nietzsche frequently addresses — was a phrase he preferred to the more rationalist notion of the "freethinker."[22]

Nietzsche desired to cultivate a readership, especially of young men, who might transform the socialist version of free spirits which argued that misery is caused by social ills, toward a new tragic worldview in which natural differences and capacities determine rank ordering. Not only would the tragic worldview reject the optimistic worldview, if successful it would reveal new value judgments that have hitherto guided the history of thought but which have been hidden because of egalitarian leveling. The concealment of these value judgments exceeded reason and rationality, and they had to be rediscovered in heredity, physiology, and biological dispositions. Rationalism and dialectics were mob doctrines that threatened to upend the natural order of rank and hierarchy, and as such Nietzsche's later turn to studies of physiology and eventually to the hard sciences must be linked to this fundamental political agenda. In order to purge the optimistic worldview from mankind, Losurdo notes that it was "necessary to go back by a long and devastating path and to ensure that the natural and unbridgeable differences that existed among human beings were once again fully acknowledged by the division of society into 'castes.'"[23]

While the socialist movements were the most dangerous expression of Socratism in Nietzsche's time, elements of liberalism had also become infected with the same optimistic worldview, and the Rousseauist tendency was also evident in the bourgeois American Revolution, specifically in its call for universal happiness. Although Nietzsche celebrated the persistence of slavery in America after European societies had abolished it, the call for "the pursuit of happiness" at the heart of the American Revolution reeked of Socratism and would only lead to vulgarity in the wider culture. Happiness for all was both a moral problem for Nietzsche — it led to a society

in which resentment and pity were elevated to noble virtues
— but more significantly, the optimism of the revolutionaries
disrupted the rank ordering of society, specifically slave
hierarchies, which Nietzsche saw as necessary features of any
social order.

A society of rank ordering was necessary because only in
such a society would *otium* — or leisure time for the wealthy —
be properly distributed such that "those whose lives turned out
well" could come into the full innocence of nature. Socratism,
manifested in the socialist movements of Nietzsche's time, not
only threatened a disruption of the moral fabric of European
society, but its ideology also risked upsetting the rank ordering
necessary for individual greatness to emerge. Societies of rank
ordering were slowly escaping Europe and America as it was
concluding a bloody civil war over the abolishment of slavery.
It was this crisis of the collapse of non-egalitarian social
structures that led to several of Nietzsche's most important
philosophical insights. As he once wrote, "In general the
tendency of socialism, like that of nationalism, is a reaction
against becoming individual. One has difficulties with the ego,
the immature, crazy ego: they want to put it back under the
bell."[24]

The closest thinker within Europe who understood the
tragic worldview was Schopenhauer, the only European
who could "see Europe from Oriental eyes."[25] Although
Schopenhauer did not share the same aristocratic political
agenda as Nietzsche, his fascination with Indian caste society
was of particular importance for Nietzsche, as Indian society
represented a form of rank ordering that Europe and America
were losing. A society of rank ordering committed to *otium* for
those whose lives turned out well avoided massification and
left room for the brilliant individual to emerge. Nietzsche's

important idea of perspectivism emerged at this precise nexus of political concern.

Irrationalism and Hyper-Nominalism

Thus far, we can summarize our argument as follows: the liberal bourgeoisie during the time of Nietzsche, just as in the present, possessed a nominalist orientation toward political truths. This political epistemology is part and parcel of liberalism and Nietzsche aimed to radicalize it. What drives it is the contradictions of capitalism, and specifically the class struggle, and due to liberals' embrace of capitalism, they are forced to abandon their commitment to rationalist universalism, especially for the working class.

The Napoleonic reaction to the egalitarian leveling of the more militant Jacobin movements of the French Revolution successfully restricted the three value spheres of society: liberty (market), fraternity (nation), and equality (state). It is the sphere of the market that erodes the other two spheres of freedom most centrally, and in this sense, from a Marxist point of view, the market *overdetermines* the other two spheres. This overdetermination is what Marx elaborates on in the first chapters of the first volume of *Capital* under the logic of the commodity form. The commodity relation determines not only the forms of consumer exchanges in capitalist society, it also determines and erodes the wider social relations that make up that society.

The pernicious effects of the capitalist market sphere must be nominally covered over in liberal capitalist social life for the stability of the status quo and for power relations to remain fluid. The fact that the market dominates over the other spheres of social life means that any demands for its abolishment from the working class had to be met with a nominalist solution. Over time, the very promise of the bourgeois revolution had betrayed itself because the market had to be defended for the class dominance of the bourgeoisie to continue unabated. Thus, in political epistemology, nominalism names a compromised position in the class struggle; it points to the refusal to complete the revolutionary aims established in the French Revolution.

Let us now turn to see how nominalism functioned in liberal political thought. For the liberal historian Alexis de Tocqueville, the concept of political realism was "synonymous with socialism and despotism, with the absolutization of the whole with respect to the parts and therefore, in today's language, with holism."[26] If nominalism is synonymous with liberalism and realism with socialism, how did this play out within philosophy? It was Hegel's philosophy that stood as the most sophisticated rebuke of liberal nominalism.

During the Napoleonic Restoration up to the Revolutions of 1848 — when Nietzsche was a young boy — the establishment of bourgeois political rule across Europe spawned a highly unstable social and political set of events, which reached a crescendo with the workers' uprisings of 1848. To deploy a concept that Nietzsche was quite fond of, the bourgeois social order was undergoing "decadence," a crisis which accelerated and gave ground to liberal nominalism. It is important to note that Germany never fully underwent the bourgeois revolution as France did, and that it faced particularly acute social misery and deprivation over the course of the post-Revolution period. But importantly, Germany's backwardness did not prevent its philosophical community from refining a system of thought out of this oppression.

From a historical-materialist point of view, Lukács's *The*

Destruction of Reason describes Germany as both the place where a complete solution to philosophy was developed — as found in Hegel — and as the site where philosophy, specifically German idealism as founded by Goethe, Kant, and Jacobi, became perverted. Schelling, Schopenhauer, and Nietzsche are the most central examples of the irrationalist tendency in the history of modern German philosophy, although there are of course others. Irrationalist philosophy has three key aspects: it first begins with an embrace of the Kantian epistemological limit to knowing objective reality. Kant posits an unknowable residue or noumenon that resists all efforts at knowledge, and philosophers take this proposal in all sorts of different directions. The danger lies in the tendency for the irrationalist philosopher to abandon the idea that the world can be grasped practically by means of a rational point or perspective on objective reality. When they maintain this view, they replace a rational perspective with one that sees this unknowable thing (the Kantian noumenon) as only being graspable by myth or intuition or through the clairvoyance of the philosopher himself.

Secondly, irrationalism is borne from the philosopher's drawing out the consequences of this epistemological orientation to a theory of the subject. If objective reality cannot be known, and this condition cannot be overcome, irrationalist philosophy harkens back to an aristocratic theory of the subject and the philosopher develops an aristocratic epistemology. Not only can objective reality not be known or grasped, it must also be negated, and out of that negation comes a new source of truth. With an irrationalist orientation, philosophers end up creating a theory in which access to knowledge is supra-rational, and thus only a select few have access to insight or great intuition. Most often, as we find in Schelling, Schopenhauer, and Nietzsche, the philosopher concocts an epistemology in which there are unbridgeable differences across human beings, which is again tied into the way the philosopher has worked with and embraced this fundamental unknowability. An irrationalist epistemology — such as we find in Nietzsche — will extend this emphasis on unbridgeable differences among human beings and argue philosophically that these differences must be acknowledged in the field of politics, ethics, aesthetics, and morality. This second tendency is what Lukács calls an "aristocratic epistemology." Aristocratic epistemology connects to politics in the following way: in the irrationalist philosopher's insistence on absolutizing differences across humans' access to the truth, they concoct justifications for that absolutization in science or philosophy. This is then used as justification for the perpetuation of relations of domination in society.

A third tendency of irrationalism is that the philosopher abandons dialectics and history as knowable categories of thought. For the irrationalist philosopher, the only way to grasp historical truth or mediation is via a *supra-rational* solution. Once the philosopher decides that arriving at a coherent understanding of the antagonisms and the contradictions that make up the bourgeois world is impossible, history no longer provides the means to discern or resolve problems in the present. We will revisit Nietzsche's complicated assault on the tradition of dialectical thinking in philosophy from Socrates to Hegel, especially when we consider the French Nietzschean philosopher Gilles Deleuze, who sought to continue and further Nietzsche's critique of dialectics.

With this overview of the key features of irrationalism in philosophy, we can now pinpoint one of the political consequences that stem from the adoption of irrationalist orientations. While there may be exceptions, it is important that we note, following Lukács's insights, that irrationalism tends to lead philosophers to abandon the prospect of a coherent understanding of the antagonisms and contradictions that make up bourgeois society. As such, philosophy falls into an apologetics for the bourgeois social order. This apologetics can take two forms: a direct apologetics in which the philosopher aims to champion the unjust social order directly, as we find in thinkers such as the libertarian writer Ayn Rand; or an indirect apologetics for capitalist exploitation, as we find in thinkers such as James Burnham or Nietzsche, in which the philosopher critiques the bourgeois social order and even aspects of capitalism, but keeps open an implicit justification of the social order. Indirect apologists often make for more effective proponents of reactionary agendas, as they incorporate an anti-capitalist critique but do not decisively champion a revolutionary position. In other words, indirect apologetics involves an obscuring or a mystification of the political and social situation. And there is no better champion of indirect apologetics than Nietzsche.

Nietzsche's irrationalism was far more explicit than Schopenhauer's because the social conditions in which he wrote were more crisis prone due to the capitalist order's entering its imperialist phase.[27] Irrationalist philosophy emerges in times of imperialism and crisis in capitalism, especially during times of economic depression and inflation. It is thus no coincidence that Heidegger became popular following the 1929 depression, when a philosophy of despair was required to speak to the wider mood of bourgeois life. Nietzsche's embrace of irrationalist strains of thought is conditioned by the imperialist stage of capitalism, a period he refers to as socially and culturally decadent.

By adopting this more engaged social and political perspective on philosophy, we can now come to see that the political stakes of adopting a realist or a nominalist position on political truths ups the ante for the intellectual. The framework we have developed should be understood as imposing a political and ethical decision on the intellectual under capitalism, especially in its crisis-prone stage: either they remain a steward or guardian of the status quo, in which case an irrationalist philosophy such as Nietzscheanism becomes highly valuable and coveted precisely because it is designed to *permit* the philosopher to evade, flee, and ignore the social and political antagonisms around them. Or the intellectual can affirm a realist position and confront the contradictions of the social order by openly acknowledging the primary contradictions of capitalism, which is bound up with the persistence of wage slavery, imperialism, and the unmet demands of the masses for a life of dignity without scarcity and austerity.

For Lukács — and for any socially-engaged intellectual — it was Hegelian philosophy that provided the comprehensive solution to the crisis of European society after the French Revolution. In this way, Hegel successfully resolved the German idealist project and brought philosophy to a comprehensive point of completion; that is, Hegelianism presented a rational account of society and history and a logical science of the new in which dialectical philosophy was now capable of addressing the contradictions of the social world through philosophy. Hegel gave philosophy a renewed social mission, which, after Marx, now implied a radical political and social mission. So successful was Hegel's and later Marx's achievement that the entire society could only be grasped with the historical and dialectical method they refined and developed. Hegel brought philosophy into a relation with the world and modern society that left the philosopher in a fundamentally public role, and Marx extends Hegel's dialectic in ways that point toward an overcoming of the contradictions of bourgeois society.

Hegel was not capable of completing his own system because he did not face the deteriorating social conditions post-1848 that a philosopher like Marx did. During this period, bourgeois philosophers did not rise to the moment and the Hegelian movement split into two warring camps: the Hegelians of the right and the Hegelians of the left. These schools of thought would debate the direction philosophy was to take after Hegel's death. Building off Frederic Engels' 1886 work *Ludwig Feuerbach and End of Classical German Philosophy*, Lukács argues that it was Marxism and the workers' movement that absorbed the Hegelian project after the bourgeois university could not apply it in the form of radicalism that the moment called for. Therefore, it is the workers' movement that must be understood as the true heir of classical German philosophy, insofar as it absorbed Marxist theory, including its philosophical aspects, and this coincided with the birth of the Second International.[28] It is not that Hegelianism ended full stop, but rather in the sense of a *sublation*; that is, it was Marxism that held the mantle of Hegelian philosophy in its fullest and most liberated form.

Hegel rejected "anthropological nominalism," and as a result, Hegelian thought stands as a great challenge to any liberal relativism or nominalist position within the field of politics. For Hegel, social freedom is marked by the progressive construction of the universal concept of man, and this includes a political definition of the subject. Hegel writes:

The fact that today man as man is considered the holder of rights is to be considered as something great, so that the human being is something superior to his status…. Now, as the source of law, universal principles are in force, and thus a new epoch has begun in the world.[29]

The Hegelian (and later socialist) commitment to achieving the unmet demands of the French Revolution insisted on the *real dimension* to the realization of political values. If these demands were realized by the proletariat, this would threaten to fundamentally alter the liberal commitment to these values.

For liberals like Taine and Tocqueville, nominalism was a move to temper the realist impulses which posed a threat to the very status of the class struggle. If the proletariat and its intellectuals inculcated a new political truth that insists on the revolutionary continuation of the Jacobins real basis for full universal demands, this would mean that exploitation and domination, such as the persistence of the institution of slavery or the system of wage labor, would meet their demise. Nominalism is a cover and shelter from realist demands, providing liberalism with a means of defending the status quo and maintaining a semblance of order and legitimacy. We thus see that liberalism is itself Janus faced, insisting that the popular demands for freedom, equality, and liberty be tempered and held back. But this covering logic requires a political philosophy that produces a series of doubles and illusions; it requires the creation of an ideology to satiate the contradictions that are produced by the liberal bourgeois social order.

Now we arrive at the heart of our argument. With the concept of perspectivism, Nietzsche aimed to radicalize liberal nominalism by forging a radical subjective nominalism (that is, perspectivism) that was meant to retain a social structure based on rank order:

> Whom among today's rabble do I hate the most? The Socialist rabble… who undermine the worker's instinct, his pleasure, his feeling of contentment with his little state of being — who make him envious, who teach him revengefulness…. Injustice never lies in equal rights, it lies in the claim to "equal" rights.[30]

It is the *claim* to rights that socialists advocate that is the heart of the problem for Nietzsche; this is to say, that a certain plebian class of people (the proletariat) would be eligible to claim rights in the first place was a scandal that must be resisted at all costs. What perspectivism emphasizes is a new strategy for creating conditions wherein exceptional and brilliant individuals serve as the main locus of the subject. This is what gives the concept the air of profound aristocratic baggage; Nietzsche was interested in returning the European social order to a time when the citizen was thought of beyond the abstract demands of rights and representation that undergird socialist realist demands.

With this framework in mind, we can now better understand the stakes of Nietzsche's genealogical method, first developed in *The Genealogy of All Morals*. As we have indicated, this highly influential text must be understood as a response to the event of the Paris Commune, which was the first seizure of state power by the proletariat in the nineteenth century. Nietzsche's genealogical method placed the problem of the human at the center of a vortex of history that stretches back to the egalitarian realism of the Jewish and Socratic ideas of the human being found in Plato and the Jewish priests who sought an idea of the human subject based on their wider social relations, that is, in consciousness.

Nietzsche split the immanent political antagonisms of his own time, namely liberal nominalism and socialist realism, into another Janus-faced division with a long and winding genealogical pre-history. In his historical treatment of this split or double — Nietzsche is an incredible thinker of the two and the double in virtually all things — he would align Cartesian rationalism, which opened the Scientific Revolution and later the Enlightenment, to the Socratic plebian philosophy. Socratism was a trans-historical expression of a certain type of human, what Nietzsche called the "theoretical human being." In his "The Problem of Socrates" lecture, Nietzsche associates Socrates with ushering nihilism and a "will to truth" into philosophy. This way of thinking about truth was a problem in Nietzsche's eyes because it ultimately suppressed a more essential truth, namely that we are not masters of the thoughts that arise in us; our thoughts do not stem from our intelligence, they rather constitute modes of reacting in which are transmitted old physiological dispositions.

Perspectivism is a polemical alternative to the crisis of the class struggle that weighed on bourgeois intellectual, cultural, and political life. It is not apparent to most readers of Nietzsche, but at the core of his doctrine of perspectivism is a vision of the subject, or the agency of the self, in which heredity and aristocratic rank can again re-emerge to determine the individual's instincts. Socratism and socialism, with all their theoretical optimism, were rooted in a realist orientation to political truths which not only threatened a disruption of the moral fabric of European society, but also risked upsetting the rank ordering necessary for individual greatness to emerge. As

Nietzsche wrote, "The categories of species and kind could be used to describe the mass but not the outstanding or even brilliant individual."[31]

Although Schopenhauer did not share the same aristocratic political agenda as Nietzsche, Losurdo shows how Schopenhauer's nominalism was the basis on which Nietzsche radicalized the idea of perspectivism. For Nietzsche, a society of rank ordering must become committed to furthering the goal of *otium* for those "whose lives turned out well." Nietzsche wrote, "In general the tendency of socialism, like that of nationalism, is a reaction against the becoming individual. One has difficulties with the ego, the immature, crazy ego: they want to put it back under the bell."[32] The realist was a "dogmatist" in Nietzsche's eyes, and perspectivism was the inescapable mode of being of a truly aristocratic nature.

As a concept, perspectivism was a way to assert the inescapability of perspective, and by extension injustice, social misery, and rank ordering, in Nietzsche's praxis. It was developed as a concept meant for the preservation of the brutal background social conditions of bourgeois social life. It is paradoxically radical in its destructive and annihilating characteristics, but this radicality conceals a reactionary political agenda underneath. The concept of perspectivism, even when shorn from its nineteenth-century context, has remained attractive to the left as it purports a radical subjective overcoming; that is, it poses as a subjective liberationist theory. But as we have aimed to demonstrate in this chapter, as a political concept it only offers a nominalist solution to the antagonisms borne from class struggle. Perspectivism is one of Nietzsche's most important contributions to the romantic anti-capitalist praxis.

CHAPTER FOUR
The Center of Nietzsche's Political Thought: A Continuous Polemic against Marxism and Socialism

Perhaps never in the history of philosophy has there been such a comprehensive anti-masses and radical aristocratic philosophy dressed up in a seemingly apolitical and anti-political veneer as Nietzsche's. But in what ways did Nietzsche's concepts and the wider cauldron of his thought interact with the socialist, feminist, and popular movements for equality of his time? The socialist and egalitarian threat was central to Nietzsche's thought, so much so that he developed his concepts with an eye toward suppressing socialism.

Although many Nietzsche scholars have argued that Nietzsche's comments on socialism and the political events of his time are marginal to understanding his thought overall, we argue that this line of inquiry is highly pertinent, especially for grasping a better idea of Nietzsche's place and function on the left.[1] Moreover, many commentators claim that Nietzsche's elitist and reactionary anti-egalitarian politics is not the core of his thought, but rather aesthetics and moral thought are. In what follows, we aim to show that such points of emphasis miss the heart of Nietzsche's thought and lead to an apolitical understanding of the philosopher. So widespread is this apolitical reading of Nietzsche that the entry on Nietzsche in the *Stanford Encyclopedia of Philosophy*, a widely read source on historical and contemporary philosophy, has no mention of Nietzsche as a "political" thinker, and as of writing this book in late 2023, the predominant Marxist and socialist critiques of Nietzsche are also missing.[2]

In this chapter, we will explore four predominant ways that Nietzsche treated socialism and left-egalitarian movements: firstly his encouraging of a strategic ignorance of socialism, which took the form of a philosophy meant for austerity and specifically austere living; secondly, his aim to pacify egalitarian political energies by accelerating the contradictions of bourgeois social life by "culturalizing politics" and fomenting a praxis of anti-politics; thirdly, his inventing of a new idea of the philosopher-intellectual who might function as an alternative to the working-class or socialist intellectual; and fourthly, and perhaps most centrally, his aim to disrupt the promise of a world wherein leisure time is widely distributed across society.

The *Otium* Wars and the Politics of Leisure Time

When Nietzsche retired at thirty-eight years of age, he lived off a family inheritance and a modest pension from the University of Basel.[3] We have already seen that for Nietzsche a higher culture can only come about on the condition that there are two castes in society: a *working* caste and an *idle* caste. The question of leisure time is what distinguishes the caste of idlers because it is idleness that makes way for a qualitatively different form of suffering.[4] From the perspective of the class struggle, we can never neglect the fact that as a young man, Nietzsche grew up in the wake of the largest working-class uprising Europe had ever seen, in 1848. Our aim is to situate Nietzsche's philosophy as being motivated by the class struggle of his time, a struggle which was constantly moving, changing direction, intensifying, and de-intensifying.

At the outset, we must recognize that Nietzsche is right to stress that free time is a necessary ingredient for the generation of culture and art, but his insistence that society be structured in such a way that the working masses are deprived of leisure time is fundamentally problematic. The socialists, with their Rousseauist yearnings for freeing man from his chains, risked only accelerating the decadence of culture in Nietzsche's view. The preservation of *otium* was not some idiosyncrasy for Nietzsche, it was a political objective of the class Nietzsche fought for in the Franco-Prussian War, the Prussian Junkers, which was composed of minor aristocrats and landed nobility. Losurdo points out that "*otium et bellum*" (which can be translated as "struggle in the cause of leisure") stood as the mantra of the Prussian Junkers. To struggle and toil in the cause of *otium* is a motto that should be placed at the very center of Nietzsche's political community-building effort. But crucially, the struggle for *otium* in the name of the interests of the Prussian aristocracy would be modified by Nietzsche into the idea of struggle for, as he puts it, "those whose lives have turned out well," to quote Nietzsche's later dedication to *The Will to Power*, written in the spring of 1888.[5]

But why did Nietzsche place such importance on leisure time in his philosophy? *Otium* has a long history in philosophical speculation, stretching back to the pre-Socratics. The concept refers to the idle time of personal leisure, in distinction to *negotium*, or public time, to which labor, civic, and family time is dedicated. *Otium*, or *skhole* in Greek, is also the time of academic reflection and leisure that forms the backbone not only of scholarly life, but of the very possibility of culture itself. *Otium* must be understood in relief from neg*otium*, or the absence of free or leisurely time, which would come to be associated with business and commerce. A social order built around affording its citizens access to *otium* is crucial for the perpetuation of culture, because *otium* produces a specific effect, namely it produces distinction. *Otium* is not an aimless or idle form of leisure, it is an active form of leisure. In fact, in *otium*, one is not passive or purely contemplative, but active in a contemplative mode. It is this combination of theory and contemplation with practice that makes *otium* so vital to the perpetuation of culture. For without a class peopled with *otium* seekers, the very possibility of culture is lost. Those who practice *otium* are thus the vanguard of the distinguished, and they allow for the possibility of a culture built on a love of difference. From distinction and rank comes difference and creativity.

The French sociologist Pierre Bourdieu argues that *otium* is what develops and distinguishes the shared worldview and culture or what he calls the "habitus" of intellectuals and especially of academics. Bourdieu argues that *otium* is based around a subtraction from the degradations and realities of wage labor. But Bourdieu points out that through this exemption from wage labor, intellectuals often develop problematic conceptions of political antagonisms. If *otium* is ideally achieved by a perfecting and combining of contemplative theory and practice, Bourdieu diagnoses academic leisure as completely aloof from such a conception. He writes that intellectuals remain ignorant, not only of what happens in the world of practice, but most especially of the economic and social conditions that make the world possible.[6]

The free time granted to the academic intellectual thus functions as a mark of distinction between the scholar and the laborer or worker. But this distinction has the effect of sheltering philosophers from the masses, and it creates unnecessary barriers to the possible fusion of philosophy with any working-class movement. While leisure time for scholarly and artistic pursuits is obviously necessary to produce quality art, Bourdieu draws attention to how, in capitalist society, the free time granted to philosophers forms a new type of knowledge that is meant to be *superfluous* to the common concerns of the people. Bourdieu says this knowledge is *meant to be irrelevant* to the masses because, in its irrelevance, the scholar forms a habitus with other scholars to effectively fortify themselves off as a closed community that speaks in a language that is only accessible to those who have undergone academic initiation.[7] While Bourdieu does not fetishize workers — and the working conditions of academics are often highly precarious, especially in the post-2008 era of austerity — what he points to is a long historical tendency of academic scholarly production which aligns very closely with an explicit political goal Nietzsche sought to further: namely, that scholarly leisure time be limited to a small crust of rare and brilliant geniuses and denied to the masses.

Otium as a form of leisure time was steadily disappearing in Nietzsche's time, which threatened Nietzsche's idea of utopia: a caste-divided society where rare geniuses are sheltered completely from dull work. In *Human, All Too Human*, Nietzsche defines the type of person for whom *otium* is meant: "It turns toward people unoppressed by crude duties, it demands refined and spoiled senses, it requires superfluity, superfluity of time, of clarity of sky and heart, of *otium*." He continues this passage by stressing that *otium* is "the only good thing that we Germans of today do not have and thus also cannot give."[8]

As we mentioned, the importance of *otium* for Nietzsche stretches back to his early volunteering to fight in the Franco-Prussian War, where his solidarity was implicitly with the Prussian Junker class of landed nobility. "Greek philosophers," Nietzsche writes in *The Gay Science*, "went through life feeling secretly that there were far more slaves than one might think — meaning that everybody who was not a philosopher was a slave."[9] At issue for Nietzsche was the problem of equality in a post-French Revolution context:

> It is different with us, who are accustomed to the doctrine of human equality, though not to equality itself. One who is not at his own disposal and who lacks leisure does not by any means seem contemptible to us for that reason; perhaps too much that is slavish in this sense sticks to each of us.[10]

The society of Nietzsche's time was approaching the point where "work and the worker are now even to the most leisurely among us!"[11] As the class struggle matured, however, Nietzsche adopted new tactics and strategies to address what he saw as the deleterious effects of the movements for equality. This is where, as we will explore shortly, Nietzsche's more creative, experimental, and radically accelerationist concepts and ideas began to emerge. As Geoff Waite has remarked, "Nietzsche's was a rhetoric — a technology — of violent speed, as well as of leisure."[12]

Nietzsche's defense of leisure time was qualified and to be limited to a select few, which he further qualified as pertaining to the rights of inheritance. A society in which *otium* is reserved for a select few had to be elevated to a new collective demand, one whereby workers must be invited to enlist in wars to assist in furthering this vision of leisure time for the bourgeois elite. Thus, Nietzsche's defense of *otium* is bound up with his community-building praxis, but how geniuses are to be granted — chosen — for leisure time would vary. For example, the Nietzschean philosopher Peter Sloterdijk will argue in the neoliberal era that when you strip the *Übermensch* of its ethos of genius, you have the contemporary capitalistic imperative to constantly relearn and retrain for new jobs. Neoliberalism has sapped the blood inheritance of leisure time and replaced it with a new demand to constantly improve one's training.

Nietzsche's aristocratic vision of the ideal social order, split by a class of winners and a class of losers would come be adopted by later Nietzscheans as the task of the market to determine. Nietzsche's own conception of the market relies on a commitment to the market that is socially constructed but *natural*, reflecting the brutality and competition of nature. This leads liberal Nietzscheans, such as Leo Strauss and Sloterdijk, to adapt Nietzsche's hyper-meritocratic vision in order to be more inclusive of the market as a site where greatness can be determined, but where there is no role for the state to foster this process of meritocracy.

The Free Spirits: An Alternative to the Proletarian Intellectual

Much has been written on the daily routines of philosophers: how they gathered their inspiration, their daily reading habits, their day-to-day schedules. According to biographers of Nietzsche, there is a debate as to how much he read, in part because he disdained the scholarly practice of collecting books for the mere sake of it. Nietzsche despised the way that modern Europeans read, and he was especially opposed to the Hegelian notion that the "newspaper replace daily prayers." Unlike Marx, who cut his teeth in politics as a journalist for the most radical news publication at the time in Germany, the *Rheinische Zeitung*, Nietzsche saw newspapers as a form of "*philistine Bildung*," or a formation of education and culture meant for the lower classes.[13] Although Nietzsche scorned the idea of reading newspapers as something the masses did, the Nietzsche biographer Thomas Brobjer has pointed out that he was a voracious reader — the young Nietzsche arose at 5:00 am each day, after going to bed at midnight, to begin his routine of reading.

Aside from these biographical details of his reading habits, at a social and political level, the issue that drove Nietzsche's thought, that informed his praxis and community-building efforts, was the rise of a new form of intellectual in European society. Nietzsche referred to this intellectual as the "philosopher-journalist," a Socratic sort of intellectual who threatened to upend the legacy of classical grammar education. "Freedom of the press ruins style, and eventually spirit. Freedom of thought ruins thinkers."[14] But there is a profound irony in Nietzsche's fear that massification was changing the standards of the intellectual in that Nietzsche himself fused his philosophy with journalism. As the French philosopher Francois Laruelle comments, Nietzsche was one of the first philosophers to practice "High Journalism," that is, he was one of the first thinkers to really fuse philosophy with current events.[15]

Let us examine the claim that Nietzsche has no politics at his core by looking at the question of the main stages of his work. One of the important contributions of Losurdo's

Aristocratic Rebel is the way that he moves beyond the three-stage — early, middle, and late — understanding of Nietzsche by proposing four stages of Nietzsche's thought, each unified by a common commitment to an anti-socialist, anti-egalitarian, and pro-slavery aristocratic agenda. The first stage is what Losurdo calls the "metaphysical" stage, which was sparked by the Paris Commune and marked by a radical anti-revolutionary agenda. Stage two, the "solitary rebel" stage, was influenced by Edmund Burke and German Romanticism, for which Schopenhauer's tragic worldview was the model. The third stage Losurdo names the "anti-moralist" stage, in which Nietzsche attacked the passions and morals of the Enlightenment, siding with Voltaire as its key figure. The fourth and most mature of Nietzsche's stages, "aristocratic radicalism," was set on affirming the innocence of becoming, and was when his more refined ideas, such as that of the eternal return, were developed. In this stage, the solitary rebel is now transformed into an explicitly anti-masses figure, incapable of calling on a popular community.[16]

To truly get at the core of Nietzsche's thought requires that we privilege the theme of revolution and see how Nietzsche developed a series of strategies for furthering reactionary political aims in his philosophy. Nietzsche was a philosopher in continuous reaction to the revolutionary tradition that found expression in the workers' struggles coming out of the 1848 uprisings, "massification," especially the problem of universal male suffrage in education, the broadening of Europe's educational institutions, women's rights, the ending of slavery, and the socialist movements of the time. Nietzsche is not a timeless thinker — he must be read as an activist, as continuously refining a metaphysics, a morality, and a series of concepts in response to political struggles.

He was a keen political observer of the current events of his time. For example, we know that in 1866 he attended a mass rally of the socialist party *Allgemeiner Deutscher Arbeiterverein* (later to become the *Sozialdemokratische Partei Deutschlands*, or SPD), founded by a friend of Marx and Engels, Ferdinand Lassalle, of which he remarked that the speakers spoke of "impotent and unreal things." We also know that Nietzsche read two of the most famous socialist works of his time, August Bebel's *Woman under Socialism* and John Stuart Mill's *Socialism*, as well as Albert Schäffle's *The Quintessence of Socialism*.

Nietzsche was also familiar with the socialism of Eugen Dühring, a famous anti-Semitic socialist whom Engels famously polemicized against in his work *Anti-Dühring*, which became a foundational text of Marxism during the period of the Second International. Although both Engels and Nietzsche found the vulgar anti-Semitism of Dühring reprehensible, this does not mean that they shared anything else in common regarding socialism and the workers' movement. It is important to emphasize that Nietzsche was fascinated by political economy, and as Geoff Waite has pointed out, he returned multiple times throughout his career to the writings of the Philadelphia-based political economist Matthew Carey.[17] It was the concept of "surplus" in the work of Carey that deeply interested Nietzsche, and we know that Nietzsche *knew of* Marx, but there is no proof that he ever seriously read him, although the two were contemporaries. In one of Nietzsche's books in his library, the name Marx is underlined, but unfortunately he never wrote anything of substance directly on Marx.

Nietzsche's familiarity with the political currents of his time, despite his seeming lack of fluency with Marxist and communist currents, has led many Marxists to consider him a thinker who is close to Marx on several social and political issues. But this seeming closeness is an illusion which upon deeper scrutiny does not hold up. From the critique of religion and ideology to the very idea of equality, we will come to see that any *seeming* alignment between the two thinkers only conceals a true diametrical opposition. Where Marx's class theory posits a fundamental schism between two primary classes, the bourgeoisie and proletariat, Nietzsche affirms the same division, but with the crucial caveat that he actively sides against the proletariat.

The heart of Nietzsche's political praxis is bent on the development of a higher civilization, but this higher civilization, as he writes, "can only come about when there are two distinct social castes: that of the working people and that of the leisured, those capable of true leisure; or, to put it more strongly, the caste of forced labour and the caste of free labour."[18] We thus see that Nietzsche's community-building praxis and the concepts that he championed, such as rank order and the pathos of distance, to name just two examples, are not to be construed in allegorical terms or as timeless concepts. It is rather more accurate to read "his whole life's work [as] a *continuous polemic against Marxism and socialism*,"[19] as Lukács once put it. Now, even though Nietzsche did not directly critique Marx, his philosophy is driven fundamentally by the situation of the class struggle of his time, that is, from a Marxist point of view "every philosophy's content and method are determined by the class struggles of its age."[20]

But what did Nietzsche actually say about socialism? Can a plausible case be made that his thought is a response to the class struggle and the threat of socialism? In what follows, we aim to show that the core of Nietzsche's thought is a response to the class struggle, and that he develops a comprehensive political praxis meant for maintaining bourgeois class rule and cultivating a new form of intellectual. In an aphorism entitled "The Victory of Democracy,"[21] Nietzsche says that the fear of socialism among the elite and rulers only strengthens democracy, and he continues to point out that socialism, if it is strengthened, leads to an idea of the "people" as omnipotent.

Nietzsche can be seen as an ally to liberals because he believed that when you fight socialism it grows stronger, which is why sometimes ignoring socialism is the best strategy for keeping it at bay. Socialism was a real threat in Europe at the time, from the communists Nietzsche feared and fantasized about in the Paris Commune, to the German Social Democratic Party. To Nietzsche, the socialist movements and the various working-class intellectuals that supported them sought to disrupt the natural division of suffering and caste order. Collectively, the socialists maintained a vision of society that was ultimately built on envy of the "better caste of society."

It was the socialists who dreamt ingeniously of "goodness, truth, beauty, and equal rights," but, Nietzsche notes, "in this age of universal suffrage I feel compelled to re-establish order of rank."[22] As Nietzsche scholar Don Dombowsky observes, Nietzsche's treatment of the "worker's problem" diagnoses it as being due to "lack of a noble presence" in employers, whose vulgarity seems to challenge the very notion of an order of rank, thereby "lending credibility to egalitarian ideals."[23] This is a crucial perspective because it shows that Nietzsche put the onus for the crisis of the working class on the bosses, rulers, and the elite. His philosophy was directed at them, and they were held responsible for allowing socialist ideas to creep into the working class. In his mature work *Thus Spoke Zarathustra*, Nietzsche writes, "And on the rulers turned I my back, when I saw what they now call ruling: to traffic and bargain for power

— with the rabble!"[24] Moreover, he all but implied the class of Marx's proletariat when he said:

> The impossible class. Poor, happy and independent! That is possible together: poor, happy and a slave! That is possible too. And I can think of no better news I could give to our factory slaves: provided they do not consider it altogether shameful to be used up as they are, as a part of a machine and as it were a stopgap to fill a hole in human inventiveness! To the devil with the belief that higher pay could abolish the essence of their miserable condition. I mean, they're impersonal, serfdom! To the devil with the idea of being persuaded into thinking that an increase in this impersonality within the mechanical operation of a new society could transform the shame of slavery into a virtue! To the devil with setting a price for which one remains a person no longer but becomes a part of a machine! Are you accomplices in a current folly of nations — the folly of wanting, above all, to produce as much as possible, and to become as rich as possible?[25]

Considering the importance of slave morality that is developed in *The Genealogy of All Morals*, a question emerges: Did Nietzsche see modern socialism as a new variation on slave morality? The answer to this question can make or break a Nietzschean-Marxist understanding of socialism, because if socialism is fundamentally corrupted by slave morality, then it can be abandoned and an ulterior Nietzschean community-building project can be undertaken. To find out if Nietzsche viewed socialism as slave morality, we need to center how Nietzsche viewed wage labor and the status of the working class in his time.

For Nietzsche, all involuntarily accepted work is a form of

slavery.[26] His radically aristocratic and reactionary view on slavery should not be lost sight of, because he lived during a time when chattel slavery was being undone, and similar to the socialists of his time, he too recognized wage labor as a form of slavery. But the crucial difference is that he concocted a philosophical vision meant to perpetuate, not abolish, wage slavery. We can thus say it is axiomatic for Nietzsche that any social order, if it aspires to aesthetic greatness, cannot function without slavery. This is a trans-historical truth which the workers' movement was threatening to undo completely. As a result of this threat coming from the optimistic worldview of the socialists, European society faced a crisis of decadence and nihilism.

The socialist intellectuals put forward a philosophy steeped in Cartesian rationalism and Rousseauist sympathy for the suffering masses, which upended Nietzsche's core idea of power and metaphysics. As he remarks in *Zarathustra*, "All living things are obeying things. Whatever cannot obey itself, is commanded.... Commanding is more difficult than obeying." He continues the aphorism with the remark, "Even in the servant have I found the will to be master — this is the will to power."[27] Socialist intellectuals, as Losurdo helpfully points out, "suppressed workers instincts and pleasures as well as their feelings of modesty," and this meant that even for Nietzsche, the supposed antagonist of Christianity believe that "religion was to be recommended if it taught the poor not to take life seriously."[28]

Socialist intellectuals were the "state-idolators of Europe" who "could easily bring things to Chinese conditions and to a Chinese 'happiness,' with their measures for the amelioration and security of life."[29] We must remember that it was the optimistic worldview that had gradually taken hold of

Europe after 1848, and at the heart of this was a skepticism toward the legitimacy of private property. As an example of Nietzsche's "High Journalism," he makes a trans-historical and philosophical connection between worker agitation and more democratic views on property and the philosophy of Plato. Plato maintained a similar anti-property position as the contemporary socialists:

> When Plato declares that egoism would be removed with the abolition of property, we may answer that, if egoism be taken away, man will no longer possess the four cardinal virtues either; as we must say that the most deadly plague could not injure mankind so terribly as if vanity were one day to disappear. Without vanity and egoism what are human virtues?[30]

For Nietzsche, "only a man of intellect should hold property; otherwise property is dangerous to the community. For the owner, not knowing how to make use of the leisure which his possessions might secure to him, will continue to strive after more property."[31] He was adamantly opposed to new distributions of property, noting that "we do not need forcible new distributions of property, but rather gradual transformations of attitude; justice must become greater in everyone, and the violent weaker."[32] The crisis of the masses and their struggle for rights and dignity called for a Machiavellian set of strategies to be cultivated. One such strategy was the importance he placed on forgetting and delegitimizing socialism among the masses and in social life more generally. The strategy of forgetting socialism was necessary for any retraining of workers' instincts and the preparation for an adjustment to a more natural brutalism determined by the market and enforced rank order. Nietzsche dreamt of a time when the masses would "forget socialism like an illness it has recovered from."[33]

What were the best strategies for forgetting and suppressing socialism? In an almost uncanny way, the strategies Nietzsche advocated are still very much the same general strategies that the liberal bourgeois order uses to maintain its rule today. The first of these is the promotion of austerity, which Nietzsche saw as offering a solution for eradicating the very desire for socialism among the masses. Austerity provided a curb on the core problem of socialism, which is its disruption of rank order and its propensity to spark desire to change of one's station and position. It is crucial we understand that Nietzsche's politics were bent on preserving a status quo in which the demands, affects, and desires of the broader working class are kept in check. Nietzsche warns that

> the only remedy against socialism that still lies in your power is to avoid provoking socialism: in other words, to live in moderation and contentment, to prevent as far as possible all lavish display and to aid the state as far as possible in its taxing of all superficialities and luxuries.[34]

Although at times Nietzsche can make himself appear as a great critic of liberalism and Christianity, we must understand that it was the specific influences of egalitarian and socialistic impulses that had infused Christianity that he felt had to be combated. Christianity in its more bourgeois and hierarchical form, and specifically its capacity to promote imperial projects abroad, were celebrated by Nietzsche.[35] Even to this day, many of Nietzsche's most famous memes and quotable phrases on social media are popular and resonate precisely because we live in a world that is fundamentally shaped by disciplined austerity. Phrases such as "You must first conquer yourselves,"[36] or "Whatever does not kill you makes you stronger," or "It is the business of the very few to be independent; it is a privilege of the strong" reveal the heart of Nietzsche's tough and austere wisdom. This wisdom is forged in the fires of a political commitment to austerity, which is why Nietzsche remains our very timely contemporary and why the liberal mainstream establishment (not just conservatives) relishes him. While these maxims are plucked by self-help gurus and young people off Google on a daily basis — Nietzsche frequently trends on Twitter and social media — so as to further a rugged individualism compatible with a bootstrap capitalist ethos, beneath these inspirational phrases lies a concerted political project.

Nietzsche would have hated the trend of "conspicuous consumption" that was practiced by many of the bourgeoisie of his time. He wanted to retain the blood heredity of his conception of the *Übermensch*; he also preached austerity, especially for the bourgeoisie and elite classes, saying, "You must first conquer yourselves"[37] and "Live as higher men and persist in doing the deeds of higher culture — then everything alive will grant you your rights, and the social order, whose peak you represent, will be preserved from any evil eye or hand."[38] In *Human, All Too Human*, Nietzsche wrote that if socialism is achieved, "man would be too feeble to produce genius any longer."[39]

We already saw how it was the theoretical human being — a new breed of intellectual — which Nietzsche associated with the socialists of his time. The emergence of this new cadre of intellectuals inspired Nietzsche to react by forging an alternative community of readers, the free spirits, a community meant to call forth would-be revolutionaries, but in completely opposite dress to the socialists. The free spirits, as Peter Bergmann has shown, closely followed and fell prey to the political fashions of an era for which they claimed to be "untimely"; they were to be a new sort of rebel that might rival the plebeian socialist intellectuals.[40]

The "danger" of socialism, in Nietzsche's view, "begins when goals become impersonal; revolutionaries whose interest is impersonal may regard all defenders of the existing order as having a personal interest and may therefore feel superior to them."[41] This impersonal dimension of the revolutionary was called into question because

> to demand equality of rights, as do the socialists of the subjugated caste, never results from justice but rather covetousness. If one shows the beast bloody pieces of meat close by and then withdraws them again until it finally roars, do you think this roar means justice?[42]

As Don Dombowsky has pointed out in his study of Nietzsche and the working class, one of the tasks of the Nietzschean new nobility was to correct the perversion of the European working class. To do so, Nietzsche proposed that the working class "'learn to feel like soldiers (soldier-workers), that they receive only an 'honorarium' and not wages," as he believed there should "be no relation between payment and achievement."[43] The core objective was a shift in attitude: "We do not need forcible new distributions of property, but rather gradual transformations of attitude; justice must become greater in everyone, and the violent weaker."[44]

Although Nietzsche has a reputation for inspiring greatness among his readers — "My formula for greatness in a human being is *amor fati*: that one wants nothing to be other than it is, not in the future, not in the past, not in all eternity"[45] — it is of crucial importance that we situate his vision of greatness as fundamentally reliant on the persistence of mass mediocrity. The Nietzschean great man breaks apart from communal ties and limits, declaring himself self-sufficient, but this radically individual philosophy in the same breath "aims at an ordering of rank: not at an individualistic morality."[46]

Crucially, instead of a desire to remove mediocrity from social life — or even better, to throw the very idea of mediocrity into question — Nietzsche aimed to determine what and who was mediocre in a capitalist society based on the pathos of distance. This meant that highly unequal access to education, resources, and opportunity were to be enshrined as norms of a modern liberal society. Nietzsche declared mediocrity indispensable for any society. Although "hatred for mediocrity is unworthy of a philosopher: What I fight against: that an exceptional type should make war on the rule — instead of grasping that the continued existence of the rule is the precondition for the value of the exception."[47]

Mediocrity must not be combated to deny its legitimacy — a sensible approach to the deeply problematic concept — but a huge swath of the masses must be passed off as merely mediocre, as possessing small lives, small desires, and small ambitions. If anything, socialism was so disruptive precisely because it called for harnessing the energies of mass excellence, not mass mediocrity. Nietzsche's vision of necessary mediocrity is akin to many common libertarian and conservative views on mediocrity today, which too often are overlooked in analyses of these political orientations. This insight hits at a common misconception about socialism that many conservatives fail to recognize, namely that socialism *does* call forth a sense of greatness within the masses, but based on an egalitarian and collective understanding of mass greatness.

It is this contradiction between the individualism of Nietzsche's *Übermensch* ethics and the collectivist basis of the left and socialism that threatens to render any left-Nietzschean project a fundamentally self-defeating one. In a more radically aristocratic statement, Nietzsche says outright that the "dwarfing of man must for a long-time count as the only goal; because a broad foundation has first to be created so that a stronger species of man can stand upon it."[48]

Nietzsche's political agenda is readable, detectable, and consistent. And we have aimed to point out its prescriptive aspects: that is, Nietzsche instructs and invents a new type of intellectual. He offers advice for rulers, bosses, and would-be rulers as much as he does to the so-called losers who read him and who are eager to be winners. Nietzsche viewed the tradition of dialectics as having opened with Socrates as a mob philosophy, stating that with dialectics, "the plebs come to the top."[49] We can understand Nietzsche's politics as engaged in a dialectical process.

A dialectical treatment of the class struggle is one which isolates the totality of the capitalist system and provides a perspective that enables a view toward the transformation of the social system. Dialectics is a method for the proper handling of contradictions, and from a socialist perspective involves the treatment of the contradictions which are unaddressed by bourgeois society. We already saw that for Nietzsche, a nominalist treatment of the contradictions of social suffering brought on by the market and wage labor was at the core of his political thought. Nietzsche's concepts — perspectivism, pathos of distance, *ressentiment*, and even the will to power —

can be read as a toolbox of strategies for overcoming — and in some cases retaining — the contradictions of capitalist society.

The Godfather of Left and Right Accelerationism

Let us remain in the social and political context of Nietzsche's time so that we can better situate the origin — and the intended function — of his concepts. We have already discussed Nietzsche's Janus-faced philosophy: at once affirming a joyful rebellious and affirmative spirit and turning toward a more brutal emphasis on discipline and cruelty. This philosophy reflected the society in which Nietzsche lived, a society that Lukács characterizes as possessing a "Jekyll-and-Hyde character." This manic style of Nietzsche's, Lukács argues, corresponded to the social existence of his time, particularly to the emotional and intellectual world of the bourgeois class. Nietzsche's class, the bourgeoisie, experienced the most acute feelings for nuance, the keenest ever sensitivity, combined with a suddenly erupting, often hysterical brutality. This is the first sign of decadence that Lukács pinpoints. The second sign of decadence is closely linked to this erratic attitude, and it is marked by a deep dissatisfaction concerning contemporary culture: an unease about culture permeates the bourgeois class. Lukács describes these manic affects and contradictory feelings in the following way:

The vast majority of the bourgeois intelligentsia clung to the illusion of living in the "best of all worlds," defending what they supposed to be the "healthy condition" and the progressive nature of their ideology. Now, however, an insight into their own decadence was becoming more and more the hub of these intellectuals' self-knowledge. This change manifested itself above all in a complacent, narcissistic, playful relativism, pessimism, nihilism, etc. But in the case of honest intellectuals, these often turned into sincere despair and a consequent mood of revolt (Messianism, etc.).[50]

Lukács pinpoints the ways that Nietzsche's philosophy linked to a wider social task of the bourgeois class, one that aimed to rescue and redeem bourgeois decadence. In this struggle, Nietzsche must be read as a dialectical thinker who recognized the "clash of class interests between bourgeoisie and proletariat" but consciously sought to remove mention of it and to suppress it in his works. Nietzsche provided a new morality for the socially militant bourgeoisie and middle-class intelligentsia of imperialism, and following his death, Lukács argues that Nietzscheanism remained a philosophy that offers a "self-criticism of the ruling and falling classes, or criticism of capitalist society from the positions of its most reactionary groups."[51]

What Nietzscheanism offers to the bourgeoisie is a road which can avoid the need for any break, or indeed any serious conflict, with the contentions and antagonisms that emerge from the wider class struggle. What Lukács points out is significant: the more the class struggle moved to the center of social events in objective reality, the more Nietzsche aimed to conceal it in his philosophy — the motif of the mask and a politics of deception are, after all, very central for Nietzsche. Understood from this dialectical perspective, Nietzscheanism is an aping and an imitation of socialist philosophy, but one that proposes "a sham revolution, a mere heightening of the reactionary contents of capitalism tricked out with revolutionary gestures."[52] Overall, Lukács argues that Nietzsche's thought was meant to assist the bourgeois transition from the liberal age of security to that of "great politics" and the struggle for control of the earth. Nietzsche is thus a prophet for what Lenin refers to as the "imperialist stage of capitalist development." Nietzsche is a prophet of great destruction to come.

Nietzsche is known as a great antagonist to dialectics, and with our perspective on his thought, we can now see that his method is more accelerationist than it is dialectical. In his autobiography, *Ecce Homo*, Nietzsche wrote, "For granted that I am a decadent, I am also the antithesis." Decadence had to be handled by accelerating its very contradictory basis. Accelerationism is a strategy for dealing with the social contradictions of capitalism distinct to dialectics which would aim to sublate or preserve and overcome the contradictions that give rise to decadence. Nietzsche rather aimed for a radical acceleration of decadence: "Even today there are parties whose goal is a dream of the crabwise retrogression of all things. But no one is free to be a crab. There is nothing for it: one has to go forward, which is to say step by step further into decadence."[53]

From the social crisis of bourgeois society in his time, Nietzsche brought forward an accelerationist politics that specifically aimed to manage social forces of decadence by accelerating brutality and exploitation, landing Europe in new wars, and immiserating the lower classes. But Nietzsche's accelerationist politics must be understood against his aristocratic politics centered on leisure time and subtraction from wage labor for the *Übermensch*. Nietzsche's insistence on a praxis of private bourgeois leisure and the preservation of *otium* is paradoxical when we consider how he also favored a politics in which the wider class struggle would be accelerated. Nietzsche's accelerationism is not to be understood as a philosophical position in support of an increase in toil for all citizens; to the contrary, it is meant to accelerate conditions of massification and egalitarian leveling backward to a class situation wherein an idle class and a toiling, exploited class are normalized. In fact, to Nietzsche's credit, he despised cultures built around constant labor such as America, a place he once described as "living in constant chase after gain [compelling] people to expend their spirit to the point of exhaustion."[54]

We can understand accelerationism more generally as an "aesthetic, cultural, and political trend that seeks to speed up the process of technology and capitalism in order to radically transform society."[55] In a historical context, accelerationism emerges from the industrial revolution of the nineteenth century and is brought about by the contradictions of capitalist society, from the immiseration of the proletarian working class under horrific labor standards to the destruction of the planet in the process. How are these contradictions to be overcome? The accelerationist solution is to harness the power of technology to transform society through an emphasis on speeding up existing capitalist processes to accelerate beyond these contradictions.

On the left, accelerationism eschews the socialist and Marxist solution of revolutionizing capitalism through wide-scale labor movements that harness the working class and aim for a revolution in the mode of production. Instead, accelerationism aims to liberate science by exceeding the bounds of existing technology. Mary Shelley's *Frankenstein: The Modern Prometheus* is an accelerationist tale *avant la lettre*. It tells the story of scientist Victor Frankenstein, who successfully defies the laws of science and overcomes the norms of God-fearing Christian civilization by creating a super-intelligent human. Frankenstein's monster is effectively an AI invention, and the very act of inventing it puts Frankenstein in the position of God. The accelerationist wager on changing society is based on the idea that the laws of science and the Enlightenment conception of God as tethered to the laws of nature can be overcome, as can cultural norms. As the philosophers Landon Frim and Harrison Fluss have pointed out, the accelerationist repudiates "lawful causality, derived from the *Principle of Sufficient Reason*, and the Cartesian notion of physically extended objects, which exist independently of human perception. In its place is set an anarchic, will-based vision of the world that is radically contingent."[56]

In more recent left-wing thought, the French philosophers Gilles Deleuze and Félix Guattari's works *Anti-Oedipus: Capitalism and Schizophrenia* and *A Thousand Plateaus* formulate an entirely new form of accelerationist politics. For Deleuze and Guattari, capital is understood as a liberating desiring-machine which can be rivaled and contested by a new praxis of nomadic rebels. Deleuze and Guattari argue that the schizophrenic stands as the closest subjective analogue to the wild accelerationist tendencies of capital and its violent flows. They theorize a "schizoid" subject who can accelerate "into the limit of capitalism, since he is the inherent tendency brought to fulfillment, its surplus product, its proletariat, and its exterminating angel."[57] Taking their cue from Nietzsche, politics is no longer about the Marxist class struggle, and they argue there is no primary schism between the bourgeoisie and proletariat, but rather that politics is now to be theorized as a confrontation of desiring-machines in a social order of depersonalized forces and flows of capital. They argue that desire is inherently multifarious and tied directly to production, and that thus capital itself resembles desire and the schizo-revolutionary subject now serves as the basis of an anarchic accelerationist politics.

Deleuze and Guattari's accelerationist politics have proven highly influential in contemporary political thought on both the right and the left. A popular buzzword of left-accelerationism is "fully automated luxury communism,"[58] a phrase that captures the ambition as well as the naïvety of the wider perspective. Left-accelerationism idealistically posits a scenario in which the capitalist class might benevolently modify its policies that immiserate the working class without any serious activation of the working class as an agent in transforming social power. Both the right and the left variants of accelerationism dream of escaping the contradictions of contemporary capitalism, with its wealth inequality and ecological devastation, with solutions that keep the existing mode of production intact.

One of the most prominent right-wing accelerationists working today is the British philosopher Nick Land. Influenced by Deleuze and Guattari, Land argues that capitalist acceleration should be used to speed genetic manipulation so that the disparities of talent between the races will become more apparent.[59] For Land, the unregulated accumulation of capital is what will lead to a biological overcoming of the human, and this situation is one where ubiquitous social fragmentation along ethnic and racial lines will only intensify. Land already sees capitalism fomenting this fragmentation, and advocates a neo-confederate politics of "white exit" in response.

Accelerationists share the view that capitalism can only be surpassed by accelerating its own processes. Land's accelerationist politics is one whereby labor has been fundamentally replaced by machines, AI, and genetic manipulation. In this vision, capitalist productivity is thought of as separate from socially necessary, human-centered labor time.[60] For Deleuze and Guattari, the Marxist view that there exists a primary schism between the bourgeoisie and the proletariat is completely re-theorized as a confrontation of desiring-machines in a society of depersonalized forces and flows of capital. Since desire is inherently multifarious and is now tied directly to production, it cannot be limited by the stable nature of a human subject. But this presents a fundamental conflict with the Marxist conception that class-based struggle against capitalist processes must be centered on leveraging the labor power of the working class. Marx's understanding of the revolutionary power of the working class is not to be understood

> as a mechanical reflex of technological development, whose "historic task" is nothing more than (automatically) to appropriate collectively the forces of production created by capitalism, but rather a class which contains the possibility of a classless society because its own interests cannot be fully served without the abolition of class and because its strategic location in the production of capital gives it a unique capability to destroy capitalism.[61]

Accelerationism is a fundamentally flawed strategy for overcoming capitalist processes, whether it is construed as a right-wing, neo-confederate racist politics as with Land, or as a libertine, countercultural politics as with Deleuze and Guattari. In reality, the basic premise of accelerationist politics already serves as the guiding ethos of the venture capitalist firms that fund the high-tech industry, and is encapsulated in popular buzzwords such as "creative destruction." The faith placed in cybernetic and algorithmic technologies to liberate humanity by the prominent libertarian entrepreneur Elon Musk, founder of the electric car company Tesla Motors and SpaceX, offers an example of how accelerationism is ultimately a highly standard form of capitalist politics. But the edginess and seemingly subversive basis of the mantra of creative destruction are not benign. Musk aims to open new human settlement on Mars, but he opposes modest wealth-redistribution policies. Left-accelerationism emphasizes strategies of full automation and universal basic income, as well as others to manipulate the instruments of financial capitalism in order to more democratically bring about socialistic changes in society.

Nietzsche is a godfather of accelerationist politics on both the right and the left. In fact, even Nietzsche's most infamous declaration of the "death of God" contains an accelerationist proposition at its core. The proposal that God is dead contains an invitation to the reader to accelerate beyond the weak morals of compassion, egalitarianism, and other soft values.[62] It is important that we historically contextualize Nietzsche's accelerationist tendencies. For example, when Nietzsche says that his philosophy will only take place after "great socialistic wars," we can see this as both a premonition and as direct support for accelerating the contradictions of bourgeois society so that a great war can give way to a new age for the triumph of the *Übermensch*. Nietzsche aimed to accelerate beyond the "degeneration" that was sapping the vitality and life drive of truly great individuals in his time.

In his effort to pacify the masses, Nietzsche aimed to accelerate and heighten "cultural politics" as a deterrent to socialist politics. Ever a careful observer of politics, Nietzsche concluded that "culture owes its highest achievement to politically weakened times,"[63] which means that egalitarian politics must be tamped down by promoting a distinctive form of anti-politics. Nietzsche's anti-politics faces the crisis of class-based decadence and the supposed ossification of culture and aesthetics that it brings about by advocating new forms of barbarism: "[Europe] requires not only wars, but the greatest and most terrible wars - and thus, temporary relapses into barbarism - if the means of culture are not to cost them their culture and their very existence."[64] He argued that "modern democracy is the historical form of the decline of the state," and much of his philosophy was bent on predicting and calibrating what an even more expedient form of the state may be. One thing is clear, however: when the conditions of culture ossify, it is necessary that times of barbarism return.

CHAPTER FIVE
Nietzsche within the Left

First: I only attack causes that are victorious; I may even wait until they become victorious.
Second: I only attack causes against which I would not find allies, so that I stand alone... I have never taken a step publicly that did not compromise me: that is my criterion of doing right.

Nietzsche, Ecce Homo[1]

When Nietzsche is read in the historical context of his time and not as a timeless philosopher, we uncover a deeper and more comprehensive reactionary philosophy bent on suppressing egalitarian working-class movements for liberation. Although Nietzsche emphasizes the importance of brutality, cruelty, rank order, and even the annihilation of the weak, these darker sides of his philosophy have been systematically sidelined, censored, removed, and de-emphasized by translators such as Walter Kaufmann, the most widely read English translator of Nietzsche in the post-war period. Kaufmann removed words such as "extermination" and "breeding" in Nietzsche's work and systematically de-emphasized Nietzsche's reactionary politics. Let us take one example from Kaufmann's translation of *Ecce Homo*, aphorisms 193-194. In this passage, Nietzsche discusses the brutal measures which his readers must take in order to accelerate beyond the degeneracy and decadence of the social order:

Let us look ahead a century and assume the case that my attempt to assassinate two millennia of antinature and human disfiguration has succeeded. That new party of life which would take the greatest of all tasks into its hands, the higher breeding (*Höherzuchtung*) of humanity, including the merciless extermination (*schonungslose Vernichtung*) of everything degenerating and parasitic, would make possible again that excess of life in earth from which the Dionysian state will grow again.[2]

Kaufmann translates "*schonunglose Vernichtung*" as "relentless destruction," replacing the more direct translation of "extermination" with the ahistorical and more abstract idea of "destruction." He also translates the "*Hiherzüchtung der Menscheit*" as "to raise humanity higher." These translation choices reflect an effort to dehistoricize and dissociate Nietzsche from Nazism and other far-right appropriations. But by replacing these terms, Kaufmann participates in a distortion of the reactionary radicalism of Nietzsche, and this leads readers to approach Nietzsche in a fundamentally metaphorical and allegorical way. Such readings not only promote what Losurdo calls the hermeneutics of innocence, they also defang the potency of Nietzsche's true political radicalism and thus lead readers to assume that he effectively can be read as devoid of explicit politics. By whitewashing Nietzsche's politics, the result is an intensification of his already esoteric political agenda.

The effect of Kaufmann's whitewashing has been to make Nietzsche untimely both to the world immediately following World War II and to Nietzsche's own social context. In Kaufmann's treatment of Nietzsche, the philosopher is given a radically apolitical makeover. The passage we have selected is one of countless examples across Kaufmann's translations, and it indicates the appeal that the Nazi ideologues found in Nietzsche, which they sought to misuse toward their own ends. But their misuse of Nietzsche is not entirely without foundation, and it is crucial that we be exposed to this pillar of aristocratic radicalism, because in the post-war period Kaufmann's translations have sought to completely expunge the true nature of Nietzsche's political sentiments.

Despite Kaufmann's whitewashing, his translations have influenced many left-wing readers of Nietzsche, and his portrayal of Nietzschean ideas has led many on the left to de-emphasize the reactionary agendas that are embedded into the core of Nietzsche's thought. When we remove or downplay his obsession with rank order and frequent celebration of brutality, we lose the real Nietzsche. Indeed, it is the other side of the Janus face that we must rediscover to fully appreciate the function of his thought, especially when we incorporate it on the left. An immediate question emerges: What is the use of rediscovering this other Nietzsche? Why not leave the reactionary Nietzsche buried in the dustbins of his nineteenth-century context? Perhaps Nietzsche should remain untimely to us because we no longer face similar social and political conflicts to those of his time. But this is not true. As we have shown, Nietzsche is our contemporary in two primary ways: Firstly, his thought has fundamentally shaped our culture and we have still not fully recognized how Nietzschean concepts are meant to function when they are adopted. Secondly, he is also our contemporary in that the social struggles of the working class, the class struggle and socialism remain remain the primary and most significant political struggle of our time, as they were in his.

In this chapter, we examine several exemplary case

studies of how Nietzsche is incorporated on the left, from the American context prior to and immediately following World War I, to the post-war period in the context of the Civil Rights movement and in liberatory upheaval of May 1968. We then consider Nietzsche in the context of the core of the Bolshevik movement in Russia, where his presence and influence generated much controversy and misunderstanding. Throughout this chapter, we continuously ask how Nietzscheanism — a philosophy which so many on the left have found transformative and even essential— works to undermine collective liberation. How do Nietzsche's anti-egalitarian tactics for the suppression of socialism become transvalued and rerouted into a left-wing project? What is lost in this transposition? Does Nietzsche, once he is on the left, in fact undermine left-oriented, liberatory projects?

We have argued that Nietzsche's concepts and ideas cannot be read as separate from the design and the program that informed his praxis and community-building aims. The cultivation of a particular type of intellectual is no different here. Nietzsche aimed to seduce young people, writing: "I aimed to seduce young readers," and "I wished to capture people with deep, rich and serene souls.... Later I thought to 'seduce' German youth."[3] In his later period, Nietzsche reflected on his community-building efforts to find "new philosophers" with a far more explicit political agenda in mind:

My need for new philosophers. Where will they come from? Only where a noble way of thinking reigns, one that believes in slavery and in many degrees of bondage as the prerequisite of any higher culture; where a creative way of thinking reigns, which does not set the world's goal as the happiness of repose — this lie is called "equality of human beings."[4]

Very shortly after his death, Nietzsche's appeal for young people began to grow. In Russia, prior to the Bolshevik Revolution of 1917, the father of Russian socialism, Georgi Plekhanov, notes in his work *Art and Social Life* that

> there is not, I think, a single country in the modern civilized world where the bourgeois youth is not sympathetic to the ideas of Friedrich Nietzsche. Nietzsche, perhaps, despised his "sleepy" (*schläfrigen*) contemporaries even more than Théophile Gautier despised the "bourgeois" of his time. But what, in Nietzsche's eyes, was wrong with his "sleepy" contemporaries? What was their principal defect, the source of all the others? It was that they could not think, feel and — chiefly — act as befits people who hold the predominant position in society. In the present historical conditions, this is tantamount to the reproach that they did not display sufficient energy and consistency in defending the bourgeois order against the revolutionary attacks of the proletariat. Witness the anger with which Nietzsche spoke of the Socialists. But, again, see what we get.[5]

Plekhanov captures what is a central goal for Nietzsche — the development of a cadre of readers who will be prepared to rule. In Germany at the turn of the century, Nietzsche attracted a particular class of followers: young people who tended to be "without constructive engagement or employment in urban centers like Copenhagen, Munich, and Berlin."[6] Nietzsche promoted what we will call a "de-classed" conception of the intellectual, joyously rebelling against a social order understood to be composed of impersonal reactive forces. Nietzsche still appeals to the youth today, and his appeal has grown considerably from the time that Plekhanov was writing in the early twentieth century. Nietzsche finds a sympathetic audience on the left because he draws readers into this de-classed position, where they tend to abandon any commitment to parties or class solidarity and instead opt for a hyper-individualist idea of liberation.

The French philosopher Gilles Deleuze aimed to transform Nietzsche's praxis into a philosophy that could help the left decode the repressive conditions of capitalist life and contribute to a new countercultural strategy for radical liberation. As we will see, in his landmark work *Nietzsche and Philosophy*, written in 1963, Deleuze redefines Nietzsche's toolbox of concepts, including the noble, *ressentiment*, the pathos of distance, and many others. But as the philosopher Matthew Sharpe has pointed out, Deleuze systematically overlooked Nietzsche's reactionary agenda. Does Deleuze's omission of Nietzsche's political core matter? We will argue that it does. And moreover, what concerns us is what we will call the de-classed basis of the Nietzschean liberation theory that Deleuze puts forward. The almost exclusive emphasis placed on culture, and not politics, as the site of liberation ends up eradicating commitments to socialism, party building, and the working class. As the philosopher Jan Rehmann notes of the French Nietzschean thinkers Deleuze and Foucault, "They banished, to a greater or lesser degree, obsolete egalitarian humanism to extract a much greater value from irrationality, pessimism, vitalism, and ultraist individualism."[7]

Nietzsche's praxis is fundamentally anti-revolutionary at its core, and this reactionary agenda is often overlooked or missed by the left. Yet, perhaps surprisingly, even though the left misreads Nietzsche's reactionary politics, or completely glosses over it, there have been many important — and complex — left-Nietzscheans, from Huey Newton of the Black Panther Party, to several of the Bolshevik philosophers during the Russian Revolution, to the American revolutionary socialist and novelist Jack London and the French philosopher Gilles Deleuze. There are many reasons for Nietzsche's appeal on the left, the first being that he has attracted a wide lay audience of working-class readers.

We know from surveys of late-nineteenth-century German workers that Nietzsche was the most read philosophical thinker, with Marx fifth on the list.[8] In one survey of these workers, they reflected on the ways that Nietzsche's *Übermensch* mythology could be applied to themselves. As a function of the doctrine of perspectivism, people tend to read Nietzsche on *their* terms. Even when we come to know the political Nietzsche and come to see his true agenda, he still cannot be easily excised from any intellectual project on the left. As such, our argument is not that Nietzsche should be canceled full stop, but that his thought forms the bedrock of a dominant, spontaneous life philosophy of contemporary capitalism; that is, his influence is paramount, and his ideas offer a theoretical surplus for politics which is so diametrically opposed to any left-wing project that it is mandatory we read him well and read him seriously. Before any operation that might seek to remove Nietzsche's thought from the left, we must understand how the left has incorporated — and continues to incorporate — Nietzsche.

As Nietzsche rose to fame in his later years, his philosophy began to be taken very seriously by the most underground political and artistic rebels. This is a trend which has been repeated from the moment he began to be read widely up to the student movements in the 1960s and 1970s and on through to today's fascination with Nietzsche on the part of young people the world over. Nietzsche himself recognized his appeal in his later years; he wrote in a letter to a friend, "A strange fact, which comes more and more to my attention. I have gradually come to have some 'influence' — all underground of course. Among all the radical parties (Socialists, Nihilists, Anti-Semitists, Christian-Orthodox, Wagnerians) I enjoy an amazing and almost mysterious esteem."[9]

Nietzsche's influence was felt across the political spectrum, and he especially appealed to political groups that professed a radical or liberationist agenda. Nietzsche's influence on these political movements, however, as the German sociologist Ferdinand Tönnies put it, was ultimately "pseudoliberational." Those converted to the Nietzschean doctrine, Tönnies notes, "were captivated by the promise of the release of creative powers, the appeal to overcome narrow-minded authority and conventional opinions, and free self-expression."[10] At the same time that Nietzsche was appealing to workers and even to socialist intellectuals around the turn of the twentieth century, there were also many socialist critics of Nietzsche who began to see the burgeoning interest in his work on the left as a problem, critiquing his influence as a deterrent to the cause of collective worker liberation from the degradations of capitalism. In the eyes of the socialist thinker Kurt Eisner, Nietzsche practiced "the ultimate in bourgeois pseudoradicalism, never touching the real bases of exploitation and always keeping the socioeconomic structure and class distinctions firmly intact."[11]

Because he preached a "philosophy for the future" that was meant for an exclusive caste of supra-individuals who would distinguish themselves from the masses, this had a certain individualizing effect on readers of Nietzsche. Eisner notes that "only when everyone attempts to represent their own personal relationship to Nietzsche, his thoughts and feelings, the suppositions and notions which make up the 'Nietzsche Problem,' will one be able to master it."[12]

Nietzsche appeals to a particular class of readers who have an ambivalent and often detrimental relation to the working class and to the wider class struggle. Nietzsche tends to appeal to what in Marxist class theory is called the petit-bourgeoisie, a contradictory class position defined by its non-relation to productive labor. One of the reasons that Nietzsche appeals to this class of intellectuals, as Leela Gandhi has pointed out, is because he provides a way for them to "bolster their onslaught on the epistemological narcissism of Western culture."[13] Nietzsche's philosophy gives fodder to a class of intellectuals who are fed up with the contradictions of their own class and the decadent culture in which they operate. Nietzscheanism is a philosophy perfectly suited to a de-classed radical philosopher, ideal for petit-bourgeois thinkers who are hungry for a critique of their culture, their class, and "the system" that will effectively not change anything.

Before the Hermeneutics of Innocence: H.L. Mencken and Jack London

When Nietzsche is read and absorbed by left-wing thinkers, whether anarchists, socialists, or even progressive liberals, he is often molded into something quite distinct and at times idiosyncratic. There is no one Nietzschean mode of interpretation, and there are multiple, often contradictory readings of his work. There are also many Nietzscheans, even on the left. But the context in which we read Nietzsche matters, and there are some contexts, for example the French and American post-war contexts, in which the aristocratic and political weight of Nietzsche was often under-emphasized, if not outright ignored. Losurdo's idea of the hermeneutics of innocence does not point to an arbitrary decision by postmodern academics and French theorists to turn Nietzsche's aristocratic concepts into allegories and metaphors. The hermeneutics of innocence points to the ways that interpretations and translations of Nietzsche, including left-Nietzschean scholars, actively de-center his reactionary politics in their appropriations of his ideas and concepts.

But what exactly is Nietzsche guilty of, given that other major philosophers also expressed reactionary political commitments? For example, Hegel and Kant theorized black people and Africans as being incapable of reason. Aristotle held favorable views of slavery. Isn't every philosopher guilty of reflecting a reactionary political view and even embodying certain backward political views of their time? No doubt this is the case, and that is why philosophers must be read in an immanent way; that is, we must read Plato, for example, in the context of a genealogy of Platonism and Neo-Platonism. Philosophers are not separate monads whose thought must remain pure. No one is purely innocent, and no one is purely guilty. But at the same time, reactionary political views do matter in any assessment of a philosopher, and they matter particularly for the left and especially in the case of Nietzsche, since he, unlike Hobbes, Rousseau, Machiavelli, or Hegel, wrote about and commented on political struggles – socialism, Bonapartism, imperialism, to name just a few – that have *direct* bearing on the political struggles that make up our contemporary political struggles.

The question becomes this: How do appropriations of

Nietzsche that ignore the centrality of his reactionary politics as merely incidental or marginal end up reproducing those very same reactionary agendas? The hermeneutics of innocence is the tendency to assume that Nietzsche's reactionary politics is marginal to his thought and that appropriations of his thought can thus sidestep deeper considerations of how it functions. Creative appropriations of reactionary philosophers can and should be enacted, but this must be done with attention to the consequences of reactionary concepts in philosophy, especially when they are applied to a project of left-wing liberation. When it comes to Nietzsche's reactionary thought, we are dealing with commitments which are more than a mere reflection of his times. As we have shown in the last chapter, Nietzsche's Janus-faced politics is more sophisticated than a direct alignment with a political tendency or party; his politics is hardwired into any deployment of his concepts, and his thought thus molds a distinctive Nietzschean orientation which carries with it a reactionary agenda.

Therefore, any creative philosophical and political appropriation of Nietzsche must be done with a careful understanding, not merely of his reactionary agenda, but of his Janus-faced intentions that imbue his concepts. As we explored in the pathos of distance, the concept clearly transcends just a right-wing or a conservative political community and can easily be applied to the left, but when it is applied to the left it will have the tendency to lead to a particular way of managing hierarchy and a sense of elitist leadership. As we will see in Chapter Seven, the concept of *ressentiment* plays a similar function to the pathos of distance, when it is accepted and embraced as a plausible way of understanding social suffering, it has the tendency to shut down political solidarity with the group accused and it thus works to reinforce existing social hierarchies.

A philosopher or thinker working with Nietzsche did not need to think about a creative appropriation of his thought prior to the rise of the post-World War II academic industry of Nietzsche interpreters who sought to defang his aristocratic radicalism. In the pre-World War I American context, Nietzsche's anti-democratic, anti-working-class agenda was not pushed to the side but centered in analyses by Nietzscheans on both the right and the left. We will now turn to two exemplary Nietzschean philosophers who wrote in the early twentieth-century American context: H.L. Mencken and Jack London.

There is no better example of a dyed-in-the-wool Nietzschean than the American literary critic H.L. Mencken, whose work served as a major inspiration for the wildly popular conservative libertarian writer Ayn Rand. Rand even dedicated her best-selling work *Atlas Shrugged* to Mencken and sought to imitate his pugilistic style in her own writing and public persona, and of course she also expressed fond admiration for Nietzsche herself. Mencken was a polemical, literary gadfly in early twentieth-century American belles lettres, writing from the 1910s through the 1940s, making his mark on literary culture as a prolific essayist and cultural critic. Writing before the Red Scare and McCarthyism targeted socialism and communism during the Cold War, Mencken polemicized against Bolshevism and the Russian Revolution.

A fervent Nietzschean, Mencken was quite unabashed in his open acknowledgment of Nietzsche's aristocratic radicalism. He argued that Bolshevism represented the most significant threat to Western civilization, and affirmed that Nietzsche's moral philosophy, specifically *The Genealogy of Morals*, must be read as a polemic against the socialist and communist movements initiated by the Paris Commune. Mencken thus shared and extended Nietzsche's own anti-socialist views, and he argued that Nietzsche was immediately applicable to his own political and social context: "The coming century is likely to be convulsed in more than one spot, and the Paris Commune... will seem to have been but a slight indigestion compared with what is to come."[14] In his introduction to the English translation of *The Antichrist* by Oscar Levy, Mencken expressed his views on democracy, which closely resembled Nietzsche's own:

> The face of democracy, suddenly seen hideously close, has scared the guardians of the reigning plutocracy half to death, and they have gone to the devil himself for aid.... What is called Bolshevism today he saw clearly a generation ago and described for what it was and is — democracy in another aspect, the old *ressentiment* of the lower orders in free function once more.[15]

Mencken also wrote a widely read biography of Nietzsche — which is still considered a popular introduction to Nietzsche even today — in which Nietzsche is presented as the center of all intellectual life. "There is no escaping him," he wrote. Nietzsche has "colored the thought and literature, the speculation and theorizing, the politics and superstition of the time. He reigns as king in the German universities — where, since Luther's day, all the world's most painful thinking has been done."[16] Mencken read Nietzsche with a toxic and virulent anti-Semitism, writing in the introduction to the English translation of *Thus Spoke Zarathustra*, "The case against the Jews is long and damning; it would justify ten thousand times as many pogroms as now go on in the world."[17]

Mencken was an undiluted Nietzschean. He argued that social and political divisions were to be thought of based on a primordial split between winners and losers, and thus as in Nietzsche's own sadomasochist vision, Mencken saw humanity as organized by an ascending and a declining line of the superior *Übermensch* and the stultified masses. Mencken also applied Nietzsche's hyper-individualist philosophy to his analysis and commentary on American literature. What Nietzsche helped Mencken envision was a theory of the American individual uncorrupted by the degenerate and stultifying masses, and from this point of view he developed a theory of the misunderstood hero who functions as a gadfly to his own people, reigning superior over the resentful and envious masses. For Mencken, Nietzschean *ressentiment* is not a nuanced or insightful concept for understanding political attachments, it rather informed Mencken's view that "envy supplies all the issues of politics in a democracy" and "it is the desire on the part of the peasants to rob the superior classes of rewards unattainable by themselves or to restrain them from the enjoyment of activities that they are unable to understand."[18]

The American socialist literary critic Edmund Wilson portrays Mencken's worldview as follows: "The superior classes embody all the learning, all the taste, all the fortitude, all the intelligence, all the sense of personal honor and all the sense of social obligation."[19] Wilson wrote that Mencken's book *Notes on Democracy* could be seen as "a sort of obverse of [Whitman's] *Leaves of Grass*." He also called Mencken's Nietzschean style melodramatic:

It is Mencken's same old melodrama, with the gentleman, the man of honor, pitted against the peasant and the boob. We are not told what makes people gentlemen or what makes people boobs, or of how it is that both these species happen to belong to the same human race, or of how it is that we often find them merging or becoming transformed into one another.[20]

In his reading, Mencken affirms that Nietzsche is

pre-eminently for the man who is not of the mass, for the man whose head is lifted, however little, above the common level. They justify the success of that man, as Christianity justifies the failure of the man below. And so they give no promise of winning the race in general from its old idols, despite the fact that the pull of natural laws and of elemental appetites is on their side.[21]

Nietzsche informed Mencken's pugilistic attitude toward the herd mentality of America's working class, which he held in disdain. Nietzsche's philosophy, for Mencken, was the most superior in its ability to move the *Übermensch* away from the "sentimentalism" enshrined in Christian culture, which only foments envy.

In his reading of *ressentiment*, Mencken argues it is primarily envy for "superior" individuals that stands as the true scandal of democracy. The true victims of democracy are those who are wrongly oppressed and disdained by their own communities but nevertheless distinguished by their will and personal achievement, not by race or birth. In an essay entitled "The Nietzschean Line," Wilson argues that Mencken has "a diluted and inconsistent Nietzscheanism." He affirms that

Mencken "believes that the illiterate should be left illiterate; that the poor should be left poor; that the socially inferior should be kept in their places." Mencken literalized the Nietzschean *Übermensch* ethos without any pressure to dilute its potency.

Mencken's undiluted Nietzschean radicalism had popular appeal at the time. The famous 1926 criminal case of Leopold and Loeb testifies to a general Nietzschean radicalism that was in the air. Leopold and Loeb were two wealthy students at the University of Chicago who committed the murder of a fourteen-year-old boy, an event that received major press attention and came to be known as the "crime of the century." The Nietzschean motivation for the crime is found in the fact that the two men committed the murder to prove they were of higher intelligence. The case was defended by the famous trial lawyer Clarence Darrow, who had argued cases in front of the Supreme Court and was among the most famous trial lawyers in all of America at the time.

Darrow argued that the two men had read Nietzsche at too young of an age: "At seventeen, at sixteen, at eighteen, while healthy boys were playing baseball or working on the farm, or doing odd jobs, Babe was reading Nietzsche, a boy who never should have seen it, at that early age."[22] Over the course of several hours, Darrow pleaded with the court that Nietzsche held a contemptuous, scornful attitude toward all those things which the young are taught are important in life, constituting "a fixing of new values which are not the values by which any normal child has ever yet been reared. Nietzsche's attitude is but a philosophical dream, containing more or less truth, that was not meant by anyone to be applied to life."[23]

Darrow's deposition resembles much of the same warnings that Carl Jung offered regarding Nietzsche's reactionary radicalism in his seminars on *Zarathustra*. Darrow read Nietzsche's morals in a far more undiluted way than post-war Nietzscheans such as Deleuze when he argued that "the morality of the master class is irritating to the taste of the present day because of its fundamental principle that a man has obligation only to his equals; that he may act to all of lower rank and to all that are foreign, as he pleases."[24] Such a sentiment was also imbued in Mencken's Nietzschean perspective, which led Leopold and Loeb, as well as Mencken, to believe they belonged to a "rare superior order of beings; that they are, in fact, 'aristocratic,' and that the other people don't matter."[25]

But while there were undiluted Nietzscheans such as Mencken in pre-World War II America, there were also left-Nietzscheans as well. The socialist magazine the *New Masses*, which had a wide readership in the 1920s, took to making fun of Mencken's Nietzscheanism in one issue. In a cartoon Mencken is portrayed as "The American Superman," but he appears as a man-child being milked by a large androgynous mother-like figure like a full-grown adult baby. In the background are the famous "asses" from Nietzsche's "The Ass Festival" in *Thus Spoke Zarathustra*. In this parable, Zarathustra interacts with the masses, who piously rehearse a celebration in front of Zarathustra's cave — the Ass Festival is a sort of reversal of the repetition of Christian congregation. It enacts a different form of religious ceremony in which the aristocratic community-founder, Zarathustra, welcomes the "convalescent," or those who are in the process of healing from the degenerate faith of the moralistic religious ceremony, and it ends with a new Ass Festival centered around adoration of Zarathustra, showing the new, mythical power of Nietzsche's conversionary agenda. This cartoon poking fun of Mencken, published by a prominent socialist magazine, shows the degree to which socialists at the time read Nietzsche as an explicit enemy of the masses and working-class liberation.

If Mencken stood as the pinnacle of undiluted Nietzschean intellectuals, Jack London, the famous American novelist, stood at the radical opposite end of the Nietzschean political spectrum. London was not an anti-Nietzschean in any straightforward sense, he rather aimed for a reversal of Nietzscheanism. London's appropriation was common among many working-class readers of Nietzsche — recall the survey data of German workers who read Nietzsche's Superman ethics during the turn of the twentieth century as speaking to them as workers, not to their bosses. Thus, even though Nietzsche wrote for "rulers," he also preached the doctrine of perspectivism, and this meant that workers could find themselves in a receptive position relative to his philosophy more generally.

London was a charismatic socialist with Bolshevik affinities. He was one of the primary spokespeople for the Socialist Party of America under the leadership of Eugene Debs. While London is known to middle-school students across America to this day for his famous novels such as *White Fang* and *Call of the Wild*, these were side projects to make money. London's true passion was class struggle. As a committed socialist, he raised money for the Bolsheviks prior to the Russian Revolution in 1917. He grew up in abject poverty but was admitted to U.C. Berkeley after experiencing homelessness and working backbreaking jobs most of his young life. Shortly after he stepped foot on the elite campus of U.C. Berkeley, he experienced such liminal dissonance — due to the predominantly bourgeois class experiences of the student body — that he soon dropped out.

DRAWING BY M. A. T.

AMONG THE ASSES

or, the Immaculate Conception of the American Superman

Figure 1. A cartoon making fun of H.L. Mencken's Nietzschean contempt for the masses. Published in the most widely read socialist magazine in America at the time, The New Masses, 1927.

The scholar Ishay Landa has painted London as fundamentally caught between an attachment to Nietzschean heroic individualism and a socialist commitment to worker liberation. London was indeed split by an ambivalent attachment to Nietzsche, and he underwent two intellectual conversions in his life, one to Nietzsche's mythology of the glorious "blond beast" and *Übermensch*, and the other to socialism. But like a fellow socialist agitator of London's time, the great "Big Bill" Haywood of the Industrial Workers of the World, who once remarked, "I've never read Marx's *Capital*, but I've got the marks of capital all over my body," London developed a hardscrabble idea of socialism based on his direct experience of wage labor in all its discipline and grueling drudgery. "I became a Socialist in a fashion somewhat similar to the way in which the Teutonic pagans became Christians — it was hammered into me."[26]

It is important that we note that London read far more Nietzsche than Marx, and he was really only fluent in *The Communist Manifesto*. Ishay Landa claims that London's project never resolved the profound incompatibility of Marx and Nietzsche, and he argues that although London expresses a set of views critical of Nietzsche's heroic individualism, he ultimately sought to fuse Nietzsche with socialism. That is, London could not shrug Nietzsche off entirely, and he remained fundamentally Nietzschean, even when he sought to overcome him. But London's struggle with reconciling the philosophy of Marx and Nietzsche is more complex than this, and his philosophical struggles between Marx and Nietzsche cannot be reduced to one or the other. London provides a parasitical reading of Nietzsche, not a full embrace of his thought. He sought to work through Nietzsche as a cultural influence within the class struggle by taking Nietzsche's radically aristocratic notions of superiority, strength, and ascending and descending lines of humanity in order to activate the will to fight in the proletariat.

But London's parasitism of Nietzsche was never fully understood, even by the socialists his political writings were meant to inspire. In his biography of London, the American labor historian Philip Foner notes that the final statement London wrote before his death was this: "*Martin Eden* and *Sea Wolf*, attacks on Nietzschean philosophy, which even the socialists missed the point of."[27] Arguably, the most important proletarian work that London wrote concerned the plight of the lumpenproletariat and factory proletariat in London, England, and Cannery Row in Alaska. It is no surprise that Nietzsche seized London so deeply, because he experienced the realities of proletarian existence not in books but in his life. In his youth, London experienced a hardscrabble and daunting life, full of hunger, homelessness, and abject poverty. Once London made enough money from his popular novel writing, he pursued his true passion, which was to document the conditions of the proletariat and to organize international working-class revolution. London's proletariat works are journalistic and anthropological. He wrote of the workers he encountered in these conditions, "They refuse to be the 'glad perishers' so glowingly described by Nietzsche," and he said, "I found all sorts of men, many of whom had once been as good as myself and just as blond-beastly; sailor men, soldier-men, labor-men, all wrenched and distorted and twisted out of shape by toil and hardship and accident, and cast adrift by their masters like so many old horses."[28]

During the pre-World War I period, London became a chief propagandist and popular speaker for Eugene Debs's

Socialist Party of America. In 1906, he went on a speaking tour of Ivy League universities to raise money to send to the Bolsheviks, during which he preached socialism with a verve and charisma that made him one of the most vocal and visible champions of the socialist worldview in America at the time. At a talk London gave at Yale, he ended his speech with a rousing class-conscious message to the elite students gathered there: "If you cannot fight for the socialist cause, we want you to fight against us. Fight for us or fight against us! Raise your voices one way or the other; be alive!" The students carried London out of the auditorium on their shoulders as if he were a star quarterback.

It is no surprise that London's works were among some of the first that the Nazis burned, especially given the centrality of Nietzsche for the fascist regime. But although London preached socialism, he had absorbed Nietzsche's understanding of the class system in capitalism as fundamentally divided between the noble and the passive, lower plebeian. London's Manichean Nietzscheanism, however, was a reversal of Nietzsche's own class views, which sought solidarity with bourgeois interests:

> It was the same everywhere, crime and betrayal, betrayal and crime — men who were alive, but who were neither clean nor noble, men who were clean and noble by who were not alive. Then there was a great, hopeless mass, neither noble nor alive, but merely clean. It did not sin positively nor deliberately; but it did sin passively and ignorantly by acquiescing in the current immorality and profiting by it. Had it been noble and alive it would not have been ignorant and it would have refused to share in the profits of betrayal and crime. I discovered I did not like it on the parlor floor of

society. Intellectually I was bored. Morally and spiritually I was sickened.[29]

This passage reveals London's socialist reversal of Nietzsche: the workers are the clean, while the wealthy bourgeoisie of high society are the dirty. But within this division some are alive, and some are passive and effectively dead. To be alive is to fight, to struggle. London enacts a reversal of the predominant Social Darwinism of Herbert Spencer by placing the worker and the proletarian in the position of strength. In his study of Nietzsche and popular mass culture, Ishay Landa is right to point out that "the ultimate problem as far as Nietzsche was concerned were the modern masses becoming a sovereign political power,"[30] and London understood this problem just as well as Nietzsche. But he sought to reverse the victors of the struggle. In so doing, London adopted a fundamentally Nietzschean idea of race and class.

London's racism has recently come under scrutiny following the Black Lives Matter protests of 2020. There were calls for London Square in Oakland, California, to be renamed due to suspicions of London's racist past. These calls for a racial reckoning, even with a figure such as London, are extremely important, as is getting a clearer picture of what sort of racism London in fact practiced. The story of London's racism is complex and ultimately reflective of his engagement with Nietzsche's thought. For London, racial and class identity were intertwined, both autobiographically and in his Nietzschean-Marxist understanding of race and class. London came from a proletarian family and his biological mother was an outright racist herself, even encouraging London to look down on white people with brown hair. However, London was also raised by an African American wet nurse and proxy mother named Virginia Prentiss who had previously been enslaved. London fought against his mother's racist views and ended up buying Virginia Prentiss a home after enjoying some financial success from his novels. In his later years, London also participated in Japanese-American cultural exchange programs and expressed a cosmopolitan, even liberal, idea of cross-ethnic and cross-racial harmony. But despite these personal experiences with the complexity of race in Reconstruction-era America, London's idea of race is best understood through his Nietzschean attachments.

For Nietzsche, race was understood as intertwined with class in such a way that racial differences were to be transversally composed. Racial differences were thus turned on their head in Nietzsche's vision — race was incorporated into his vision of a coming future society where great men would contend for dominance. Nietzsche's understanding of race, perhaps paradoxically, should therefore be decoupled from the more vulgar biological conception of difference that informed Wagnerian and most social-Darwinist frameworks of race, which insisted on

Figure 2. The famous anti-fascist Hollywood actor Edward G. Robinson as Captain Wolf Larsen, the brutal Nietzschean Übermensch *in the 1941 film* The Sea Wolf. *Written and produced by Robert Rossen and adapted from Jack London's novel of the same name.*

the existence of racial genetic and intellectual deficiencies. Nietzsche shifts the very basis of racial difference to the "well-formed/ill-formed" distinction, and it is important to note that he advocated eugenics not merely for the "malformed" — Losurdo and other scholars have shown that Nietzsche went even further and advocated for the annihilation of the "decadent races."[31]

Nietzsche broke with the Christian-based anti-Semitism of Richard Wagner in his transversal racialization approach, which stemmed from an anti-Christian and neo-pagan line of continuity. It is also crucial to understand that the new pan-European elite made up of the master *Übermensch* which Nietzsche called for was also one that could be composed on a cross-racial solidarity, which could include Aryan, European, white, Jewish, and black races. What is essential is the well-formed/ill-formed dichotomy, and furthermore the notion of an ever-immanent, ascending and declining Manichean split within humanity:

Commerce and industry, the circulation of books and letters, the commonality of all high culture [*Kultur*], rapid changes of place and of scenery, the present nomadic existence of all those who do not own land — these conditions are inevitably bringing along with them a weakening and finally a destruction of nations, at least of the European ones: so that as a consequence of these changes and the continual crossbreeding that they occasion, a mixed race, the European, must come into being.[32]

Nietzsche de-essentializes racial difference and couches the question of race in terms of a grand racial struggle whereby crossbreeding creates new physiological and reactionary tendencies and new "herd-species" get developed. In an unpublished fragment from 1885, he writes, "Whoever has a strong commanding and daring will definitely achieves supremacy in such times."[33]

For, however heterodox Nietzsche's vision of racial struggle may have been, it is crucial that we recognize his vision does not challenge a liberal capitalist vision of race. Although he did not live to witness our society, Nietzsche's conception of racial conflict *describes* the neoliberal functioning of racialized capitalism in surprisingly accurate ways. Nietzsche's racism is one whereby winners and losers are immanently decided and divvied up, but according to which the basis of that division is not pre-determined by race as such. It is this quasi-cosmopolitan, elitist racism that informed Jack London's idea that the class struggle would require the noble and the clean to unite — across class positions, importantly — and to forge solidarity for the cause of proletarian revolution. But such a socialist praxis leads to a fundamentally voluntarist understanding of the class struggle and praxis of revolution.

When Nietzsche prophetically states that only "from you that have chosen yourselves will grow the Overman,"[34] what he means is that the class struggle is ultimately decided on the basis of an unavoidable heroism that must sprout from the scene of contesting wills, where a passive mass of workers are dead and asleep, mired in *ressentiment*, but among whom is the rare and heroic *Übermensch* capable of deciding their greatness.

Is there an alternative vision to such a conception of heroic voluntarism in revolutionary socialist thought? Is Nietzsche's cultural influence so great that no synthesis of Nietzsche and Marx can be accomplished that would be capable of overcoming this conundrum? These questions lead us to consider how Nietzsche is read by the working class. Is the danger of Nietzsche on the left that he seeks to seduce working-class readers into his romantic but ultimately bourgeois-supporting project? Does reading Nietzsche force us to abandon the working class all together and result in a tribe of intellectual *Übermenschen* uncommitted to collective solidarity? Are such readings of Nietzsche inevitable? The challenge that London raises is precisely centered on whether a synthesis of Nietzsche with Marx can be plausibly achieved such that this synthesis does not undermine the Marxist core goal of proletarian liberation.

The sociologist Adolf Levenstein wrote an important work entitled *Friedrich Nietzsche in the Judgment of the Working Class*, which performed a sociological analysis of how Nietzsche was read and interpreted by German workers around the turn of the century. What Levenstein discovered in this study, perhaps unsurprisingly, is that Nietzsche's seductive style attracted what Geoff Waite calls a "proletarian reading formation," which was quite critical of Nietzsche. In other words, much of what Nietzsche "really meant," namely his overt reactionary politics and anti-masses message, was intimated by working-class readers as a reactionary philosophy that could be converted toward working-class ends. Levenstein polled German workers once in 1912 and again in 1919, immediately after the war. He discovered that Nietzsche resonated with the workers, and whether they were educated or non-educated, Nietzsche connected to their lives, especially to their sense of "tragic isolation," and he sparked a need to cultivate an "inner life" among these working-class readers. The workers tended to connect with Nietzsche as the "quintessential outsider," and even though Nietzsche's philosophy was hostile to the working class, his thought worked "strongly and bindingly on the most neglected core of society."[35]

Nietzsche was a highly familiar intellectual point of reference for the working class, just as he remains today. But Nietzsche didn't attract a certain readership so much as he created it. If, as Lou Salomé writes, Nietzsche did not write to convince, he wrote to convert, this means that Nietzsche's popularity has effects and does more than just offer a sense of individual purpose. In the class struggle, Nietzsche directs his readers to take a position that can be detrimental. Among the literary establishment and socialist writers in the pre-World War I period, Nietzsche's reactionary philosophy and the possibility of his converting working-class readers away from collective solidarity was acknowledged by socialist thinkers such as London and Leon Trotsky.

Trotsky published his first major article in 1900, "On the Philosophy of the Superman." Written in part to mark the occasion of Nietzsche's death, in it Trotsky points out that Nietzsche's philosophy of radical individualism did not only appeal to the bourgeoisie or to the men of Wall Street and high finance. Trotsky pinpoints the problem of Nietzsche for working-class politics when he notes that Nietzsche "became the ideologue of a group living like a bird of prey at the expense of society, but under conditions more fortunate than those of the miserable lumpenproletariat: they are a *parasitenproletariat* of a higher caliber."[36] Trotsky identifies a particular deleterious class formation that emerges as the chief expositor of the Nietzschean philosophy, a class formation which was unconsciously furthering a bourgeois, heroic, individualist conception of themselves — influenced by Nietzsche's thought — while at the same time appealing to a socialist movement and its values.

Like Jack London and Huey Newton — who we will explore at the end of this chapter — Nietzsche divides intellectuals on the left. Is a synthesis possible with Marx and Nietzsche? This question draws one into the more fundamental question of how to activate the working class in the class struggle; that is, the question of how to incorporate Nietzsche on the left revolves around waking the working class up from its apolitical slumber. But what comes after one uses Nietzsche for class consciousness is what matters even more. An *Übermensch* ethics was brought into the left to foment a revolt against a decadent and stultified bourgeois class, and its function — during the turn of the century up to World War I — was to spark radical consciousness among the working class.

Bolshevism and the Inescapability of Nietzscheanism

Nietzsche was not an optional figure at the turn of the twentieth century. The fin de siècle was a turning point in capitalist social relations, and the coming Great War would stage a series of revolutions against the vestiges of the aristocracy and monarchial elements within the European ruling classes. Revolutions took many forms across Europe, and not all of them were successful; however, none proved more consequential and world-transforming than the Russian Revolution of 1917. Reflecting on its one-hundred-year anniversary in 2017, Alain Badiou referred to it as "an unprecedented event in the history of the human species."[37]

Antonio Gramsci characterized the Russian Revolution as "the great revolution against '*Capital*.'"[38] By this curious statement, Gramsci means that Bolshevism tapped into a form of Marxism that proved — by the success of the revolution — that the determinant of history is not lifeless economics, but "man; societies made up of men, men who have something in common, who get along together, and because of this (civility) they develop a collective social will."[39] The mature Marx of *Capital* had a conception of transition from capitalism to communism such that some interpreted him to be arguing that revolution will emerge from the sheer weight of capitalism's own internal contradictions. Whether Marx put such a rather vulgar idea forward or not is not of interest to us, but what is of interest are the conditions under which the Bolshevik Revolution actually occurred. Its first notable feature was that it was forged through a collective will in the face of great catastrophe — a world war the likes of which humanity had never experienced — and the second feature is that the Bolsheviks overthrew the bourgeoisie in a society which had not yet undergone a full-on liberal bourgeois revolution.

Gramsci is correct to point out that the Bolsheviks defied the implied theory of revolution in Marx's *Capital* — Marx, after all, did not develop or predict the course of proletarian revolution — by harnessing the will power of the proletariat in a country which was still dominated by the aristocracy. In such a context, where revolution was so vitally dependent on the organization of the proletariat, it should come as no surprise that Nietzsche's thought, as well as Nietzscheanism, would prove decisive. When compared to the mature Marx, Nietzsche's prognostications of future "great socialistic wars" proved more prescient than Marx's rather scant ideas of future conflict. The question that must be asked is: How did the Bolsheviks treat the "Nietzsche virus" in the culture at the time? How did they read Nietzsche and how was Nietzsche incorporated *within* the Bolshevik movement?

Nietzsche was among the most popular writers for the working class in Germany, and among the literati and educated classes in Russia reading him was an essential rite of passage. As we saw in Levenstein's study, the reading habits of the working class expressed a critical reading method. Nietzsche was read as appropriable for working-class experiences, but at the same time, the problem remained that Nietzsche's liberationist philosophy was not easily transferable to socialist or collectivist ends. A hyphenated "Nietzschean-socialism" or "Nietzschean-Marxism" required the mediation of intellectuals; it required Nietzsche to enter the polemics on the left. Someone like Jack London would likely have rejected the idea that his attempt to critique Nietzsche resulted in a Marxist-Nietzscheanism. For London, Nietzscheanism as a general cultural presence had to be combated by the working class, and this required a working through of Nietzsche so that the working class could shrug off his elitist philosophy.

Nietzsche played a formative role in Bolshevik thought running up to and especially in the wake of the revolution, when a new myth for the proletariat had to be invented. Bernice Glatzer's *New Myth, New World: From Nietzsche to Stalinism* offers the most in-depth study of how Nietzscheanism functioned in Russian culture prior to 1917, and of how Nietzsche's thought forged the post-revolutionary sequence through to Stalin's rise and ascension to power. It is also a well-researched survey of the ways Nietzsche was read by Bolshevik intellectuals and leaders. But Glatzer's argument ends up assigning Nietzsche an outsized influence on Bolshevism and fails to differentiate the ways that Bolshevik thinkers worked to isolate the problematic aspects of Nietzsche's philosophy via strategies that Trotsky had noted in his early 1900 essay.

According to Glatzer, Bolshevism *as such* was Nietzschean.

Nietzsche's concepts were inescapable for the Bolsheviks. The mythology of the *Übermensch*, the emphasis on hardness and cruelty, and the very idea of a transvaluation of values were all adopted *fait accompli*. But it is not clear whether Nietzsche was adopted because Nietzschean ideas were "in the air" or if the Bolsheviks were capable of a discerning judgment of Nietzsche; that is if they were capable of distancing themselves from him. If Nietzsche, or more accurately Nietzscheanism, was truly an inescapable influence at each of the stages of the Russian Revolution — from the pre-revolutionary period, to the domestic civil war between the Bolsheviks and the White Army, to the New Economic Policy, all the way up to Stalin's rise to power and the introduction of his bureaucratic regime — this means that in the realm of theory, Nietzscheanism was *mandatory* for the Bolsheviks. But was Nietzsche mandatory for the major Bolshevik theorists like Lenin, Bukharin, Gorky, and Trotsky?

A closer analysis of these thinkers' works reveals that while Nietzsche was certainly embraced outright by a faction within the Bolsheviks, Nietzsche's philosophy split the Bolshevik movement. He was not a fatalist presence within Bolshevism; rather, the Bolsheviks show that the theory of Nietzsche as a general cultural ideology can be contested and worked through. The reality is that these thinkers sought to distance themselves from Nietzsche time and again. Although Nietzsche does not appear in Lenin's treatise against Machist philosophy in the Bolshevik movement, *Empirio Criticism: Critical Comments on a Reactionary Philosophy* was an implicit critique of subjectivist and irrationalist philosophy. Yet, Glatzer insists that Nietzsche's "values and attitudes" were "imprinted in the foundational myth"[40] of Bolshevism. Nietzsche's was a philosophy of "hardness" and "cruelty" that justified the Bolsheviks' more brutal policies toward their enemies.

Glatzer argues that Bolshevism was not able to escape the ideology of Nietzscheanism and that it provided the sort of philosophy needed to pierce the rigid Christian-orthodox establishment morality, to harness the gritty toughness of proletarian revolutionary energy, and ultimately to forge a new myth for the new communist state after the success of 1917. We already saw that, at the time, Nietzsche's presence in Western intellectual circles was practically inescapable, but just as his philosophy was so widely adopted, Marxist and socialist detractors were certainly present within the Bolshevik movement. This is a view that Geoff Waite also adopts in his reading of Lenin: "[Lenin] had no choice except to confront the ever growing phenomenon of Nietzscheanism as 'popular' phenomenon."[41] In one survey of an anonymous worker circa 1912, they wrote: "For the person who can look further into the distance, the way goes through socialism to the possibility of individuality in Nietzsche."[42]

Where Glatzer is most convincing is in her discussion of Nietzschean ideals that were infused into the *Proletkult* working-class cultural movement and the ways that self-avowed Bolshevik Nietzscheans such as Bogdanov, Lunacharsky, and Ivanov indeed worked with Nietzschean concepts in their writings and advocacy for new cultural and mythical festivals to build proletarian pride and ludic consciousness-raising. Glatzer notes that Lunacharsky called for and helped to invent the concept of new mass festivals, which he saw as "a powerful agitational tool" meant to "excite the feelings of the audience and readers and [have] a direct influence on their will."[43] But Glatzer misses the very real danger that Bolshevik thinkers identified in Nietzsche, including leading thinkers like Lenin, Trotsky, and Bukharin. From his jail cell, Bukharin wrote of Nietzsche, in a poem entitled "Mad Prophet":

Your sanguinary delirium
> *About the "will to power"*
> *Morality of the master caste,*
> *The blonde menagerie*
> *That subjugates the people;*
> *Above smoke and blood and bonfires,*
> *About wars without end;*
> *And the Dionysian orgies*
> *Of the predatory beasts.*

Your ravings about the "Superman"
> *Above the slaves, "the herd"*
> *Of those who under him will kiss*
> *The dust from aeon to aeon.*

All of Zarathustra's aphorisms,
> *The Virgin soil of paradox,*
> *Are elegant, subtle sophisms*
> *Turning everything to blood.*

And it's no accident that now
> *War, robbery and every vice*
> *In your high pride are blessed by you,*
> Prophet of the Lunatic Asylum.[44]

Bukharin recognized Nietzsche as an inescapable cultural force that had wreaked havoc on the very prospect of revolution. He pinpoints the madness of Nietzsche not in the standard bourgeois liberal conception of Nietzsche's mental illness, but as stemming from the cultural and political success of his reactionary philosophy in society. Nietzsche, the "Mad Prophet," is made mad precisely by the success of his attempts to retain a feudal rank order amid a social moment that witnessed the collapse of the aristocracy.

In Glatzer's analysis of Nietzsche's role in the Bolshevik movement, Nietzscheanism was victorious and spelled the defeat of Bolshevism. Glatzer thus hints at the cryptic statement made by Georges Bataille that "Nietzsche is the only philosopher outside of communism."[45] Glatzer's implied argument is something like Bataille's premonition: no true overcoming of Nietzsche was possible in the Bolshevik movement and on through to Stalinism. The times required the brutality; the justification for the invention of a new man demanded the violent catastrophe that came with Stalin's "socialism in one country."

The Bolshevik revolution remains a lesson to the left today, precisely due to the theoretical ingenuity of the Bolsheviks' practice. Trotsky, Lenin, and Bukharin each rejected Nietzscheanism. They did not aim to synthesize Nietzsche within a socialist worldview; that is, there was no elective affinity on offer. Nietzsche was recognized as an enemy to the left whose cultural hegemony had to be worked though. But what happens when no enmity is recognized at all? What happens when Nietzsche is placed in the theoretical driver's seat of the left?

Deleuze's Nietzsche: The Counterculture Rebel

One of the most influential incorporations of Nietzsche on the left is found in the work of post-war French philosopher

Gilles Deleuze. Deleuze's embrace of Nietzsche is different than that of any of the thinkers on the left we are discussing in this chapter in that he sought to center Nietzsche as the primary philosopher. But Deleuze read Nietzsche in a highly idiosyncratic and singular way as offering a toolbox of concepts for experimentation. Deleuze affirms that the greatness of Nietzsche is not found in how he interprets history or philosophy and nor does he offer any source of meaning. This leads Deleuze to develop a highly creative appropriation of Nietzsche, which he applies to the history of philosophy, and places Nietzsche at the center of his political thought.

We will begin by assessing Deleuze's Nietzsche in an essay called "Nomad Thought," published in 1962, the same year as his major work *Nietzsche and Philosophy*. In it, Deleuze lays out the political function of his Nietzsche more explicitly than in any of his other works. "Nomad Thought" is Deleuze's Nietzschean manifesto, a text that celebrates Nietzsche as the pre-eminent thinker of the counterculture, usurping both Marx and Freud in importance for the left. Deleuze declares Nietzsche the most vital philosopher for liberation. Just six years after this essay was published, the May '68 uprising occurred. Deleuze begins the essay by arguing that it is Nietzsche's method and style that makes him so revolutionary:

> It is at the level of methodology that the question of Nietzsche's revolutionary character arises: the Nietzschean method itself makes the text something about which we should no longer ask ourselves, "is it fascistic, bourgeois or revolutionary rather it is a field of per se"; externality where fascistic, bourgeois and revolutionary forces confront one another.[46]

It is important that we identify what Deleuze stresses as

most vital in Nietzsche's thought. For Deleuze, the will to power reduces relations to what he calls their "disembodied forces," which means that Nietzsche's style becomes a "political instrument" for decoding repressive social codes imposed by the family and capitalist social life. Thus, it is not a synthesis of Marx with Nietzsche that Deleuze is after. "Marx and Freud may be the dawn of our culture, but with Nietzsche, something altogether different occurs: the dawn of a counterculture."[47]

In Deleuze's view, Nietzsche is all the left needs. And it is Nietzsche's style that is the key to his liberatory offerings, specifically his use of the aphorism. The aphorism is so valuable because it represents a play of impersonal forces that is "always outside the others." Nietzsche's aphorisms "mean nothing" and "signify nothing," and thus have no more a signifier than a signified element. Nietzsche's dramatic personae, the Antichrist, Zarathustra, and Dionysus, are transhistorical figures who are invoked as "neither signifier nor signified elements, they are rather designations of intensity upon a body which can be the body of the Earth, the body of the book, but also the suffering body of Nietzsche: I am all the names of history."

Marx's class analysis and the centrality of the proletariat or the working class as the agent of emancipation are thrown out the window in Deleuze's thought, making Nietzsche the main philosopher of the left. The historical context of Deleuze's political situation must be noted in this analysis. Deleuze was writing at the peak of the Cold War and the war in Vietnam, as well as of the reactionary state communism of Stalin's regime. In a reference to the more senior French Nietzschean philosophy of Pierre Klossowski, Deleuze states that Nietzsche's subversive power is in the fact that he "plotted against his own class." Nietzsche is the thinker of liberation in the most fundamental ways because his philosophy exceeds the repressive traps that language imposes on our bodies; it is only Nietzsche's philosophy that circumvents the bureaucratic stagnation that Marxism and Freudianism had fallen sway to in the era of Stalinism. Deleuze writes, "We clearly know that the revolutionary problem today is that of finding a unity of localized struggle without falling back into the despotic and bureaucratic organization of the Party or the State."[48] Nietzsche thinks beyond the state, beyond institutions; he *de-classes* his readers. Deleuze finds these decoding and de-territorializing gestures liberatory. Nietzsche collapses the very distinction between left and right.

Yet why is the counterculture offered up as the primary — and desired — site of liberation for Deleuze? A look at Deleuze's *Nietzsche and Philosophy* helps to shed light on the central role of culture. For Nietzsche, culture is made up of the "morality of customs," which can include torture, "iron collars," and everything that is obeyed by a people, class, or race. That which is obeyed is always what Nietzsche calls a "reactive force," but in the act of obeying laws there emerges a generic adherence to them. Culture is a battleground where reactive forces, some arbitrary, some cruel, and some stupid, are all played out. But the principal object of culture is to "reinforce consciousness." And the function of culture is to make man into a promising being, a subject of the creditor-debtor relation from which the archaic cultural conflict of the master and the slave emerges. When man is made to feel responsible for his reactive forces, the state of bad conscience occurs in which he also feels culpable for these reactive forces. Deleuze writes that, "however we consider culture or justice we always see in them the exercise of a formative activity, the opposite of *ressentiment* and bad conscience."[49]

Nietzsche's historical analysis of the origin of culture tracks the emergence of the "free and active man," or the man who can promise, in distinction to the slave, who is adjusted to normative constraints and "codes of repression." For Deleuze, this means that Nietzsche identifies a higher figure who appears "at the end of the tremendous process" of culture: "The sovereign individual, like only to himself, liberated again from morality of customs, autonomous and supramoral." This man "has his own independent, protracted will and the right to make promises,"[50] as Nietzsche remarks. "The product of culture is not the man who obeys the law, but the sovereign legislative individual who defines himself by power over himself, over destiny, over the law: the free, the light, the *irresponsible*."[51]

But culture also triumphs in a reactive form, precisely in what Nietzsche famously calls the "herd" — which he defines as history itself. Deleuze reads Nietzsche with a highly selective lens when he portrays Nietzsche's idea of the herd as the very core of universal history. Deleuze writes, "History thus appears as the act by which reactive forces take possession of culture or divert its course in their favour."[52] This framework for understanding history completely sidesteps the historical context in which Nietzsche wrote and how his very idea of what constitutes "reactive" elements in culture is fundamentally bound up with the egalitarian universalist socialist struggle of his time. It should now be clear why culture emerges as the site of emancipation for Deleuze. Nietzsche's conception of history leads to an understanding that all institutions of culture — including contemporary culture — are born from reactionary forces. In a way, like Foucault's Nietzschean understanding of power as a ubiquitous force that animates all social relations, Deleuze sees all of culture as covered in reactionary, impersonal forces.

The Nietzsche scholar Matthew Dill has shown that Deleuze's conception of the will to power is misleading as it misrepresents both Nietzsche's and Deleuze's own use of the terms. Nietzsche tends to reserve the terms "active" and "reactive" for his descriptions of force (*Kraft*), and Deleuze uses different terminology when describing modes of power (*Macht*). Deleuze flips this association and applies "active" and "reactive" to his descriptions of force while using the terms "affirmative" and "negative" for his descriptions of will to power.[53] What is at issue is two different meanings of the will to power, one as force and the other as power. Dill points out that by flipping these associations, Deleuze ends up with an instrumentalist theory of power qua power as domination, and that he transposes weakness and strength onto force, not power, which is the opposite of how these terms function in Nietzsche's usage.

But even with this reversal of force and power at work, Zarathustra's teachings on the "transvaluation of values" insists on a total break, which occurs at the moment of a destructive transmutation. Nietzsche writes in *Ecce Homo*, "I know the pleasure in destroying to a degree that accords to my power to destroy."[54] Importantly, Nietzsche stressed that the market and economic struggle are not the site for the transvaluation; it is culture. As he states in *Zarathustra*, "Away from the marketplace and from fame have ever dwelt the devisers of new values."[55] Deleuze follows this emphasis on culture as the site of politics, and this shapes his views, especially in the '68 period and arguably throughout his work. It is well known that, for Deleuze, Nietzsche's radicalism is found in his opposition to dialectics and in his embrace of Nietzsche's will to power. Dialectics, to which socialism, Christianity, and egalitarian traditions are all beholden, do not realize that "a will does not want an end or a telos — those are essences and weak forces."[56]

Nietzsche is incorporated as the main philosopher of the left to overcome the weak and the passive "codings" that are imposed on individuals — irrespective of class — which means that socialist parties, working-class organizations, and institutions which may further the ends of a more patient revolutionary situation all come under suspicion. The problem with Deleuze's Nietzsche is in this ubiquitous notion that "culture comes to serve reactive forces which pervert it."[57] There is no historical reconstruction of Nietzsche's times and the political context that shaped his thought. Deleuze's Nietzsche omits any mention of the significance of the French Revolution for Nietzsche's thought on social and political matters.

In the final estimation, Deleuze's Nietzsche does not allow us to detect liberal bourgeois forces as reactionary forces because this reading of culture construes it as *totally* reactive. Nietzsche emerges as a counterculture rebel who points to abstract reactionary forces that are ultimately indiscernible in society. Deleuze's Nietzsche takes up a trend in the wider field of French Nietzscheanism after World War II: he systematically sidelines any association with Nietzsche's aristocratic radicalism in relation to his interpretation of Nietzschean concepts.

As Jan Rehmann has convincingly shown in his study of both Deleuze and Foucault, Nietzsche's concept of the pathos of distance is read by Deleuze with no attention to the fact that the concept is meant to differentiate noble from plebeian. Rehmann notes that "for Deleuze in the origin there is only 'active' and 'reactive,' 'affirming' and 'negating' forces, which are called allegorically 'noble' and 'base.'"[58] Deleuze's Nietzsche whitewashes the aristocratic Janus face of Nietzsche, leaving only an ultra-leftist rebel who smells reactionary forces in everything. The problem with the proposition that everything is reactionary is that leftist struggles lose their capacity to confront specific fascist threats when they appear. It is not clear whether everything is bourgeois, everything is fascist, or if everything bourgeois is already fascist.

Nietzsche within the Black Panthers

Huey Newton was the co-founder and one of the most important theorists of the Black Panthers, a Marxist-Leninist black-power organization that was catalytic in shaping black struggle in America. Newton was fluent in Marxist schools of thought from Leninism and Maoism to Stalinism, and he read widely in Western literature and philosophy. Inspired by Third World struggles and revolutions that shrugged off colonial occupation and oppression, Newton combined a tactical and strategic vision with theoretical sophistication.

For Newton, as for the Panthers overall, philosophy and theory were invaluable tools for the struggle. The main challenge was a cultural one; namely, how to revolutionize and spark proletarian consciousness, especially among black Americans. Decades and generations of segregationist, white-supremacist oppression was formally coming to an end with the success of the Civil Rights movement, but these concessions were half measures, and the mainstream Civil Rights movement was a far cry from the class-struggle revolutionary politics that the Panthers championed.

The Panthers' tactics differed from the more mainstream civil rights strategies of nonviolent agitation spearheaded by Martin Luther King Jr., which sought to mobilize large-scale consciousness toward legislative and policy changes. The Panthers instead set their sights on mobilizing inner-city black populations into cadres primed for revolutionary agitation. But this revolutionary energy did not exist inertly within the people, it had to be cultivated and brought out. For Newton, this is where Nietzsche came into the picture, precisely regarding the question of the internalized value system of both blacks and whites in American culture.

Newton was raised in a left-wing family and was named after the left-populist leader Huey Long, who famously criticized F.D.R.'s New Deal as being too moderate. A true autodidact intellectual, Newton was committed to Marxist revolutionary thought in the Leninist tradition, and he worked especially with the insights of Maoism and the Chinese Cultural Revolution. Newton's class analysis was fundamental to his worldview, and it shaped the way he saw white supremacy in America, even as a young boy:

I felt that white people were criminals because they plundered the world. It was more, however, than a simple antiwhite feeling, because I never wanted to hurt poor whites, even though I had met some in school who called me "nigger" and other names. I fought them, but I never took their lunches or money because I knew that they had nothing to start with. With those who had money it was a different story. I still equated having money with whiteness, and to take what was mine and what the white criminals called theirs gave me a feeling of real freedom.[59]

Along with the other co-founder of the Black Panthers, Eldridge Cleaver, Newton formulated the theory that late capitalism had undermined the revolutionary agency of the industrial working class and that any true revolutionary agitation in America — and globally — lay with those proletarians who had been formally barred from wage labor and marginalized from any of the promises of the post-war American welfare state. The Panthers aimed to spark a new consciousness of racial and class oppression among inner-city black populations who were experiencing the brunt of American imperial aggression in their everyday lives. How did the treatment of America's — mostly black — lumpenproletariat differ from that of the colonized in Southeast Asia, where America's war in Vietnam was raging? The problem revolved around the cultural and the psychological conditioning of the people, and this is precisely where Nietzsche's philosophy proved so influential to Newton's thinking. What are the strategies for promoting a fundamental shift in black consciousness toward militancy and radicalization? For Newton, this would not be achieved through cultural empowerment symbols such as "natural hair styles" and African nationalist pride symbols. Rather, Newton realized that it was necessary to fundamentally change the word "black."

While not citing Nietzsche explicitly, as early as 1971, the fifth year of the party's existence, Nietzsche's influence can be seen in Newton's article "Black Capitalist," where he writes:

When we coined the expression "All power to the people," we had in mind emphasizing the word "power" for we recognize that the will to power is the basic drive of man. But it is incorrect to seek power over people. We have been subjected to the dehumanizing power of exploitation and racism for

Figure 3. Huey Newton speaking at a conference in 1971 after returning from a visit to Mao's China. He would meet the psychoanalyst Erik Erikson at Boston University for a dialogue and exchange just a few months after this event.

hundreds of years; and the Black community has its will to power also. What we seek, however, is not power over people, but the power of control of our own destiny.[60]

The will to power is not theorized here as the possession of the more powerful group, but as capable of being realized by a subjugated community. Nor is the concern here a ubiquitous idea of power, such as we find in many contemporary academic studies of power, especially in the wake of the Nietzschean philosopher Michel Foucault. At a time when most left-Nietzscheans tend to see power everywhere, in the field of speech, language, culture, art, and style, the legacy of

Nietzsche's will to power has distorted our capacity to discern power and to rationally diagnose power relations in the world.

The error of seeing power in everything is owed to a certain reading of Nietzsche. As Nicos Poulantzas has remarked,

> It is often said that one can deduce from Foucault nothing more than a guerrilla war and scattered acts of harassment of power; but in fact, no kind of resistance is possible if we follow Foucault's analyses. For if power is always already there, if every power situation is immanent, why should there ever be resistance? From where would resistance come, and how would it be even possible?[61]

The Panthers stand out from this more recent trend in left-Nietzschean analysis of power because they linked all of their political activity to the prospect of global revolution informed by revolutionary Marxist doctrine.

Although the prospect of global revolution did not materialize in the West, the most lasting impact of Nietzsche on the Panthers came from the struggle in the cultural field. Newton's left-Nietzscheanism is a major factor in the radicalization of America's understanding of the police — namely, the Panthers made the police a fundamentally political category. In "Truth and Lying in an Extramoral Sense," Nietzsche writes of truth as

> a mobile army of metaphors, metonyms, and anthropomorphisms — in short, a sum of human relations which have been enhanced, transposed, and embellished poetically and rhetorically, and which after long use seem firm, canonical, and obligatory to *a people*: truths are illusions about which one has forgotten that this is what they are;

metaphors which are worn out and without sensuous power; coins which have lost their pictures and now matter only as metal, no longer as coins.[62]

American blacks are an exploited group, forced to accept a reality that pacifies their resolve for collective action and atomizes their general condition. Thus, what Newton realized was that in order to spark a revolutionary consciousness of this situation, it was necessary to "unhinge existing identities" and "to change their consciousness of themselves and to be less accepting of the white man's version of God — the God of the downtrodden, the weak, and the undeserving."[63] Reminiscent of Jack London's great attempt to reverse and appropriate Nietzsche's aristocratic praxis for the proletariat, Newton aimed for a *lumpen* transvaluation of black identity. Newton's aim was to foster a shift in consciousness among black people, particularly lumpenized blacks, toward seeing themselves as the called, the chosen, and the salt of the earth.[64]

For the ground to be laid for something like a revolutionary transformation in black identity, the field of struggle would be the site of language, where the meaning of common terms could be contested. Thus, in ways reminiscent of later "discourse theory," which grew to prominence in academia in the 1980s, Newton experimented with the very symbol of the police in the minds of Americans. Toward this end, the Panthers advocated the extreme slur "pig" for cops, a choice in terminology that was calculated and intended. Newton writes that use of the term "pig" was perfect for several reasons. First of all, words like "swine," "hog," "sow," and "pig" have always had unpleasant connotations. The reason for this probably has theological roots, since the pig is considered an unclean animal in Semitic religions. In the English language, well-established "pig" epithets are numerous — we say that someone "eats like a hog," is "a filthy swine," and so on."[65]

The Black Panther Party's use of the word "pig" was intended to strip the oppressors, namely the police, of their invincibility in the eyes of the black community. The word "pig" evokes a detestable image that takes away the image of omnipotence. A pig brings the theater of ordinary oppression — which is muted by the status quo of capitalist social life — out into the open. The term, in all its hyperbole, names what the unconscious of the oppressors refuses to say outright, which is that they see the poor black man as an animal, a pig. It is thus a reversal that is at work in the use of the term, and the association it evokes in the minds of people — both white and black — is meant to connect the man "running loose in the ghetto with a gun" with the man "sitting on Wall Street or in the White House." Both men, after all, "can bleed like a man and fall like a man."[66] The deployment of "pig" was an attempt to alter the consciousness of black people by removing them from the super-egoistic force of the police state. For white people, it was meant to shock and dissimulate: What would it mean for such a term to become normalized in common parlance?

If a transvaluation of the very meaning of the police were to transpire, such a movement would alter the very meaning of what the police stand for in society. In his dialogue with Newton, the psychoanalyst Erik Erikson points to this attempted transvaluation of the meaning of the police, from "armed technicians" meant to serve and protect to a completely different understanding of the police as fundamentally hostile and oppositional to the very values of the society. If such a transvaluation in the very meaning of the police were to be successful, it would affect the "frontier of the whole society's identity consciousness." Such a transvaluation would not necessarily be a "political victory," but a "propagandistic impact" if there was a "universal actualization of new images and symbols."[67]

Newton's appropriation of Nietzsche's idea of the transvaluation of values is an incredible testament to the creative ways that Nietzsche can be read by the left. Newton acknowledged that he did not agree with *everything* in Nietzsche's thought, which must mean that he was aware of the reactionary political core to Nietzsche. This led Newton to creatively misread Nietzsche. For example, he remarks that Nietzsche said the transvaluation of values was a political tactic implemented by the Christians in Ancient Roman society. Initially, the Christians were weak, but they understood how to transform this weakness through the power of language.

> By using phrases like "the meek shall inherit the earth," they imposed a new idea on the Romans, one that gave rise to doubt and led to defections to the new sect. Once the Christians stated that the meek shall inherit the earth and won over members, they weakened the strength of those in power."[68]

Thus, while Newton acknowledged that Nietzsche's ideas "had a great impact on the development of the Black Panther philosophy,"[69] we must understand this as a brilliant appropriation of Nietzsche that shows the pertinent use of his thought for leftist political ends.

Given that Newton and the Panthers are best situated in twentieth-century anti-colonial struggles, it is important that we pinpoint how Nietzsche treated non-European and nonwhite subjectivity. Tim Brennan has shown that Nietzsche's treatment of non-European (including nonwhite) subjectivity is premised on a series of ambivalent Orientalist clichés. As a great philologist, Nietzsche tried to show how the Oriental texts of antiquity, just as the decadent culture of Socrates in Ancient Greece, related to the conflicts of his day. In terms of the Oriental connections, Nietzsche embraced the brutalist nature of the Indian Laws of Manu for the capacity they gave adherents to "name your enemies."[70] Christianity and modern-day socialism are associated with Indian Chandala values, and the very category of the proletariat, especially that of the lumpenproletariat, is made akin to the untouchable caste in Indian history and culture. A core reason why Nietzsche is read by anti-colonial thinkers in the context of militant armed struggle is because he prophesizes a situation of generalized civil war: "As soon as it is no longer a matter of preserving nations, but rather of producing the strongest possible mixed European race, the Jew becomes a useful and desirable an ingredient as any other national quantity."[71]

Nietzsche's insights are a mixed bag for colonial struggles, as this passage reveals. In any given colonial struggle — whether that be a civil war or general class struggle — Nietzsche appears has an allure for every side. Elective affinity with Nietzsche thus works and is often more effective the more a group experiences its own condition as marginal. Nietzsche invites those on the margins of society, such as Jews, into a struggle wherein they might prove themselves. The Nietzschean field of struggle can be construed or read as the field of battle, from the modern capitalist stock market to fighting fascist "pigs" on the streets. Nietzsche preached a distancing from European bourgeois decadence and narcissism, and he distanced himself from the leveling spirit of the Europe of his time. The very definition of the self that Nietzsche develops, because it is thought of as a recent creation based on "historical forgetting,"[72] as Brennan notes, made Nietzsche attractive to the academic field of postcolonial studies. We see now how Nietzsche has been adopted by revolutionaries, academics, and radicals who are eager to define themselves by their distance from European culture.

The Black Panther Party was not a Nietzschean organization by any means; rather, they appropriated Nietzsche's views on power and the transvaluation of values to address their more fundamental predicament — how to intensify the contradictions of the American police state at the very beginning of the collapse of the post-war welfare state. The FBI, in tandem with the American security apparatus, imprisoned many of the most central Panther organizers and assassinated the charismatic young leader Fred Hampton right as he was truly beginning to rise in prominence. As the neoliberal era set in following the election of Ronald Reagan in 1980, the Black Panther Party abandoned its radical Marxist doctrines and adopted a black nationalist approach to political organizing. If we draw up a balance sheet of the Panthers to gauge their lasting impact, we must recognize that while the anti-colonial *lumpen*-directed revolution did not materialize, they did dramatically change the cultural zeitgeist.

Newton's ability to appropriate Nietzsche's ideas of power and the transvaluation of values thus disproves Trotsky's suspicion that when Nietzsche is brought into the class struggle, he only attracts the "parasitenproletariat." Newton appropriated Nietzsche at a distance from his doctrines, working with his ideas as if he were molding them for the distinct challenges facing the black lumpenproletariat. By combining a class-centered analysis of the American situation with an attention to the ways that power and language shape perception, Newton left an indelible mark on American consciousness and the relation between cops and black Americans. Indeed, the Panthers altered both white and black Americans' perceptions of the police in significant ways. The lasting imprint of this alteration is evident in the wake of the single largest anti-police protest movement in the summer of 2020, which was sparked by the murder of George Floyd.

Although very few commentators have pointed it out, George Floyd was a member of the lumpenproletariat — a black man excluded from formal wage labor and forced into the black-market illicit economy. Floyd was killed by the police in Minneapolis, Minnesota, as he was selling cigarettes on a street corner. Whether we agree with Newton that the lumpenproletariat still possess a revolutionary potential, the fact that the "Floyd Uprising" grew to such prominence is a testament to the persistence of the lumpenproletariat as a class, which must be considered via Marxist and socialist analysis.

Newton's lumpen-Nietzscheanism looks very different today, precisely because the left has generally abandoned Newton's class analysis, a focus that mediated his otherwise bourgeois application of Nietzschean *Übermensch* ethics. There are numerous strategies for developing positive self-affirmation, from liberal identity politics, which centers the rare and brilliant handful of entrepreneurs who realize their greatness on the field of the market, to the New Age spiritualist variety, which identifies with the wisdom of the ancients as a means of greater self-awareness and realization. But what distinguishes Nietzsche's *Übermensch* ethics is the elitist and exclusive air of aristocratic leadership that it implies. Nietzsche emerges here as a perverse educator for the left, but the education that he offers is found in the fact that some version of self-help discourse is necessary for left leadership and political organizing. That Nietzsche explicitly distances his ethics form the marketplace — the transvaluation of values occurs "away from the marketplace and from fame"[73] — means that when Nietzsche is brought within the left, the tendency is to reproduce a certain type of revolutionary subjectivity which drifts far from working-class politics.

Moreover, we can identify many left-Nietzschean protagonists — Deleuze's "counterculture rebel," Newton's "*lumpen*-revolutionary," Jack London's "hardscrabble working-class revolutionary." These subjective protagonists molded or appropriated Nietzschean insights. Our argument is as follows: these left-Nietzschean radicals are only sensible for any left-oriented project that is stridently anti-capitalist if they are given a healthy dose of Marxist class analysis. Without a firm commitment to class analysis, any Nietzschean subjective protagonist risks being seized by market instrumentalization or elitist individualism. Even when a class perspective is combined with a Nietzschean *Übermensch* ethics, as was the case with Newton, Nietzsche's aristocratic insistence on hierarchy and rare exceptional leadership undermines the organizational culture, which ends up as a mirror of the already existing hierarchies found in capitalist institutions. Nietzsche bypasses the question of equality entirely on the left, thus making the very prospect and legacy of the egalitarian demand of the people into a catastrophic blind spot for the revolutionary cadre. It is only by returning to Marx and his own radical critique of equality that this blindness can be corrected.

When the left reads Nietzsche without the agendas of the hermeneutics of innocence, Nietzsche forces them to face the problem of elitism within their own leadership head on. For

Newton and the Panthers, Nietzsche's doctrines of power and the transvaluation of values were essential for creating a cultural understanding of the police that has materially altered consciousness in radical ways. But this was only the case because Newton's legacy and the entirety of his thought and praxis exceeds Nietzsche. Newton advocated social revolution in ways that are fundamentally anti-Nietzschean: his lifelong commitment to global revolution centered the lumpenproletariat as the core revolutionary class. This is a vision of what Newton, in his late work, named "intercommunalism" — an attempt to retain the utopian revolutionary vision through a class-directed understanding of revolution centered on the Global South. That Nietzsche would render a negative judgment on any such global revolutionary desires, rejecting it as a movement of *ressentiment*, does not detract from the lessons Newton derived from his writings.

CHAPTER SIX
Elective Enmities: Marx and Nietzsche

Better an enmity from one block
Than a friendship held together by glue.

Nietzsche, *The Gay Science*[1]

In 1809, Goethe wrote a novel entitled *Elective Affinities*, which applied the scientific concept of the mixing of two chemical compounds as a metaphor for love and marriage. The novel plays with the idea that human relationships, and by extension social ones too, can be thought of as a reaction akin to the mixing of vastly different chemical compounds. Not every mixture produces the expected chemical reaction, and some mixtures gel together like water and wine. As a substance, Nietzscheanism mixes with politics on the right and the left, producing certain types of actors, from the lumpen revolutionary to the counterculture rebel. As we saw in the last chapter, the mixing of Marx and Nietzsche in political struggles produces certain reactions which are conditioned by the level of crisis the capitalist social order is facing. Nietzsche appears in the situation of post-war consumer capitalism differently than how he appeared in the period from 1890–1945, when he was an inevitable figure for the left to face and work through.

In what follows, we will begin with an experiment in mixing the two compounds of Marx and Nietzsche by looking at how they address the problem of religion. Despite the stereotypes that have been built up about the two philosophers, they did not aim to negate religion outright. The clichés about Nietzsche's anti-Christian atheism and the common quip from conservatives that Marx was a communist atheist who reduced religion to a vulgar "opium of the people" are just that — clichés. Upon closer examination, both thinkers bring a wealth of insight to religion and diagnose it as a social form wherein both ideology and power intersect in crucial ways. But this seeming resemblance on the question of religion conceals an irresolvable impasse that will lead us to the very heart of the enmity between Marx and Nietzsche: the proletariat and revolution.

Marx vs. Nietzsche I: Religion, Ideology, Suffering

An entire monograph could be written on religion in Nietzsche and Marx, but we aim to drive more directly into the heart of our mixing experiment by separating the core of both thinkers' views on the subject. We will begin with the concept of ideology, which both thinkers used to describe Christianity and by extension any religious system or institution. Although Nietzsche did not have a well-developed theory of ideology, Marx developed a highly sophisticated one. In his early work, prior to the development of ideology in *Capital*, Marx theorized ideology as a type of "false consciousness" that bourgeois society drills into us.

An ideology of false consciousness is one in which the dominated class develops an *imaginary* relationship toward their *real* conditions of social existence. False consciousness was summed up by the American novelist John Steinbeck when he remarked that "socialism never took root in America because the poor see themselves not as an exploited proletariat, but as temporarily embarrassed millionaires." False consciousness involves an imaginary covering-over of social reality, and there is no more effective force for such a process of covering-over than religion.

For Marx, the primary form of religion was the Christian church of his time. In what way did people believe in God and seek solace from the teachings of the church? For Marx, belief in Christianity concealed a real longing for unity with humankind and universal brotherhood, a longing for a more humane world, what he called the "fantastic realization of the human essence." But he thought the real social basis of religious beliefs is grounded in an illusion, or "an opium," which is "the sigh of the oppressed creature, the heart of a heartless world, and the soul of soulless conditions."[2]

Religious belief contains a real longing for a utopian form of tranquility and equality in the world, which means that religion articulates a relation to the common and the universal that is not able to be fulfilled in bourgeois capitalist society. This longing that religious beliefs represent is negated by class society and the relations of domination and exploitation that people face every day. Marx links this real longing for the universal that religion conceals to the popular demands that the French Revolution opened in social life: equality, liberty, and fraternity. These demands are to be understood as *universal* categories of social life that are also collective — not merely individual — demands of the masses. They capture something essential and worth furthering, but which capitalist society blocks any fuller realization of in the material relations of actual social life. Religious community appeals to this similar universal longing.

Marx recognized that these demands cannot be fully met due to the contradictions of capitalist society, and this would lead him to declare bourgeois equality to be a limited, and ultimately parochial, concept that did not speak to the realities of exploitation and oppression that the working class experiences under capitalism. Appeals to bourgeois equality occlude and hinder the possibility for universal equality to be realized. In a brilliant analysis of Marx's theory of religion, Losurdo points out how Marx saw in bourgeois equality a continuity with Christianity. Marx wrote that equality appeals to "the unity of human essence, for man's consciousness of his species and his attitude towards his species, for the practical identity of man with man, i.e., for the social or human relation of man to man."[3]

Nietzsche also analyzed religion as an ideological force in modern society. Nietzsche scholar Mark Warren notes of Nietzsche's critique of Christianity that Nietzsche saw Christianity as an ideology that "served the Machiavellian political function of teaching obedience and thus served both the priestly and aristocratic classes."[4] Thus, both Marx and Nietzsche argued that religious believers turned to religion to express and protest real distress and suffering.[5] Religion is a means for the concealment of suffering that goes unacknowledged in the modern world, according to both philosophers. But here lies the crucial difference in our mixing of the two thinkers: Marx criticized the illusoriness of religious transcendence that came with the working class's attachments to religion, which he theorized as a yearning for unmet ideals of brotherhood and equality that bourgeois society was incapable of delivering. While

Nietzsche criticized this desire for transcendence to which this dream and illusion, however confused and unrealistic, gave expression.[6]

We thus have a *seeming* similarity emerge between the two thinkers: their critiques of ideology aimed to expose how religion puts "flowers on chains," to adopt a phrase from Losurdo. Religion concealed a common universal yearning but prevented the believer from assigning its real status to capitalist exploitation and domination. That is why religion was an ideology in Marx's eyes. Nietzsche sought a completely different solution to the problem of religion and ideology than Marx did — he aimed to legitimize the chains of suffering that religious attachment sought to remediate. Nietzsche was thus only a partial critic of Christianity; so long as Christianity could enforce a non-egalitarian form untainted by socialism and mass leveling, Nietzsche found it admirable.

Marx sought to blow apart the false transcendence of the "flowers" of religious ideology entirely, including its promises of heavenly paradise and calls for brotherhood, by exposing them as an opium that sought to conceal the chains of capitalist exploitation. Nietzsche's critique of religion, on the other hand, aimed to legitimate the oppression perpetrated by the ruling class and transform it into an ideology that treated this violence and oppression as natural. Marx's critique of ideology sought to delegitimate the basis of ruling-class ideology entirely. As he writes in *Capital*:

To abolish religion as the illusory happiness of the people is to demand the real happiness. The demand to give up illusions about the existing state of affairs is the demand to give up a state of affairs which needs illusions. The criticism of religion is therefore in embryo the criticism of the vale of tears, the halo of which is religion.[7]

Marx understood that the realist dimension of Christianity and its promise of "flowers" were false and ultimately limited, but even in their falseness, they express a real form of suffering in the world. This partial basis of Christian accounts of social suffering did not lead Marx to abandon the promise of the universal dimension within the class struggle. Indeed, Christianity was an "opium" for the masses, a consoling technique, and Losurdo notes that for Marx, "heavenly equality confirmed or risked confirming worldly inequalities, which was the real target of Marx's critique."[8] Engels suggests a similar view on religion to that of Marx in a letter to the Young Hegelian thinker Arnold Ruge:

> The reform of consciousness only resides in letting the world perceive its own consciousness, to awaken it out of the dream of itself, to explain its actions to itself. Our whole purpose — as in the case of Feuerbach's critique of religion — is nothing else but the bringing of religious and political questions into self-conscious human form. Hence our maxim must be: do not reform consciousness through dogma, but through the analysis of the mystical, self-confused consciousness let it be explicated as either religious or political.[9]

For both Marx and Nietzsche, the form of ideology that religion fostered had a far stronger density than ignorance, which is why ideology cannot simply be overturned by an act of enlightenment. Emancipation from false consciousness requires an act which would fundamentally break from bourgeois morals, values, and religion. For Nietzsche, "metaphysics, morality, religion, science — they are... considered only as different forms of the lie: with their assistance there is faith in life."[10] Unlike Marx, Nietzsche argued that there is nothing worth preserving in the appeal to universal values — the universal dimension of these appeals represents the Rousseauist and Socratic "spirit of revenge."

We can now get a clearer idea of the political significance behind Nietzsche's declaration of the death of God. If Christianity had lost both its capacity for maintaining rank order and the very universal — or the supernatural — as a justification of the social order, this means that an entirely new form of community-building was called for in its wake. As the scholar Ishay Landa has pointed out, the death of God called for a community-building response and alternative, for if God died, Nietzsche says, "Dear are all the Gods: now do we desire the Superman to live."[11] The task of the *Übermensch* was nothing short of a total and radical transvaluation of the egalitarian values left in the wake of the demise of Christianity as an institutional force capable of fending off the egalitarian threat. The *Übermensch* was meant to accelerate beyond the very category of "man" that was left over following the death of God. Marx faced a similar crisis of modern atheism in his work, but there is a crucial difference. For Marx, "the criticism of religion ends with the teaching that man is the highest being for man."[12] Landa points out that if God is indeed dead, then the Marxist corresponding claim must be, "Long live man!" We see here a diametrically opposed conception between Marx and Nietzsche regarding the question of the consequences of the death of God.

But yet we can see how, for both thinkers, the critique of Christianity and ideology brings about the need to wrestle with the categories of "man," "consciousness," "the universal," "the herd," and "the masses." Let's take the example of how both thinkers treat the concept of consciousness. For Nietzsche, consciousness "belongs not to man's existence as an individual but rather to the community and herd — aspects of his nature; that accordingly, it is finely developed only in relation to its usefulness to community or herd."[13] The very category of consciousness is traced back to Socrates, the Abrahamic religious tradition, and Cartesian rationalism. For Marx, on the other hand, consciousness is not to be discarded as a fundamentally fictional or illusory basis of social reality. In *Theses on Feuerbach*, Marx claims consciousness is founded in the "ensemble of social relations," that is, consciousness is what exists between individuals. It does not arise from any essence or genus of the human being, nor is consciousness tied to the herd such as the nation, the state, or culture.

To better understand what Marx means by consciousness, we can turn to the Marxist philosopher Lucien Goldmann, who developed the idea of what he calls "potential consciousness" to describe the theory of consciousness in Marxist thought. Goldmann distinguishes potential consciousness from "real consciousness," which is found in the concepts of space, time, good, evil, history, causality — these are the elements of perception that structure consciousness. Potential consciousness, on the other hand, is what concerns the praxis of Marxist thought; it is founded in the ensemble of social relations, that is, it is consciousness that is found in the splits within the dominant class and the interstices of its unrepresentable basis. As we saw above, there is only a partial and ultimately unfulfilled dimension to the values of equality and justice, including the values of religion, in bourgeois social life. But the false basis of universal bourgeois values such as equality is only truly realizable as false from the proletarian standpoint. The proletarian, working-class standpoint possesses a unique epistemological advantage due to its deprivation of these so-called universal values. What is at stake in the class struggle is the conscious self-determination of the "We" of the proletariat. The proletariat is thus an agent which destroys the false ideological consciousness of bourgeois class society. Goldmann writes:

> Because the proletariat is the act of practical negation of all ideology, there is no such thing as a proletarian ideology, or an ideology of the proletariat, just as we have seen that it would be absurd to talk about a materialist ideology. The proletariat is precisely the mass of concrete individuals, inasmuch as, and under the effect of their conditions of existence, these individuals destroy all ideological consciousness.[14]

Here we see that Nietzsche and Marx *seem* to align, as both thinkers aim for the destruction of ideological consciousness. But Marx theorizes a practical and revolutionary break with bourgeois ideological consciousness through an act of political organization toward revolutionizing social life, whereas Nietzsche theorizes this destruction as furthered by the crisis of nihilism and decadence in bourgeois society after the death of God. What comes in the wake of this crisis is a new conception of nature in place of the Christian transcendent basis of meaning. As Landa remarks,

> It is not enough for Nietzsche to claim that the universe and nature are indifferent and meaningless, that the universe "does not by any means strive to imitate man"; he rather

insists, in effect, that humans imitate the universe, should bow before the indifference and absurdity of existence and rearrange their lives accordingly."[15]

The crisis of European values that Nietzsche identifies also calls for a new philosopher to legislate the transvaluation of this crisis. But it is precisely in his attempt to transform our understanding of man and nature in the wake of the death of God that "Nietzsche projected an aggressive variant of bourgeois private egoism onto human nature," according to Rehmann.[16] In other words, Nietzsche's *Übermensch* community-building project should be understood as an attempt to preserve a class standpoint of the private bourgeois individual.

Eternal Return: The First Religion of Modern Capitalism

Nietzsche intended his "philosophy of the future" to transform and to overcome humanity in the wake of the death of God, and as we have argued, his philosophy is best understood as a community-building project. But Nietzsche's work is also to be understood, in a perhaps paradoxical way, as a new secular religion. Although it may seem odd for the philosopher known for the death of God and an all-out assault on Christian morals to also be the inventor of a new religion, this is exactly what Nietzsche did, and many of his closest readers and scholars have found agreement in the notion that his philosophy represents a new sort of religion.[17] The philosopher Walter Benjamin captured this paradox in a short but highly influential essay entitled "Capitalism as Religion":

Capitalism is entirely without precedent, in that it is a religion which offers not the reform of existence but its complete destruction. It is the expansion of despair, until despair becomes a religious state of the world in the hope that this will lead to salvation. God's transcendence is at an end. But he is not dead; he has been incorporated into human existence. This passage of the planet "Human" through the house of despair in the absolute loneliness of his trajectory is the ethos that Nietzsche defined. This man is the superman, the first to recognize the religion of capitalism and begin to bring it to fulfillment.[18]

Benjamin hits at the heart of the argument we have sought to drive home throughout this book; namely, that the enduring legacy of Nietzsche is found in the community-building aspects of his thought. We can now add a crucial twist — a big part of what explains the enduring relevance of Nietzsche's philosophy is found in the fact that his concepts are designed to fulfill capitalist imperatives.

One of the most definitive imperatives of capitalism is change. Capitalism operates on what Marx identifies as the valuation cycle of commodities. In order to reproduce itself, capital must undergo a rapid movement through the valuation cycle, what Marx refers to as M-C-M: money gets converted into a commodity, exchanges with other commodities, and then is sold again for money. It is this cycle which includes, crucially, the commodity of labor power, which means that while the worker sells their labor power, they are not only at the whim of the payment of the capitalist (wage), which is set both by the whim of the capitalist and by the state, the worker is also vulnerable to the randomness of capital and its need to leave the physical location of its reproduction (the factory, the corporation, and so forth) and undergo a new valuation cycle.

This continual necessity of movement and change leads capital to constantly relocate and reinvest from one locale to another. In fact, we can say that the staying power of a life philosophy such as Nietzscheanism in capitalist society is precisely due to the ever-changing and accelerating basis of capitalist social life. And this drive toward the frenetic movement of capital has only intensified in our epoch of hyper-finance-driven capitalism. For example, in the 1960s, valuation cycles had an average length of three years; this is to say, capital would hang around in one place for an average of three years before moving on. But by the 1990s, the average capital valuation cycle was reduced to just three months. This hyper-financialization of capital produced a highly unstable worker and brought with it the rise of an increasingly insecure working class that is promised very little job protection and lower and lower wages for their work.

At a cultural level — which is precisely where Nietzscheanism has remained so salient — capitalism requires that workers be prepared for "permanent change." This is a reality that Nietzsche incorporates into his philosophy, and it helps to explain why he has been influential in self-help and positive psychology, which focus on the importance of adaptation to a life of *constant* change. It is in this context that we must come to understand the enduring popularity and function of Nietzsche's most important concept: the eternal return. As a doctrine, the eternal return was meant to retain an explicit political function; specifically, it was "meant for those in power [to] use as a weapon"[19] Losurdo describes the eternal return as the "counter-revenge of the ruling classes, who now deride the hopes and illusions of the subaltern classes."[20]

The eternal return is best understood in the context of this inseparable nexus of class power that Nietzsche aimed to retain, and through the category of nature which he aimed to re-theorize in the wake of the death of God. The eternal return is a doctrine in alignment with a naturalization of capitalism. One way to understand this doctrine is through the accelerating dynamics of capitalist social life, wherein subjects must submit to constant and brutal exploitation and this submission must be elevated as the eternal condition of man. As a concept, the eternal return is among Nietzsche's more obscure ideas, which is why he frequently remarked that the very act of conceiving of the eternal return is not for everyone. We see here the very core of Nietzsche's aristocratic epistemology at work in the doctrine of the eternal return, for if only geniuses can truly come to master the concept, those who don't master it are castigated as either weak losers or those who suffer at a different level.

As a concept, the eternal return obsessed Nietzsche later in his life, and he even desired to return to school to study what modern physics and science might inform him about this idea to enrich his understanding.[21] The core of the doctrine of the eternal return maintains that the universe deliberately evades a goal, and that a cyclical process therefore becomes an inevitability to which "all those must succumb who would like to decree upon the world the power of eternal innovation, i.e., to invest such a finite, specific, constant and immutable force as 'the world' with a miraculous capacity for the infinite shaping anew of its forms and conditions."[22] The concept is first introduced by Nietzsche as a thought experiment and a challenge to the reader:

What if some day or night a demon were to steal after you

into your loneliest loneliness, and say to you, "This life as you now live it and have lived it, you will have to live once more and innumerable times more; and there will be nothing new in it, but every pain and every joy and every thought and sigh and everything unutterably small or great in your life will have to return to you, all in the same succession and sequence"… Would you not throw yourself down and gnash your teeth and curse the demon who spoke thus? Or have you once experienced a tremendous moment when you would have answered him: "You are a god and never have I heard anything more divine."[23]

The concept draws from Stoic and Roman philosophy and has been incorporated into historical theories of cyclical time, such as the famous notion of the *saeculum*, which maintains that human civilization undergoes mutations in unilinear cycles over and over.

What is the political context of Nietzsche's doctrine of the eternal return, and how does it link up with his other notions, such as perspectivism? As we argued in Chapter Three, Nietzsche's concepts are meant to affirm the naturalism of capitalist exploitation and relations of domination. The socialists of Nietzsche's time were theorizing revolutions of industrial capitalist society with concepts of cyclical time, and they argued that cycles of capitalist time are fundamentally illusory. Louis Blanqui, an important communist leader of the Paris Commune, for example, developed an idea of the eternal return and applied his insights to revolutionary egalitarian politics. We know that Nietzsche was familiar with Blanqui's concept through reading about it in a widely popular book of secondary literature by Fritz Lange, *History of Materialism and Critique of Its Present Importance*.[24]

Losurdo points out that the notion of eternal return appeared at a time when the bourgeoisie had lost trust in the impending development of the progress of the system of capitalist production that they had set in motion. The concept emerges at a peak of bourgeois decadence, during a time in which even the bourgeoisie had lost trust in capitalism. This loss of trust in the very project of capitalist development delivering a meaningful telos represented a loss of belief in the very process of capitalism among the class who were meant to be the main champions of the social order. From this class perspective, it is not surprising that new forms of atheism grew within bourgeois culture during Nietzsche's time, and that his concept of the "transvaluation of all values" became a way for the ruling class to think of a way to change the sphere of values while leaving the productive sphere completely untouched. The Nietzsche scholar Karl Löwith once called the eternal return an "atheistic surrogate for religion,"[25] and the philosopher Leo Strauss, in his seminars on *Zarathustra*, hit on a similar point:

> What was preparing itself at this time was then something unheard of before: a political atheism of the right. This, I think, is what fascism primarily means, whatever the lip services paid by men like Mussolini and Hitler might mean. Now from a purely political point of view we can say that Nietzsche comes to sight first as the originator of the political atheism of the right; and I believe you will not find another one who is comparable in any way to Nietzsche in power, in stature, who would deserve this title, however dubious.[26]

Our argument is that the doctrine of the eternal return was meant to naturalize the historically contingent economic order and affirm its inevitability as eternal. This is why the concept is so brilliant from a political perspective, because it would prove to have staying power long after Nietzsche's epoch. Nietzsche predicted that his thought would be with humanity for the next two thousand years,[27] and this is one way to understand why it has indeed remained so formative up to our own time.

Nietzsche also meant the eternal return as a critique of all appeals to the eternal in philosophy and religious thought. As Leo Strauss comments, "All philosophies which posit something eternal are rooted, according to Nietzsche, in the spirit of revenge, the spirit of escaping, the radical perishability of everything."[28] Strauss links Nietzsche's concept of the eternal return directly to his effort to subdue the "moral tarantula" of egalitarianism that was spreading like a cancer across Europe in his time. If successful as a concept, the eternal return would lead to a new way to embrace cruelty among the *Übermensch*, and would provide an alternative form of vengeance against the Rousseauist and egalitarian spirit of revenge.[29] When Nietzsche wrote that the concept should be understood as "a weapon for those in power," we thus see how it is one additional weapon in the armory of the Nietzschean community. As Nietzsche remarks to his readers in *Human, All Too Human*: "Live as higher men and persist in doing the deeds of higher culture — then everything alive will grant you your rights, and the social order, whose peak you represent, will be preserved from any evil eye or hand."[30]

The invitation to affirm the eternal return is also to be understood as a conversionary doctrine, an invitation to separate oneself from all vestiges of the herd mentality. This invitation has had a great deal of appeal among Nietzsche's readers, and it is no surprise that the doctrine stands out as one of his most important. There is a seductive quality in the concept of the eternal return, which lies in the way that it functions as a form of religious conversion, and which has shaped our modern notions of the very idea of conversion. But we are referring to a post-"death of God" conception of conversion, namely to a type of conversation that Nietzsche opens based on the following existential conundrum: What does it mean to change your life and dedicate yourself to a cause? If we take the death of God seriously, one of the consequences that arises is that the very notion of conversion fundamentally changes.

It is therefore not surprising that Oswald Spengler, an important reactionary Nietzschean historian, sought to make a similar case in his influential work *The Decline of the West*, arguing that conversion has fundamentally altered in modernity. Spengler maintained there are only re-occupations of vacant positions in the fixed structure of a culture's field of options, but not authentic conversions. More recently, the Nietzschean philosopher Peter Sloterdijk has embraced a similar view of conversion in his work *You Must Change Your Life*. Sloterdijk argues that in postmodern society, the very experience of conversion to political or religious movements no longer inducts and transforms the subject into what Sloterdijk calls the "vertical" dimension of faith and belief.

In Sloterdijk's view, the possibility of converting to a religion or to a political cause that might portend a transformation or even a revolutionary change in the world is over. Conversion has instead been relegated to what Sloterdijk calls the "horizontal" dimension. To make this point, he invokes the notion of *metanoia*, a Greek term that means "a change of heart," as a form of conversion whereby

HOW TO READ LIKE A PARASITE

the individual merely seeks out a new point of view and does not convert on the presupposition that doing so would change the world. Sloterdijk argues that conversion has now sped up and happens all the time — we are constantly converting in a game of what he calls "ascetic acrobatics," wherein we are driven by the demand "You must change your life," which imposes itself on all of us.

Sloterdijk's argument that conversion of the vertical dimension has been evacuated in our time must be read for what it is — an all-out assault on the Marxist revolutionary position. Sloterdijk argues that the sense of conversion that would be capable of revolutionizing social relations died with the '68 generation. In its revolutionary passion to transform society, the '68 generation only came to realize that "one does not save oneself by changing the world." Sloterdijk cites Jean-Luc Godard's 1982 film *Passion*, which portrays a series of characters failing repeatedly as they attempt to radically restructure society. This is then interpreted as a proof of his Nietzschean view that conversion is fated to be a mere metanoia, or a changing of one's mind, a personal change of heart.[31] Sloterdijk claims that the possibility of a conversion that involves the idea that one's action in the world will result in a collective social transformation is over. He thinks that after May 1968, the fate of all conversion is to be reduced to purely individualist asceticism. And he is not appalled by such a closure of revolutionary conversion — as a Nietzschean thinker, he welcomes it. What Nietzsche thus opens for Marxism, which must feel compelled to respond to this crisis, is a turn to the question of political theology. While there are many fascinating schools in contemporary discussions of Marxist thought on political theology, we do not have the time to delve deeply into them at this point. But the provocation of this crisis of conversion was once well encapsulated by Jean-Paul Sartre, who stands in stark opposition to this pessimist Nietzschean idea of conversion. In his Marxist phase, Sartre argued for a revitalized idea of revolutionary conversion in the field of politics. He said that to be on the left requires that one adjust oneself to a condition of "permanent conversion," by which he meant that revolutionary commitment *must* lead to a life of constant conversion to promote the destruction of morals and existing bourgeois politics and to facilitate lasting bonds within revolutionary groups, or what Sartre called "fused groups."

A Pre-History of Marx vs. Nietzsche: Pascal vs. Pelagius

Nietzsche has a way to bring out religious concepts but in a secular and modern fashion. The concept of conversion is one way to understand what it means to develop an adherence to socialism and to Marxist principles. As a Nietzschean philosopher, Sloterdijk opens a problem that we have sought to track throughout this chapter; namely, in our attempt to mix Marx with Nietzsche, what do we encounter? Is the method of hypothesizing an elective affinity between the two thinkers adequate? Sparking an elective affinity between Marx and Nietzsche should never be done in a perfunctory fashion. We have discovered that while both thinkers are driven by common concerns and respond to the crisis in Christianity and the problem of social suffering in its wake in capitalist social life, they arrive at diametrically opposite positions. Any elective affinity inevitably runs afoul; there are serious, unresolvable bones of contention in any attempt to mix the two thinkers.

We have argued that the doctrine of the eternal return is best understood as a quasi-religious account of capitalist social life that serves to adapt subjects to a life of constant change. That Nietzsche would refer to the concept as "explosive" and that the very idea would involve a "discontinuous intensification"[32] (to use a phrase of Sloterdijk's) has only added to its paradoxical appeal. It is paradoxical in that it embraces the disorienting effects that come from hyper-movement and change, and yet it affirms that, despite these movements, the world is fundamentally unchanging. If the concept of eternal return represents Nietzsche's new religion, as Benjamin rightly points out, the embracing of it is therefore meant to have a particular function, mainly shutting down any material or revolutionary transformation of the world from below. If only an esoteric elite can truly master the eternal return, this exclusion constitutes the point where the Marxist-Nietzschean mixture falls apart. For if the premise of the Marxist wager is that philosophers have only interpreted the world, and that the point is to change it, Nietzsche's eternal return stands as an antagonist to this very prospect.

We have now pinpointed the true stakes of the Nietzsche-Marx enmity — the mixture dissolves at the point of changing the world. Nietzsche stands as the inventor of an esoteric, contemplative solution meant for the invention of a new elite, while Marx stands for the invention of a revolutionary break from class domination through a proletarian revolution from below. But is this enmity completely novel in the history of political thought? We now want to argue that the Nietzsche-Marx enmity has an historical precedent and analogue in the philosopher Blaise Pascal and his engagement with the legacy of the egalitarian thought of the theologian Pelagius in the seventeenth century.

Pascal is an important Christian philosopher who, like Nietzsche, lived during a time of profound social instability and fragmentation. Both Pascal and Nietzsche produced a philosophy that played a specific political function, aiming to preserve the status quo of a decaying Church hierarchy that was being overrun with nihilism. In Pascal's case, this crisis was brought about by the turn to rationalism during the Scientific Age in the sixteenth and seventeenth centuries. This was a period that, according to Lucien Goldmann,

> destroyed the two closely connected ideas of the community and the universe, and had replaced them by the totally different concepts of the isolated individual and of infinite space. In the history of the human mind, this represented a twin conquest of immense importance: on the social plane the values to be recognized were those of justice and individual liberty; on the intellectual plane the system as valid was that of mechanistic physics.[33]

The rationalist discoveries in science pointed to a paradox of human action in the world; specifically that, for the first time, human action could now be judged as good or evil by reference to an independent system of ethical criteria that transcends the individual. Rationalist criteria can be made into theological or social justifications, but the rationalist discovery pointed to an authority that stands outside and above the individual. This characteristic of rationalism, as Lucien Goldmann notes, "tends to abolish both God and the community, and it is this which explains why the rise of rationalism was accompanied by the disappearance of any external norm which might guide the individual in his life and actions."[34]

For Pascal, the infinite space of rational science was the space where God falls silent and man is obliged to give up any genuinely ethical norm. This prospect points to a new paradigm of tragedy in Pascal's view, and now the central problem revolves around whether values that exceed the transcendent truths of the Aristotelian and Thomist universe can indeed be guaranteed by rationalist means. The problem was whether man could still rediscover God, or put differently, whether man could rediscover the community and the universe. The rationalist revolution in science thus meant that to discover God had now come to mean the realization of a social totality in an ideal community.

The rationalist revolution in science paved the way for the philosopher Spinoza, who emerged shortly after Pascal. Spinoza would spark the pantheist controversy and locate God as immanent in nature, whereas Pascal would stick to a solution that was more in concert with the conservative Jansenist orientation toward Catholicism that he followed. Overall, what the rationalist discovery portended was beyond a mere theological discovery, it also had bearings on what Goldmann refers to as the knowability of the social totality for the first time. The quest for knowledge of the social totality rests on a faith and a conversionary potential which implies that if the social totality is knowable by man, it is indeed changeable by man. In this context, Pascal would stand, like Nietzsche, as a great antagonist to such a prospect. For if the rationalist quest for the knowability of the social totality was one of truth and the enactment of the ideal community, Pascal argued to the contrary that man must accept a fate of atomized individuality. The paradoxes of a rationalist understanding of the universe meant that man must learn to live in the paradoxical space split between nothingness and eternity.

The rationalist revolution taking place in Pascal's time posed a threat to the Church establishment as it threatened to de-sacralize the divine and dethrone the sovereign metaphysical God. This crisis must be understood as one that affected the Church authorities and the ecclesiastical class, which importantly parallels the crisis of the bourgeois class in Nietzsche's time. It is in this context of class crisis that Pascal's concept of the wager on the existence of God is best understood. Pascal's famous concept of the wager, like Nietzsche's concepts, was meant to offer a solution to the preservation of the ruling class, with which Pascal identified in his own affiliation with the conservative Jansenist tendency within the Church. The rationalist revolution was undermining the validity of God, producing a crisis within the pool of future priests, and giving way to a new generation who may not have been overtly atheist but who were losing their trust in the legitimacy of the Church. Pascal's wager develops an ingenious solution to this crisis of belief. It affirms that God is absent and hidden from human consciousness because we have grown too exhausted to know and discover God. The wager deems the world tragic, wretched, cruel, and unchanging. From this pessimistic position, Pascal then builds up an individualist philosophy which became a guiding ideology of the class system of what would become the European bourgeoisie. Pascalianism is the ideological backbone of the class known as the *noblesse de robe*, who were basically French aristocratic bureaucrats prior to the French Revolution. Pascal aligned with the Jansenist movement within the Church, a notoriously conservative strain of Catholicism which preached a commitment to predestination.

The wager is thus a concept akin to Nietzsche's eternal return in the social function that it sought to further. Like the eternal return, Pascal's wager can be read in different ways in terms of its political effect and function. The wager can be read as a reactionary ideological concept meant for the purpose of maintaining a status quo precisely by affirming — like Nietzsche's eternal return — that nothing in fact changes. But Pascal's wager has a radically other, egalitarian dimension to it which is not meant for furthering the rank order of the status quo. This egalitarian element is latent and implicit in the British theologian named Pelagius, who challenged the Augustinian Church authority by rejecting original sin and eternal damnation.

While Pelagius emerged prior to Pascal by roughly 1,200 years, he stands as the egalitarian interlocutor of the entire history of the Augustinian Church doctrine, a doctrine and class system which Pascal sought to preserve. The Pelagian wager goes beyond the atomized individual and declares that changing the world also changes the condition of mankind. This distinction draws us back to the Marx-Nietzsche enmity we explored earlier in the way that the stakes of this debate revolve around the knowability of the social totality and the possibility of changing the world. In an interesting way, Goldmann argues that twentieth-century existentialism — a movement in philosophy that saw Nietzsche as one of its philosophical godfathers — has a genealogical connection to Pascalian pessimism in the way that existentialism tends to affirm an absurd vision of the cosmos. Existentialism, like Pascal and Nietzsche's philosophy, condemns the world without putting forward any hope of transforming it in and through history. Marxism thus emerges as the genealogical successor of Pelagian universalism, offering a revamped theory of the wager that insists on a certain knowability of God, a wager that affirms meaning in history.

The contours of the Pascal and Jansenist debate with Pelagius are directly applicable to Nietzsche's own polemics against socialism, a movement he saw as constituting a profound threat to the persistence of the tragic worldview. Nietzsche viewed Socratic optimism as trans-historically reappearing in the socialist movement of his time. Thus, what both Pascal and Nietzsche offered to the contemporary ruling class was a philosophy which insisted there is no possible transcendence beyond human wretchedness through acts of revolution. Both Pascal and Nietzsche must be read as clever anti-revolutionary thinkers, fundamentally responding to the disintegration of the class they sought to defend; for Nietzsche, that class was a decaying bourgeoisie of the encroaching imperialist era.

It must be remembered that Nietzsche did not view Christianity as entirely jeopardized and that he admired aspects of it, particularly its capacity for domination and enforcement of rank order. In this way Nietzsche admired Pascal precisely for his cunning embrace of the reactionary class dominance of the church. Regarding his love for Pascal, Nietzsche's sister Elisabeth Forster-Nietzsche wrote that "he loved Pascal as a kindred spirit; he was as moved by his end as if it had been that of a beloved friend, indeed, as if he himself were threatened by it."[35] In later, unpublished fragments from the spring of 1885, Nietzsche expresses his great admiration for Pascal, offering praise for his "subtle" and "flexible" spirit, which he juxtaposes to the Roman Empire in its allowance of "freedom in faith and nonfaith."[36]

Nietzsche was fond of some aspects of the Christian church that Pascal sought to protect, precisely for the way the church practiced a "spiritualization of cruelty: the idea of hell, tortures and heretic trials."[37] From this system of cruelty, Nietzsche said, new pleasures emerge among the Christian followers, to which he credits how "good he looks" and Pascal's "supple spirit."[38] Pascal plays a considerable influence on Nietzsche which is evident in his lesser studied work *Dawn: Thoughts on the Prejudice of Morality* where Nietzsche interprets Pascal's religiosity similar to how he interprets Rousseau's philosophy and compassion, namely as a form of self-hatred. But unlike Rousseau, Pascal is considered a noble Christian philosopher who has achieved the "unification of ardor, spirit, and honesty foremost among all Christians."[39] Nietzsche also sees Pascal as a model for the sort of discipline and submission that his philosophy calls for, "don't we, like him, have our strength in beating ourselves into submission? He in aid of God, and we in aid of integrity."[40]

Pascal's response to rationalism was to carve out a space for the faith of the wager that affirmed paradox and the unknowability of the absolute. The Pelagian alternative declares that social reality is in fact thinkable, and this thinkability of the social totality links us back to the nominalist/realist distinction. The Pelagian tradition is the clear forerunner to the realist socialist tradition out of which Marxism emerged in the nineteenth century. This tradition is distinguished by its affirmative and optimistic position, which is found in the Hegelian and, above all, Marxist dialectic. The dialectic goes beyond the tragic vision and the existentialist wager by showing that man can indeed achieve authentic values by his own thoughts and actions and that collective solidarity can change the world.

In Goldmann's framework of historical-materialist analysis, Marxism does not attempt to introduce a new theory of transcendental values, but it does posit that philosophy must become a praxis, and this movement from philosophy and contemplation to practical revolution is bound up with conversion and faith in the future, a faith based on the affirmation that humanity can remake itself in history. Revolutionary Marxism requires a wager that our actions and our solidarity to transform the world will, in fact, be successful. The Nietzsche-Marx mixture on religion "leaps over six centuries of Thomist and Cartesian rationalism and renews the Augustinian tradition."[41]

Marx vs. Nietzsche II: On the Cathartic Moment of Revolution

We have aimed to demonstrate that we benefit from reading Nietzsche in the historical and political context in which he wrote rather than as an untimely thinker detached from social and political realities. Left-Nietzscheans are too often content to read Marx as conditioned by his historical context as a means of discarding many of his points of emphasis. For example, the entire theory of Bonapartism, and even parts of Marx's class theory, are often discarded by contemporary Marxists as being dated or a product of Marx's time. But they rarely propose to read Nietzsche in the same way. It is the *supposed* timelessness of Nietzsche's thought that has led so many left-Nietzscheans to attempt to fuse him with Marx, to combine these two thinkers who are otherwise diametrically opposed.

Nowhere are the stakes of this fusing of Nietzsche with Marx more significant than when it comes to the concept of revolution. We have already seen how in our attempt to mix Marx and Nietzsche in terms of religion, we were led to the problem of revolution. For Nietzsche, following a long tradition of aristocratic rebels like Pascal, the prospect of a rational revolution of the world had to be cleverly covered over through the invention of concepts meant for use by a ruling class to retain rank order amid a potentially revolutionary situation. As we saw, for Marx the bourgeois ideals of equality are embedded in the tradition of Christianity and have to be unearthed from below; that is, the proletarian revolution would destroy the ideological consciousness of bourgeois society and reinvent the egalitarian basis of these very ideals. But such a prospect terrified Nietzsche.

Lukács pinpoints the fear that drove Nietzsche when he states that "the proletariat is the first oppressed class in history that has been capable of countering the oppressors' philosophy with an independent and higher world-view of its own."[42] Nietzsche knew this himself, as we see in one of his notebook fragments from the late summer of 1873: "If the working classes ever discover that they easily could surpass us in matters of education and virtue, then it is all over for us!" He then adds a fascinating counterpoint to this reflection: "But if this does not occur, then it is really over for us."[43] This fragment reflects the seriousness with which Nietzsche treated the working class and the possibility of revolution. What we find here is a dual awareness of what a revolution from below would portend for the class position from which Nietzsche wrote — the bourgeoisie — and his fear regarding what would happen to the bourgeoisie if no proletarian revolution occurs. In both instances he makes an appeal to his bourgeois and middle-class reader; that is, he sets himself at a distance from the bourgeoisie while at the same time writing for its preservation. This is the paradoxical power of Nietzsche that his readers on the left fail to grasp — the edgy, romantic, anti-capitalist position still insists on preserving the class status quo.

But how did Nietzsche treat the threat of working-class revolution? In *The Genealogy of Morals*, he alludes to Marx's idea of the revolutionary proletariat as "a haunting spectre embodied in a class of barbaric slaves who have learned to regard their existence as an injustice, and now prepare to avenge, not only themselves, but all generations."[44] Although direct reference to the proletariat does not appear in his writing, we will argue — in line with Lukács — that Nietzsche's constant reference to the "masses" stands as an undeniable reference to Marx's notion of the proletariat.

But what is the proletariat? As Étienne Balibar notes, "Properly speaking, the bourgeoisie is the only class in history; before it there were only castes, orders, and estates (*Stünde*), which were not yet real classes. As for the proletariat, once it matches its definition, it is no longer simply a class but the masses."[45] From *The Genealogy of Morals* onward, Nietzsche remains very concerned with the masses both as a trans-historical force and, especially, as a concrete reality in Europe following the French Revolution. Importantly, he saw the French Revolution as the "last great slave rebellion," driven by *ressentiment*. Nietzsche aims to abolish not consciousness as such, but one form of consciousness: the consciousness of the proletariat.

The philosopher Howard Caygill has compared Nietzsche and Marx's divergence in their respective readings of the Paris Commune by pointing out that Nietzsche criticized the utopian dimension of the Communards and socialist utopians that led the uprising. Caygill suggests that Nietzsche might have found in the Paris Commune something more agreeable to his philosophy if he would have understood, from a philological point of view, how "the word 'commune' was itself a citation combining archaic and new, a pre- and a post-state political form."[46] In Caygill's reading of Marx's lectures on the Paris Commune, he notes that Marx, unlike Nietzsche, understood that the revolutionaries affirmed the radical future-oriented dimension of the commune, and that thus, "far from being a 'slave revolt in morals,' the Commune marked a noble resistance to the 'slave masters revolt in morals.'"[47] Caygill thus argues that Marx identifies *ressentiment* as a feature of what drove the Paris Commune, specifically through the drive for vengeance against the ruling bourgeois class. But Caygill adds a far too charitable reading of Nietzsche by suggesting that Nietzsche missed the "future-oriented" and therefore affirmative element of the revolt. In this way, Caygill attempts to make Marx and Nietzsche compatible on the question of revolution by suggesting that, if only Nietzsche had retained the proper philological attention to the affirmative aspect of the Commune, it would have been treated by him with greater favor. But such a reading seriously misdiagnoses the fact that anti-revolutionary politics were at the very center of Nietzsche's thought. Revolution is a problem for Nietzsche as it produces an inevitable pitfall: when the masses make appeals to realist universalism, such as to the value of equality, this only accelerates nihilism. We must read Nietzsche's thought in the context of the immediate aftermath of the French Revolution, from which the Paris Commune emerges as a significant egalitarian spark and a revolutionary opening.

Malcolm Bull's *Anti-Nietzsche* draws attention to the ways that, in his close reading of the French Revolution, Nietzsche identifies how the revolution bottomed out once the Jacobins began to demand what Bull refers to as "extra-egalitarianism."[48] More precisely, it was the attempt to institute full equality among wage workers that brought the fuller realist demand of equality to a screeching halt. Bull points to the law proposed by Isaac René Guy le Chapelier, who put forward a collective rather than an individual-based idea of the wage. This demand for collective wage equality ended up backfiring, as it did not allow for any association of workers based on individual economic interests, thus barring craft guilds and trade unions, and was in effect from 1791 until 1884. The Le Chapelier law is thought to offer credence to Nietzsche's skepticism about equality and its unrealizability in any revolutionary situation given that it effectively halted the egalitarian thrust of Jacobinism. In our wider framework of realism and nominalism, we remember that bourgeois society limits the realist universal expansion of equality specifically in the sphere of the market. Here we see the precise historical point at which the Jacobin insistence on universal equality falls short — the capitalist imperative hits the wall in the fairness of the wage.

But does any revolution — whether bourgeois or proletarian — face such an inevitable bottoming out? Nietzsche's views on equality are grounded in a profound skepticism, not only regarding the wage but also citizenship, property, and especially very idea of Jacobin universal equality itself. His assault on equality extends far beyond the bourgeois capitulation of the Jacobins in the case of the Le Chapelier law.

The insight of *The Genealogy of Morals* is that social inequality is the source of our value concepts and the necessary condition of value itself. As Bull notes, "Equality for equals, inequality for unequals — that would be the true voice of justice" in Nietzsche's view. But what Bull pinpoints is that extra-egalitarianism is the engine that stokes nihilism, and this drive is reflective of a weakness of will that ultimately becomes a problem because it fosters a social order that loses touch with the aesthetic dimension of life. The forces of "leveling down" thus lead to a "leveling out" of aesthetic value, and this means that for Nietzsche, the core problem of equality is that it saps human potential for higher living and art-making. Revolutions for equality sap the spirit and create a way for humans to "join together to become less than they might otherwise be."[49] What is crucial to understand in this argument is that nihilism, "the Great Beast," emerges when the "less than equal are introduced into the equation."[50]

Again, the problem with revolution for equality is its activation of a particular class whose envy, resentments, and sheer existence are then meant to be brought into a relation of equality with others not of their rank. Moreover, it is the envy of the lower classes that a revolution cannot sublate or positively transform. As the American literary critic Edmund Wilson observes in his Nietzschean reading of H.L. Mencken, "By virtue of their ineptitude [the proletariat] remain fettered to the plough and the bench, are embittered by envy of 'their betters.' It is this envy which supplies all the issues of politics in a democracy."[51] Wilson pinpoints what is at issue in any proletarian revolution from below from a Nietzschean perspective: it is the desire on the part of the peasants to rob the superior classes of "rewards unattainable by themselves or to restrain them from the enjoyment of activities that they are unable to understand."[52] In *Beyond Good and Evil*, Nietzsche writes of the plebeian class in the following way:

If one knows something about the parents, an inference about the child is permissible: any disgusting incontinence,

any nook envy, a clumsy insistence that one is always right
— these three things together have always constituted the
characteristics of the plebeian.[53]

In Nietzsche's view, the French Revolution filled the masses
with intractable envy, and it is this envy which drives the desire
of proletarian revolution. Indeed, socialism itself, which grew
out of the great revolution, was built on envy of the better
caste of society. But such a vision of proletarian desire — as
fueled fundamentally by envy — is not coherent, let alone
an accurate description of the condition of the working
masses. In Losurdo's treatment of the Nietzschean concept of
ressentiment, he locates envy as the core issue at work. Losurdo
writes that "contrary to the theory of aristocratic radicalism
and the assumption already commonplace in the tradition of
liberal thought, *ressentiment* is an instrument of reaction that
aims to divert social protest onto false targets, to fragment the
subaltern classes into countless corporate branches."[54]

As a concept, *ressentiment* poses a fundamental barrier to
proletarian solidarity, and Nietzsche weaponizes it so as to
fend off political agitation and the possibility proletarian
revolution. This is an ingenious tactic on Nietzsche's part,
because any revolution from below must rely on the creation
of solidarities and alliances across classes in order to succeed.
Thus, envy is a real problem that must be overcome by
working-through its deleterious effects. In fact, if Nietzsche is
right that envy toward the "better caste" or higher class has
merit, what this means is that Nietzsche becomes an ironic
teacher of proletarian revolution and *ressentiment* may be read
as a great warning to any would-be proletarian revolutionary.
But Nietzsche characterizes the post-French Revolution
situation of his time, and any democratic polity, as riddled

with intractable resentments that prevent and thwart a more egalitarian social order from coming about. Revolutions do not fundamentally resituate resentments in a cathartic moment, in Nietzsche's view.

But let us be more charitable to Nietzsche and ask whether his suspicion of revolution has some merit. Perhaps proletarian revolutions are driven by resentments which are never overcome. This leads us to the second pitfall of any proletarian revolution in Nietzsche's view, which is found in the fact that revolutions from below do not adequately transform humanity. If anything, Nietzsche predicted the conditions of our austerity-driven liberal capitalism when he wrote, "One day the worker will live like the bourgeois; but above him, the higher caste characterized by its frugality: thus poorer and simpler, but in possession of power."[55] The noble human being cannot be reduced to the lesser human being, and Nietzsche's political praxis, through the concept of the pathos of distance, was meant to ensure that this unbridgeable chasm is maintained. Does such a vision of a natural division and the persistence of necessary inequality among humanity square with a Marxist idea of revolution?

The Marxist philosopher Gramsci argues the opposite of Nietzsche's view when he claims that what is most vital in proletarian revolution is that revolutions produce what he calls a "cathartic moment." Contra Nietzsche's pessimism, Gramsci affirms that revolutions resituate and reorganize the common resentments and discontents of the masses. This reassortment of relations of envy and resentments that are indeed produced by class conflicts — Nietzsche rightly acknowledges this — are not destined to a bottoming-out into even more intensified forms of resentment. We once again reach a point in our elective affinity in which Marx and Nietzsche fail to hybridize. At best, Nietzsche emerges as a perverse teacher of the revolutionary tradition. A thinker whose concepts — the eternal return and *ressentiment* (to name just two) — are deployed as active deterrents to the very goal of Marx's "Thesis XI." But before we abandon any trust or faith in the prospect that revolution is destined to only intensify resentments, as Nietzsche claims, we must turn to the very concept of *ressentiment* itself.

CHAPTER SEVEN
Ressentiment and the Politics
of Social Suffering

If the prospect of revolution is fated to bottom out into interminable envy toward others, if equality as such spells the tragic fate of revolution, the Nietzschean philosopher concludes that revolution has never truly happened. If the French Revolution is construed as the great modern slave revolt, as Nietzsche insists, this means that there is nothing to salvage from its emergence in world history. If we take Nietzsche at his word, he now possesses all the cards regarding the very prospect of revolution, and the "men of *ressentiment*" are pacified. Nietzsche read the left-wing elements of the French Revolution as unleashing a wicked force onto the world, a wicked egalitarian genie let out of the bottle. When we read Nietzsche as an antagonist of the left, we see that his concepts were meant to respond to its universal and egalitarian dimensions after the French Revolution, to halt them in their tracks. This is the heart of Nietzsche's political nominalism: the refinement of concepts meant to further a particular sort of political polemic that is opposed to the wider movement of egalitarian politics.[1]

The problem of *ressentiment* is not bound up with the question of revolution alone. That any egalitarian revolutionary movement will get caught in the spider web of *ressentiment* only captures part of the problem, in Nietzsche's view. It bears noting that, as a concept, *ressentiment* was already in the air when Nietzsche first wrote about it in *The Genealogy of Morals*. In Nietzsche's time, prominent liberal political thinkers like Hippolyte Taine and Alexis de Tocqueville, as well as literary figures from Dostoevsky to Kierkegaard, developed reflections on *ressentiment*. But it is Nietzsche's reflections on it that have stood the test of time, and he has popularized the concept to such a degree that it is now taken as a common-sense idea of liberal politics.

The concept of *ressentiment* is defined as the phenomenon of suffering, which is a problem that calls for a comprehensive treatment that is both psychological and social in its diagnosis, as well as philosophical and theological in its deployment. *Ressentiment* is a valuable weapon in the arsenal of Nietzsche's political ideas. It is, arguably, next to the eternal return, Nietzsche's most important concept, specifically in the way it functions as a political polemic. The concept is meant to designate, name, and ultimately to *tame* a lower form of suffering in social life.

As we have already demonstrated, for Nietzsche the residues of slavery persist in any human society, and modern capitalist society, with its system of wage labor, is no exception. While Nietzsche does not pinpoint the class of the wage laborers as ontologically bound up with *ressentiment*, he recognizes that *ressentiment* is a general condition of modern life which has the potential to infect anyone. But there is an implied class application of *ressentiment* in Nietzsche's thought which emerges within the "pastoral" discourse of the modern Socratic "priests." The category of the priest includes egalitarian Christians, socialist intellectuals, and liberal utilitarian's — figures who allegedly preach a doctrine that all suffering must be brought to a halt, especially extreme suffering. The pastoral discourse sees the problem of suffering as one in which they (the intellectuals) are elected to manage and mitigate the suffering of those who already suffer at a lower level.

It is the socialist intellectuals who teach the proletariat to protest their lot in life, that they ought to be outraged at their material conditions. How else would the scandal of the proper distribution of suffering become a problem in the first place, if not for the socialist intellectuals who tell the working class that they can expect more from life? It is this mediation of the socialist "priest" that has to be combated, and against which Nietzscheanism deploys the weapon of *ressentiment*, a concept which invokes a polemic that is meant to ensure that nothing is changed. Read in this light, *ressentiment* is now elevated to a theological concept; that is, it addresses the problem of human suffering, which makes up an entire field of inquiry in theological studies called theodicy, which is the attempt to offer a spiritual rationale for human suffering in the world.

Is human suffering divinely ordained? On what basis is the existence of suffering valid in the eyes of God? Is human suffering to be understood in a strict atheistic way, as a fundamentally man-made phenomenon which we can control and mitigate? The philosophical tradition of utilitarianism places the problem of human suffering at the very core of what is most vital about political life, and suggests that all social problems must be analyzed and redressed with an eye toward the lessening of human suffering as the primary benchmark of political decision-making. In the liberal political philosophy of utilitarianism, the problem of suffering is mapped onto the rubrics of pain and pleasure, and political action must be aimed toward maximizing pleasure and minimizing pain. Nietzsche was familiar with the liberal utilitarian philosopher John Stuart Mill, and even read his work *Socialism*, published in 1879. Nietzsche viewed utilitarianism as a modern form of slave morality that aims to spread the sort of pleasures that are expressive of the very opposite of master morality.

In Nietzsche's critique of utilitarianism, we see his ambivalent views regarding the poor: "Peasants and the poor have less to envy in a king than a king in the poor, so they are happier." The problem does not lie with them, it lies with the intellectuals who preach philosophies such as utilitarianism and socialism; they are the ones who disrupt the contentment of the peasant's morality and happiness. They do so by aiming to universalize a conception of pleasure that is of the herd mentality, that levels down. The problem with socialist intellectuals is that "many of them have suffered too much, so they want to make others suffer."[2] Modern philosophers and "freethinkers" are "without solitude," and are "levelers" who long for "an easier life for everyone,"[3] and the two doctrines they repeat most often are "equality of rights" and "sympathy for all that suffers."[4]

As we saw in Chapter Four, in Nietzsche's view mediocrity is necessary in any society and should be fostered. What many scholars have missed in their understanding of Nietzsche's critique of utilitarianism, however, is the problem of work and precisely the problem of "extrawork" under modern capitalism. In his view, mediocrity must go unquestioned for the class of those who perform the necessary slave labor of extrawork in capitalist society, and this is where the problem of pain emerges. Pain must not be minimized for this class of laborers, but must rather be reserved for new experimental directions by an aristocratic class who would come to experience pain in their leisure time.

The problem of the suffering of the proletariat is thus not found in the empirical fact that they suffer, it is rather found in how this suffering is treated as a class and how the problem of *excessive suffering* is to be experienced by this class. Nietzsche asks, "Is the rabble also necessary for life? Are poisoned fountains necessary, and stinking fires, and filthy dreams, and maggots in the bread of life?"[5] and he continues, "For their number is always small: but the others, the suffering, have nothing that heals them to that degree from the negative consequences of much suffering."[6] We see here an important acknowledgement that there are forms of pain which fundamentally disrupt any remediation, and therefore excessive pain and suffering must be muted and sedimented into the natural order of social life. Nietzsche's theodicy is thus bent on molding the social order in such a way that excessive suffering — which is necessary for the social order to produce high art and aesthetics — must come to be completely accepted and unquestioned by the working masses.

Quite simply, the proletariat must learn to suffer in such a way that their excessive suffering is not internalized as excessive, and moreover, their suffering must be experienced as a lower level of refinement and complexity. With his characteristic proleptic style, Nietzsche writes in *Zarathustra*, "But thou, profound one, thou sufferest too profoundly even from small wounds."[7] Here we see an invocation to the cultivation of a new community wherein suffering aesthetically from "small wounds" is taken as qualitatively more refined and significant than the suffering brought on by social oppression.

Nietzsche is known as a thinker who *personally* suffered greatly, from his lifelong sicknesses to his often self-imposed ascetic suffering, such as when he would write in the frigid Swiss mountains until his fingers became frostbitten and blue.

But rarely do Nietzsche scholars consider the social dimension of suffering that concerned him in his theory of *ressentiment*. Let us remember Nietzsche's idea of utopia as

> a social order in which the hard work and misery of life will be allotted to the man who suffers least from it, that is, to the dullest man, and so on step by step upwards to the man who is most sensitive to the highest, most sublimated kind of suffering and therefore suffers even when life is most greatly eased.[8]

Christianity is the world-historical force and culprit that brought out the problem of extreme suffering and named it as a social problem which Nietzsche recognizes "was never a Hellenic problem."[9]

> Religion has the same effect which an Epicurean philosophy has on sufferers of a higher rank: it is refreshing, refining, makes, as it were, the most of suffering, and in the end even sanctifies and justifies. Perhaps nothing in Christianity or Buddhism is as venerable as their art of teaching even the lowliest how to place themselves through piety.[10]

The question of suffering exceeded the private bourgeois individual and was thought of by Nietzsche as a fundamentally social question, tied directly to the pathos of distance. For example, Nietzsche argues that the concept of "grace" has no meaning or good odor "*inter pares* [among equals]."[11] Indeed, "profound suffering makes noble; it separates."[12] In his early lectures on the Greek state, Nietzsche celebrates it as an "ingenious barbarism" wherein "war, slavery and pain connected to it, found 'justification.'"[13] According to the

Greek vision of the cosmos, the persistence of extreme and even senseless suffering in the world did not need an external justification or a mysterious divine will to make sense of this evil. Therefore, for Nietzsche, instead of a theodicy that describes a spiritual or divine rationale for the persistence of suffering, Losurdo points out that Nietzsche preferred to speak of a "cosmodicy." This is the inverse of a theodicy, which describes how suffering is *justified* in the universe.

The attempt to enact a cosmodicy explains the intent of Nietzsche's reflections on pain, suffering, and *ressentiment*, as it shows how they emerge from the politics of extreme suffering in social life. It is important to point out that Nietzsche's reflections on suffering exceed political concerns alone, and his existentialist reflections on the dynamics of pain and suffering from a poetic and aesthetic perspective are often deeply insightful and valuable, particularly due to the fact that Nietzsche himself dealt with and learned to manage extreme suffering on a day-to-day basis. But the backbone of these reflections is to be located in Nietzsche's tragic cosmodicy, which was premised on the view that only the strong can become who they are. But more pointedly, the strong must be capable of a refined cruelty and get used to it with a resolute heart, as he writes: "If his force is even higher in the rank-ordering of forces, he himself is one of the creators and not just a spectator: so it is not enough that he is capable of cruelty only in seeing so much suffering, so much extinction, so much destruction; such a human being must be able to create pain with pleasure, to be cruel with hand and deed (and not just with the eyes of the spirit)."[14]

While the problem of suffering exceeded personal reflections and touched on the social context, it was also implicated in Nietzsche's community-building project. In *The Gay Science*,

Nietzsche writes of his ideal disciple, whom he contrasts with the Socratic disciple who cannot say no and says to everything, "Half and half." Such a disciple, "supposing that they adopted my doctrine," would "suffer too much, for my way of thinking requires a warlike soul, a desire to hurt, a delight in saying No, a hard skin; he would slowly die of open and internal wounds."[15] The emphasis on suffering and pain can be philosophically assessed from an aesthetic and artistic perspective in Nietzsche, but it should not be understood as reducible to an individualist set of reflections on the deep pain that he personally experienced. While these subjective experiences no doubt color his reflections on pain and suffering, we will examine Nietzsche's conception of them from this more socially mediated point of view.

Given that suffering is considered in this socially mediated perspective, the category of pain is also thought of as political before it is considered as an individual or aesthetic experience. The category of the aesthetic in Nietzsche's thought is best understood as based on a prior political separation — the pathos of distance — between those who suffer at more refined levels and plebeians who suffer in more vulgar terms.

But as with most of Nietzsche's concepts, his reflections on suffering and pain contain insights and even wisdom. We have aimed to demonstrate that we gain more from his insights when we prioritize the reactionary political thrust that is at the center of his thought. This centering of Nietzsche's politics does not negate these insights, but instead adds greater depth and nuance to them. In fact, Nietzsche understood something about pain that is close to what the poet Emily Dickinson once observed:

Pain has an element of blank;

It cannot recollect
When it began, or if there were
A day when it was not.
It has no future but itself,
Its infinite realms contain
Its past, enlightened to perceive
New periods of pain.[16]

Dickinson recognizes that pain is universal and repetitive, "It has no future but itself," but Nietzsche understood pain as being born from social power and labor. Both Nietzsche and Dickinson understood that the "infinite realms" of pain contained an element of the eternal, that they returned, that pain in some sense knows no future. But unlike Dickinson, Nietzsche's musings on pain were forged in a reactionary political direction that was centered on the scandal of the social suffering of the working class.

Ressentiment and Christianity

Although the political dynamics of post-French Revolution Europe were at the center of Nietzsche's thought, he also defined *ressentiment* as a form of social suffering that exists trans-historically. The origin of *ressentiment* is found in the teachings of Jewish priests and subsequently in the Abrahamic religions — primarily Judaism and Christianity. The problem of *ressentiment* in religion, especially Christianity and Christian moralism, has been a common touchstone for interpreters of Nietzsche's famous concept.[17] But is Nietzsche's assessment of Christianity as a religion that generates *ressentiment* accurate?

The German philosopher Max Scheler's 1913 work *ressentiment* offers a rebuttal to Nietzsche's historical genealogy of *ressentiment* as tied to Christianity. For starters, Scheler agrees with Nietzsche that the specter of the "man of *ressentiment*" — a man whose life and values are turned upside down — looms large as a historical phenomenon that must be diagnosed and identified. But Scheler disagrees with the historical origin of such a social creature. He argues that Christian ethics has not "grown on the soil of *ressentiment*,"[18] but that bourgeois morality is the primary generator of *ressentiment* in social life. Christian compassion, the very cornerstone of what Schopenhauer criticized in Christianity, which criticism Nietzsche continued in his reading of *ressentiment*, is not to be understood as an outgrowth of slave morality. The Christian is not afraid, like the ancient, that he might lose something or that it might impair his own nobility when he acts out of compassion.

As a protagonist of Christianity, Scheler maintains that the religion "acts in the peculiarly pious conviction that through this 'condescension,' through this self-abasement and 'self-renunciation' he [the Christian] gains the highest good and becomes equal to God."[19] Scheler thus disables Nietzsche's fetish for the slave-noble distinction as a total fabrication that is not pertinent to Christianity precisely because Christian morality has a consistent historical aristocratic ethos, not a weak slave morality. Scheler's critique of Nietzsche opens a new source of solidarity between Nietzsche and any Christian reader of his work, because what appears as a condescending act — self-renunciation, compassion toward the meek and poor, and so forth — is now revealed as an affirmative and noble act for the Christian. In exerting Christian-inspired compassion, the believer "becomes equal to God,"[20] according to Scheler. Scheler thus rejects Nietzsche's dualistic theory of the strong and the weak as applying at all to Christian morality, and this means that Christianity does not contain the germs of modern socialism that Nietzsche accuses of *ressentiment*. Scheler thus defends Christianity as an anti-egalitarian institution that accords its morals in line with "aristocratic codes and mores."[21]

Similar to Nietzsche's fondness for Pascal, Scheler celebrated the aristocratic aspects of bourgeois Christianity, as evidenced by his support for the rank order of some elements of the modern Church and in his support for Christianity in imperial conquests in the Far East. But these aristocratic elements were aberrations; if the core of Christian moral discourse was a slave morality, this was only truly visible in Europe after the French Revolution had fallen sway to egalitarianism. Scheler argues against such claims, showing how the Church never had a major problem with private property throughout its existence. Nor is Christianity to be understood as a precursor to state-directed communism.

Scheler pinpoints modern liberal humanitarianism, not Christian morals, as being responsible for a form of egalitarian love which he sees as a cause of modern *ressentiment*. Liberal humanitarian thought, with its origins in the post-French Revolution period, is "not based on a positive value but on a protest and negation (hatred, envy, revenge) against ruling authorities."[22] August Comte, the great liberal positivist, is the inventor of the term "altruism," a concept which Scheler links directly to the perpetuation of modern bourgeois *ressentiment*. Altruism is problematic, in Scheler's view, because it is pays no mind — as Christianity does — to altering the state of those it supposes to uplift.

In Scheler's pro-Christian account of modern *ressentiment*, it is liberal philosophies that preach an equality that pays no attention to any spiritual alteration of the condition of the human and that stand out as the engine of *ressentiment*. These modern liberal doctrines promote degeneration, nihilism, and *ressentiment*. The problem with Scheler's embrace of *ressentiment* is that it affirms — just as Nietzsche intended — a sadomasochist vision of social and political conflict. Scheler and Nietzsche both see *ressentiment* emerge as a general social feature of modern liberal capitalism: "Only the man who is afraid of losing demands equality as a general principle."[23] Scheler shares Nietzsche's problematic framing of *ressentiment* as a tendency to "degrade the superior persons, those who represent a higher value, to the level of the low."[24]

Where Scheler's insights into *ressentiment* are most valuable, however, is in the way that he elaborates on some of the psychological and affective dimensions of the condition and how it affects values. For example, Scheler shows that subjects who are overrun by *ressentiment* end up subjectivizing values and morals to the imperatives of capitalist life. Because the man of *ressentiment* is "narrowed to his own desire and objectives," this has the effect of relativizing values based on race, tribe, nation, and so forth.[25] There thus emerges a false universalism inherent to bourgeois liberal culture that accelerates a value relativism and identity politics wherein values are based only on one's "factual existence."

The subject of *ressentiment* is drawn into an existential vicious circle where they end up reversing the hierarchy of values as they exist. This means that they can only posit values from the position of their own subjective complaint and passive negation of the other's values. This vicious circle means that values end up being derived purely from the capitalist world, that is, from the standpoint of each individual consumer or atomized worker. Scheler offers a critique of modern bourgeois morality and nihilism whereby modern bourgeois life is subject to a condition of generalized *ressentiment* that leads to a reversal of values which only reinforces parochial communities of the aggrieved. *Ressentiment* is caught in the field of the other's values and is unable to break free from its strictures, a sign of which is that the subject of *ressentiment* "imitates genuine modesty by means of prudery."[26]

Ultimately, *ressentiment* is a problem for Scheler — a thinker who wants to preserve the moral codes of Christianity in the modern world, precisely because they have their origin in strong aristocratic values — because it distorts our understanding of moral values. This distortion of moral values leads to a spiral which forces us to lose our capacity to apprehend the virtues, which then leads to a situation in which our desires and our convictions are "not arrived at by direct contact with the world and the objects themselves, but indirectly through a critique of the opinions of others."[27] *Ressentiment* thus perverts the subject's moral agency to invent new values. The confluence of affects that make up *ressentiment* — envy, anger, and jealousy — name a condition in which the subject is unable to *work through* the repression of these affects. Scheler fails to point to any viable way out of this situation other than through an embrace of a Christian moral worldview.

Ressentiment in Neoliberal Times

Nietzsche's strategic concept of *ressentiment* has a certain function when deployed in the class struggle: it rigidifies and intensifies what we will name a liberal polemical form of politics that designates boundaries of insider/outsider and thus shuts down the possibility of solidarity across groups and classes. For Nietzsche, the thinker who is supposedly *beyond* good and evil, the function of *ressentiment* is to resituate moral distinctions even more forcefully and polemically than before.

To name one's opponent to be in a condition "of *ressentiment*" establishes a particular liberal form of polemic: it fortifies a boundary of communication and interaction with the other. When this label is assigned to a person or group, they are marked as damned, as outside, other.

When an individual or group is to be designated as possessing or being in a state of *ressentiment*, it functions a bit like modern cancel culture today. The act isolates communities or individuals as ineligible for any redress or solidarity. As Scheler has shown, *ressentiment* can only be grasped as a psycho-political concept, and the prospect of receiving any promise of relief from the "inner torment" of *ressentiment* is rarely if ever addressed in Nietzschean thought. When the concept is deployed, its function is to shut down and paralyze whoever it is that is called out. It is as unclear to those who use the label to describe others, just as it is to those who receive that label themselves, whether the accused might ever reasonably escape *ressentiment*.

Is *ressentiment* an escapable condition for those thought to be imbued with it? Nietzsche addresses this possibility and sets a very high bar for any possible overcoming of *ressentiment*, which involves a community-building conversion: "For man to be redeemed from revenge — that is for me the bridge to the highest hope, and a rainbow after long storms."[28] As we articulated above, *ressentiment* names a condition of an overwhelming confluence of resentful feelings — revenge, envy, jealousy, and shame — which come together to create a brutal vortex of bad conscience and a stunted relation to the outside world and others.

But why do we choose to name this vicious combination "*ressentiment*"? What does this naming procedure in fact do to our supposed enemies? What is the effect of naming *ressentiment*? This brings us to a core problem with the very concept of *ressentiment* itself; it assigns an *ontological* condition to an individual or a community. To hurl the label onto someone generates a political paralysis. In this way, *ressentiment* shuts down discourse because it implies an ontological status which severely affects the agency of the accused. In declaring someone to be of *ressentiment*, you name a state of being, not a temporary affect. This is different than saying the other is acting resentful, which would name their actions as a transient affect with a possibility of being cured or overcome.

Nietzsche's historical genealogy of *ressentiment* assigns the phenomenon to entire religious communities, and transversally to individuals. This transversal application of *ressentiment* to individuals has the advantage — for the liberal Nietzschean — that it allows those subjects to be identified based on the immanent performative metrics of capitalist competition. With transversal *ressentiment*, the "losers" in capitalist society can easily be identified based on how their lives have turned out, on how successful they are. If you are deemed a loser by objective standards of success, you are of *ressentiment*. Did you not receive tenure? Did you not get that promotion? The liberal Nietzschean has all the empirical proof they need to work with.

Transversal *ressentiment* is assigned to a community or group and interacts with and mediates the other, more generalized social form of *ressentiment* which is a condition any individual may find themselves in. With transversal *ressentiment*, anyone can be assigned and thus any one individual can fall victim to it, but it tends to affect groups. When one is declared to be of *ressentiment*, the label assigns you to those others of the same condition. In this way, the social order naturally produces transversal communities of *ressentiment*, and from that, their own sense of habits and character can be identified. This coding system of *ressentiment* has an important political function — it shuts down solidarity with that group and it enacts a barrier, a distance.

The idea of *ressentiment* is crucial to any liberal entrepreneurial society, in that it allows for a Nietzschean commitment to the *Übermensch* to be tied to the imperative of success. Whether liberal, libertarian, or neoconservative, the concept of *ressentiment* is an invaluable tool for retrenching the ideology of meritocracy. Given that liberal capitalist society is so profoundly unequal at its very core, those who are not in the elite positions or who are struggling to make ends meet can be qualified as subjects of *ressentiment*. Just as we saw with Nietzsche's treatment of the working class, the concept of *ressentiment*, when it is deployed to describe those who have supposedly lost in their careers or occupation, works to pacify and ultimately mute the social suffering of those it accuses.

Ressentiment is an irrationalist concept in Lukács's sense of the term. It names an interminable maelstrom of negative affects and in the very act of naming shuts down any resolution. This irrational basis of *ressentiment* is bound up with the fact that it remains unclear why the philosopher, or anyone who hurls the name at an individual or group, would not use the term "resentment" instead. After all, if your perceived enemy is resentful, and not of *ressentiment*, this implies that your enemy can change, that they can be worked with and even transformed, possibly even by your ideas and initiative. This irrational effect of the application of *ressentiment* to one's enemies has the potential to close that other off, signaling a total rejection of the other.

In this way, *ressentiment* relies on and upholds a conception of politics informed by the Nazi jurist Carl Schmitt, who argued that politics only truly begins after the "friend-enemy distinction" has been established. *Ressentiment* is a tried-and-true liberal polemic on the right, and is used by everyone from the populist right to neoconservatives and libertarians. Although the word "*ressentiment*" itself is rarely used by the contemporary right — with all its pretentiousness — it still deeply affects the right's intellectual culture. The *function* of *ressentiment* is deployed daily across conservative cable news and in the halls of power. This is a sign of the profound cultural success of Nietzscheanism.

What is this common sense that Nietzsche has bequeathed to contemporary political discourse on the right? It's a story we know too well, a nauseating and vulgar idea, namely that any demands for egalitarian justice or "rights" from an aggrieved group, or for even universal social policies like healthcare and college-debt forgiveness, all constitute a disruption to the natural harmony of capitalist competition and individual property rights. While the right has long been defined by its hostility to universalism, it has also been defined by its hostility to demands that come from aggrieved or marginalized groups, who the right construe as "victims," including women, minorities, or racialized groups. Demands for egalitarian justice from below are interpreted by the right as driven by envy and jealousy for those whose lives have turned out better. We thus see that the two forms of *ressentiment* — transversal and generalized social *ressentiment* — are fused as one by the right.

The right shares the Nietzschean view that communism and socialism are fundamentally movements of *ressentiment* because they legitimate collective *ressentiment*, the main culprits of which are the intellectuals who seek to legitimate and shepherd whole hordes of aggrieved victims and resentful people. But on both the right and on the left, the use of *ressentiment* is always polemical, precisely because it names something more than mere resentment — it names an interminable misery. *Ressentiment* names a condition whereby a toxic intersection of negative affects overwhelms a person. For a person or group in such a condition, this condition is thought to be inescapable; the subject seized by *ressentiment* is other, morally outside, an enemy.

How have philosophers on the left wielded the accusation of *ressentiment*? Those philosophers who buy in to the discourse and who use the concept as a hammer on their supposed enemies do so in two ways: first, they assume a socio-psychological disposition and type of person or group; and secondly, precisely because the consequence of naming someone or some group as being of *ressentiment* has the paralyzing function that it does, the application of *ressentiment* makes the accusation into a paradoxically *moral* claim. That there is a moral quality to *ressentiment* in political discourse should come as a shock, especially to Nietzschean philosophers who pride themselves on surgically removing moral concerns from politics entirely.

It is worth asking what it means to wield the claim that one group is of *ressentiment* or that another is not. The concept possesses a disciplinary function in the sense that, once it is deployed, it works to set the boundaries of permissible social suffering and grievance by cordoning off *those* subjects as fundamentally lost in the quagmire of their own passive resistance. How does the philosopher — whether they are of the left or the right — discern whether a protest movement, a group of workers on strike, an oppressed racial group advocating for justice, or members of an entire political party are driven by *ressentiment* and not resentment?

We must seriously ask: Is it even worth continuing to wield

the concept of *ressentiment* anymore? With all its ontological baggage, its fatalistic, quasi-religious, and moralistic connotations, its capacity to shut down those it names as irredeemable to any politics of solidarity or even dialogue, what does it allow us to achieve in the management and processing of social suffering? *Ressentiment* has hyperbolic baggage that must be avoided. It is instead far more productive to the project of political solidarity and to socialist and emancipatory politics that we incorporate an understanding of resentment as being a common affect of social life in capitalism. What we are advocating here is rather modest; we argue that the distinction between resentment and *ressentiment* is too often overlooked, and that this is a result of the long shadow that Nietzsche has cast over contemporary politics. The philosopher Sjoerd van Tuinen points to this problem as the "resentment-*ressentiment* complex" of liberal politics, wherein the wielding of the *ressentiment* label functions to exclude certain communities from the possibility of proper justice.

It is common for Nietzschean-inspired liberals to wield the *ressentiment* label when describing particular social and political movements, from the Black Lives Matter movement and Occupy Wall Street to the followers of Donald Trump who stormed the US Capitol on January 6th. If these actors were driven by resentment, an otherwise healthy virtue, the demands and agonism they bring to the body politic could be worked with and they would not become an enemy. The assigning of the label of *ressentiment* to any group has the function of solidifying and making apparent the friend-enemy distinction. Within this complex, we can now see how *ressentiment* is closely linked to Nietzschean perspectivism in the sense that when the philosopher wields the label, they are choosing a perspective, but the twist with *ressentiment* that is so crucial to understand is that in deploying the label, the philosopher adopts a moralized understanding of social suffering and conflict.

Nietzsche never cared to make a distinction between resentment and *ressentiment*, and this has led to the conception that culture itself is an engine of *ressentiment*. Søren Kierkegaard held a similar view to Nietzsche, although he did not situate *ressentiment* in the class system and in relation to labor, as Nietzsche did. For Kierkegaard, *ressentiment* is the condition of the "age of reflection," which came after the turbulent and "passionate" revolutionary age ushered in by the French Revolution. But Kierkegaard understood the perpetuation of *ressentiment* in an inverse fashion to Nietzsche.

For Nietzsche, it was the French Revolution and its spreading of egalitarianism throughout culture that ushered in modern *ressentiment*, whereas for Kierkegaard, it is the overly reflective and self-obsessed bourgeois age that accelerated feelings of *ressentiment*. But importantly, as van Tuinen has pointed out, both Kierkegaard and Nietzsche ended up taking these modern pathologies of *ressentiment* — hysteria, anxiety, boredom, and so on — which are affects distinct to the bourgeois class and its culture, and universalized them to all classes.[29] Following Nietzsche and Kierkegaard, the entire discourse on *ressentiment* replaces an understanding of class opposition with a failure of individual character. As van Tuinen says, the concept of *ressentiment* is premised on the perspective that "capital is not bad, humans are bad."[30] It is this Nietzschean perspectival shift from the structure onto the group or the individual that makes any deployment of *ressentiment* fundamentally bound up with a moral claim.

The deployment of *ressentiment* has a specific function: it renders an immanent judgment on a class, political movement, or an individual; but what matters most is how the accusation turns them into a different sort of enemy, one for whom recognition, dialogue, or redress is impossible. Those subjects declared overwhelmed by *ressentiment* have transgressed liberal political norms, and in so doing have become a threat to the very prospect of justice. While van Tuinen is correct to point out that Nietzsche set the stakes for *ressentiment* to be wielded as a liberal moral accusation, what he misses is the way that Nietzsche also historicized *ressentiment* as a built-in feature of any culture and civilization and claimed that it is brought about primarily through the introduction of more egalitarian demands from the lower classes.

Unlike Kierkegaard, for whom *ressentiment* is a general cultural possibility affecting the entirety of bourgeois society, Nietzsche's use of the concept goes much further. *Ressentiment* has a political-epistemological end in Nietzsche's view, in that it is meant to shut down any consideration of extreme suffering. We remember that Nietzsche's nominalism works to cover over the real dimension, the real scandal, of social suffering, specifically suffering that is born from market tyranny and class oppression. *Ressentiment* plays a similar nominalist function; it is meant to further a desired social objective, that is, to pacify and to stabilize a social order so as to make way for rank order and for exceptional geniuses to emerge whose suffering can be qualitatively treated at a higher, more refined level. Those deemed to be of *ressentiment* suffer at a lower level of refinement and sophistication, but they don't know that they do. The hurling of the label reinforces the pathos of distance because the enemies are segregated and othered from any prospect of political solidarity or transformation.

There is a fatal error that drives contemporary debates about *ressentiment* and which lies in the warning that Gramsci left us that the mass's demands for equality are *not* to be understood as the engine of *ressentiment*. We must shrug off this Nietzschean suspicion of *ressentiment* as being tied fundamentally to demands for equality or to the problems of equality in capitalism. The very framework of *ressentiment* reinforces a conservative point of view that rests on the presupposition that "inequality is a fact of nature and passionate resistance in the name of justice is portrayed as mendacious and harmful."[31] Liberal Nietzscheans invoke *ressentiment* in contemporary political debates and analysis because they trust Nietzsche's historical genealogy of it as emanating from a more primordial struggle between the strong and the weak and the outgrowth of a slave morality that only foments the conditions of it. *Ressentiment* has emerged as a concept that is vital to ideologues of capitalist liberal democracy, whether of the right or the left, precisely because the social order requires "good losers." The subjects of *ressentiment* are those whose grievances are deemed irrational and thus morally problematic because they have compromised the liberal status quo.

The resentment-*ressentiment* complex, as van Tuinen calls it, concerns the philosopher or intellectual's role in the class struggle and the authority they arrogate unto themselves in labeling such and such a group or such and such an individual as being *of ressentiment*. Anytime the philosopher names or assigns *ressentiment* instead of resentment, they take a side in the class struggle. But even more problematic is the way that deeming a group to be of *ressentiment* has the tendency to reinforce liberal political mores, and this is how Nietzsche returns as a champion of the liberal status quo. The core idea of Nietzschean *ressentiment* is formed around an understanding of social suffering that aims to excise suffering that is brought on by class and market oppressions.

What does *ressentiment* look like in today's late-capitalist social order, wherein a whole number of media and political apparatuses foment and channel common resentments toward specific targets? At issue with common resentments is the problem of the repression and lack of acknowledgement of certain social sufferings. Our social order, any social order for that matter, must invent ways to channel and sublimate these common resentments, which are unconsciously processed and often difficult to work through. The limitations of liberal polemics that are hardwired into wielding *ressentiment* are evident in Wendy Brown's *Society Must Be Dismantled*, where she discusses the problem of *ressentiment* in the post-Fordist, neoliberal era.

In a sweeping analysis of the Fordist era (1945–1973), Brown acknowledges that this was a period of relative stability for the working class, especially in the West, and in America in particular. The post-war New Deal era had raised egalitarian prospects for all social classes, and racially subjugated groups, especially the American black population, had experienced a sizable improvement in their quality of life. But the post-Fordist, neoliberal era is now marked by a ransacking of this former stability, which is evidenced by the decline in real wages since the late 1970s, the gutting of social services, especially in former industrial-belt areas, and the decline in life expectancy among the former industrial working class in America.

Within this situation of general class struggle, Brown locates and identifies a particularly egregious expression of resentments in white men, most of whom are former working class. What marks this social class as bound to *ressentiment* is that they formulate their grievances through a "loss of entitlement" framework; that is, they are aware of their former supremacy and dominance, but the way this rage is expressed misses the material economic loss of that entitlement. The white working class thus nominalizes its own situation of social suffering through cultural registers of resentment, and projects these resentments onto false targets: the Mexicans at the border, the lazy black welfare mothers, and the globalist elites who have left everyday Americans behind. Trump is the perverse shepherd of this white, male, supremacist loss of entitlement, and is the primary architect and political mediator of these resentments.

Brown wields a hammer in her diagnosis of *ressentiment* in this social class, and argues that it is the neoliberal deterioration of the social sphere that is a major cause of this situation. The social is "the essential modern site of emancipation, justice, and democracy," and neoliberalism only foments this *ressentiment* because it guts social protections that promised a more egalitarian distribution of goods and resources. Neoliberalism encourages an antidemocratic culture from below while "building and legitimating antidemocratic forms of state power from above."[32] The social is an important achievement of the Fordist, post-New Deal social order, a zone of social life that was ideally meant to be a protector of "market instrumentalization." The social is what binds us in ways that exceed personal ties, market exchanges, or abstract citizenship.

Margaret Thatcher's mantra that "society does not exist, only families and individuals" must be understood as the structural engine of neoliberal *ressentiment* as it erodes the social fabric and converts all social relations to the brutal logic of market instrumentalization. This destruction of the promise of the social "permits the effective political disenfranchisement (and not only the suffering) produced by homelessness, lack of health care, and lack of education. And it permits assaults on whatever remains of the social fabric in the name of freedom."[33]

This domain of collective life that Brown calls the social is where democratic rights were gained for minorities, women, and other marginalized groups, but neoliberalism has shifted the social to a more market-instrumentalized sphere of social life. The social is now overwrought with inequalities, abjections, and exclusions. It is crucial that we understand the way this process has been internalized by those who benefited from the Fordist-era stability of the social — namely, white men — who stand as the linchpin of the most potent form of *ressentiment* today. Yet Brown does not analyze this *ressentiment* as primarily immanent to class conflict, seeing it rather as being born from a crisis of norms and a deviation from the new norms of neoliberalism, which are antinormative at their core (that is, neoliberalism invites the working class to participate in their own immiseration through austerity, budget cuts, and the curtailing of basic social services such as healthcare and retirement). Moreover, Brown's reading of *ressentiment* is based on an ahistorical account of Nietzsche's own theories of it, as she argues that "Nietzsche reflected on the nihilism emanating from the accidental human toppling of the divine; he did not explore formations of power that do not merely trivialize, but openly defile and defy moral values."[34]

Nietzsche *did* theorize *ressentiment* beyond an immanent critique of Christian moralism. In fact, any left-wing appraisal of Nietzsche must center his metacritique of liberalism and socialism during his own time, and do so by recognizing that he theorized *ressentiment* as a problem of the laboring class in capitalism. Moreover, the concept dealt with a political, epistemological problem that was centered on how to manage the extreme suffering of this class of people. Brown argues that white men in the post-Fordist, neoliberal era practice a historically unique form of *ressentiment* which stems from a "loss of entitlement" rather than from weakness. According to Brown, nineteenth-century Christian *ressentiment* was driven by a weakness of the lower classes, a point that is not qualified by any convincing reference to Nietzsche, but simply accepted. Moving the analysis away from a structural class analysis, she goes on to suggest that the primary site of this new *ressentiment* is identity conflicts and a culturalization of grievance politics.

Brown's framework for understanding modern day *ressentiment* sets the stage for the perpetuation of an ongoing struggle between two wider social groups vying for power: an oppressed assortment of minorities, women, and immigrants who suffer the most from the neoliberal assault on the social, and white male supremacists who suffer from the same destruction but whose resentments are deemed ontologically inferior. Brown thus wields the concept of *ressentiment* to cohere and circumscribe the terms of social struggle based on the very routing mechanisms that bourgeois class rule seeks to reinforce. By identifying *ressentiment* as a coherent phenomenon that describes this otherwise nebulous social class — aggrieved white men — Brown contributes to a framework that takes this liberal cliché at face value and does not challenge it.

In other words, the problem in Brown's analysis of *ressentiment* is that it produces a liberal Manichean division wherein one form of resentment is authentic and others are not. It is this dualism that the concept of *ressentiment* reproduces; an account of social conflict that has completely abandoned any class analysis of resentment. Brown's framework retrenches a cultural politics as the primary site of contemporary social conflict, a framework that is clearly indebted to the failure of the New Left to fight off the rise of pernicious neoliberalism. The aggrieved, white, male, formerly working-class subject may have a particularly loud microphone, but does this mean that other political coalitions are immune from falling sway to the *ressentiment* trap?

What is missing in Brown's framework of *ressentiment* is any prospect that such a dynamic might ever change, that this class — or is this cohort something more nebulous than a class? — might be capable of an egalitarian or even socialist form of politics. Instead of a broad, class-based politics that might work to undo the neoliberal system that foments resentments across class and racial divides alike, Brown identifies one group who has sunk to the depths of *ressentiment* and others who remain at a more righteous level of resentment. It is not clear what work is involved or even what value there is in isolating one set of resentments as morally superior to others, other than its serving up an understanding of social conflict as situated around an intractable culture war. Socialist politics must rather pierce the belly of the beast to identify and isolate the structural forces that make these culture-war polemics the only site in which social antagonisms are eligible to be experienced. To shift the ground of Nietzschean culture-war strategies — it is important to remember that Nietzsche himself deployed culture-war tactics as a weapon against socialism — we must interrogate the resentments and the common affects of the working class instead of relying on a partial and limited culture-war framework of analysis.

If *ressentiment* is stoked by situations that are "injurious" but beyond one's control, or situations wherein, as Scheler puts it, "injury is experienced as a destiny," this invites the question as to what the resentments of the working class look like today.

As Scheler notes, *ressentiment* tends to be confined to those who serve and are dominated; it is these subjects who "fruitlessly resent the sting of authority."[35] Liberal capitalism is a system that requires that the working class accept their domination without resentment. When they fall into the more problematic condition of *ressentiment*, the Nietzschean philosopher enters the fray and begins to carve out the boundaries of engagement with such untouchable and deplorable groups.

When we analyze a phenomenon such as Trumpism, it is far more accurate to speak of the resentments that emerge from this movement as emanating from what the Marxist sociologist Eric Olin Wright calls the "contradictory class position," or what in classical Marxism is called the petit-bourgeoisie, than from the working class. Scheler rightly pointed out that under industrial capitalism, the petit-bourgeoisie are more prone to envy of the bourgeoisie precisely because of their proximity to that class, whereas the working class is less prone to such political affects of envy or jealousy. At Trump's infamous January 6th storming of the US Capitol Building in 2021, less than 10 percent of the rioters were from a working-class background. The majority that make up Trump's core base of supporters are petit-bourgeois small-business owners (for example, real-estate developers) and downwardly mobile petit-bourgeois. Regardless of what Brown may think, Trumpism does not predominantly draw from the working class.

Yet at the same time, the working class is not free of resentments, nor is it made up of pure souls who have sublimated the toxic brew of envy, jealousy, and pity that makes up *ressentiment*. What is needed is a more coherent and sober understanding of the political affects of today's working class. What affects, passions, and yearnings drive the working class today? What makes them tick? Do they in fact see themselves as working class?

In *Coming Up Short: Working Class Adulthood in an Age of Uncertainty*, an important ethnographic study of the American millennial working class by Jennifer Silva, we are presented with a complex picture of the everyday life and challenges of working-class young people. Silva's study is nothing less than eye-opening. We learn that class disadvantage, inequality, and social power all tend to be internalized by the working class in ways that are nothing close to attitudes or feelings of resentment, let alone to the more dramatic form of *ressentiment*. Silva asks each of the working-class subjects in her study how they understand people who are more successful than they are. One participant had this to say:

> If I believe that the man I call "Sir" and who calls me by my first name started with an equal fund of powers, do not our differences, do not all signs of courtesy and attention given to him but denied me, do not his very feelings of being different in "taste" and understanding from me, show that somehow he has developed his insides more than I mine? How else can I explain inequalities? The institutions may be structured so that he wins and I lose, but this is my life…. Even though we might have been born in different stations, the fact that he is getting more means that somehow he had the power in him, the character, to "realize himself," to earn his superiority.[36]

This comment warrants several remarks: the first and most startling is the way that class advantages are taken to be *natural* features of the world, *unchangeable* dynamics that must be accepted. But not only are those inequalities structural and not to be challenged, there is thought to be an inner power drive in each of us which determines our fate. The subject accepts that they must lack the drive of someone who has been granted far more privileges by institutions than they have, thus ignoring the role that economic privilege plays entirely. This sentiment is not surprising and is reflective of a garden-variety American gritty spirit, a residue of the Protestant subconscious that tells us that capitalism is a natural order whose hierarchies should not be challenged. But most importantly, this reflection does not possess an ounce of resentment toward or envy of others. If anything, there is a glaring absence of any resentment toward "superior" people. The working class serves, but they do not "resent the sting of authority," as Scheler put it.

What allows working-class people to confront the enormity of the challenges they face and the suffering they endure? As Scheler notes, "If an ill-treated servant can vent his spleen in the antechamber, he will remain free from the inner venom of *ressentiment*, but it will engulf him if he must hide his feelings and keep his negative and hostile emotions to himself."[37] What Silva's study reveals is that working-class people are not sublimating their inner resentments and negative feelings through class struggle. There is little to no class consciousness among the people Silva interviews.

Working-class people face immense risk in their daily lives, and they are often torn from their family's due to divorce and drug and alcohol addictions. These day-to-day challenges "[leave] them with only the deep and unyielding belief that personal responsibility is the key to meaning, security, and freedom," Silva notes.[38] Instead of bearing the pains of their day-to-day struggles by externalizing their feelings of resentment onto more successful people, the working class has turned to self-help to work through their issues. In what Silva calls the "mood economy," working-class people set milestones for themselves not based on the approval of others or of social authorities; they rather seek validation for themselves by conquering their emotions and feelings. The battle of today's working class is not a Nietzschean will to power for domination, it is fought on the terrain of conquering historical and personal traumas, of proving to themselves and their immediate friends and family that they can wrest emotional control over their lives. But this struggle can also lead to what Silva calls the trap of the mood economy, wherein working-class adults are "unable to realize the visions of worthy personhood" and this becomes "the greatest injury of all."[39]

The norms of capitalist life allow only *permissible* forms of resentment, which include those brought about by market competition, such as the feeling one gets when a colleague gets a raise that feels undeserved, or a privileged person gets admission into a fancy college, or friends begin to buy homes without having worked hard for their down payments. These feelings of resentment are permissible, but if one is deemed a loser from the standpoint of the ruling ideology, then one risks falling into something more ontological than mere resentment; one risks *being* a subject of *ressentiment*. Silva's study shows that the working class does not tend to experience these more common, market-based competitive resentments because their struggles are more serious than these more superficial concerns.

The working class experience trauma, addiction, and poverty, which from the perspective of the ruling ideology might very well render them losers before they have even played the game. If a working-class person gets a chance to play to the game, that is, to attempt to move to a middle-class life, they most often discover that the game is rigged and the odds are set against them. It is therefore more accurate to say that the working-class person faces conditions that are repressive and noncommunicable, and that the alienation they experience is often not even permitted to see itself as alienated. But despite the gravity of these experiences, as Silva's study demonstrates, the concept of *ressentiment* does not apply to working-class experience.

The affect theorist Lauren Berlant has described our culture as one of "cruel optimism," by which she means that the measures of what it means to be successful are far out of reach of most people, yet they are forced to internalize these goals and aspirations as if they are viable and achievable.[40] Despite the Nietzschean presumption, our society is not one of a rampant resentment; it is one of a subdued, impermissible, quiet resentment. These dynamics are captured in what the philosopher Byung-Chul Han has called the contemporary "achievement society" — a social order in which everyone is expected to rise above the herd and realize their true self by engaging in the risks and rewards that come with this struggle.[41] The achievement society leaves no space for negative affects and common resentments to be processed or even expressed. Our society is marked by a repressive positivity, which is why our society produces, as Han remarks, "depressives and losers, it does not create madmen and criminals."[42] Our culture has lost touch with how to make room for legitimately negative or even ambivalent experiences.[43] If someone has "strong feelings of subjective inadequacy," and "he or she is unequipped to cope,"[44] they feel as if they have become a loser. But what we are arguing is that while the stakes of what it objectively means to be a winner have become fundamentally out of reach for so many, this is not creating a situation in which the masses are mired in *ressentiment*. The concept has become incoherent and it is unclear what it describes, but it should be clear by now what sort of function it plays when it is deployed as a weapon in liberal political struggles.

As both Byung-Chul Han and Andreas Reckwitz have pointed out from a sociological perspective, the "loser" is today defined as one who has failed to "self-singularize" themselves. The loser is a loser in the sense that they have failed to optimize their lives and distinguish themselves. In Reckwitz's analysis, this means that unlike the new middle classes, the underclass is now perceived as made up of losers who lack openness, empathy, and a cosmopolitan and entrepreneurial sense of style.[45] In Han's theory of the performance society, the loser is defined as a depressive who has failed to abide by the regimen of positivity and self-actualization. While Han draws our attention to the more productive forms of resistance, to the injunction of enforced positivity that losers can harness, what interests us apropos of *ressentiment* is the way that so-called losers internalize the ideology of capitalism's zero-sum game.

If we accept the premise that our society can be divided or assessed through this Manichean lens of winners and losers — an objectively idealist and faulty frame of analysis — we need to ask if the internalization of the loser takes the form of what Nietzsche called "bad conscience." Bad conscience is an internalization or repression of reactive forces. Imagine the subject who is dejected by the repetition of enforced positivity they find everywhere in society; from wage-labor service jobs to everyday relations at school, it can feel as though no one will let people be themselves. This can lead to repression and internalization whereby even genuine positivity is experienced and felt as painful because the subject has struggled for so long to meet the barrage of demands that they be positive.

In a society dictated by the injunction to constant positivity, bad conscience can easily fester. Deleuze says this becomes a problem because it can "extend *ressentiment*." Bad conscience leads *ressentiment* further into psychic entanglements where the contagion has spread. Bad conscience is understood as a metaphysics of forces whereby "active force becomes reactive, the master becomes slave."[46] The subject of bad conscience experiences pain on a frequent basis, but they must transform this pain into an entirely different rationale in order to tolerate it. It is this transformation through which values and culture enter the picture, because Nietzsche's claim in *The Genealogy of Morals* is that entire cultures, such as Judaism and Christianity, develop values out of this condition of bad conscience. The value of compassion toward the stranger and the poor in Christianity is theorized as a submission to reactive forces. This reading has it that Christianity developed a spiritualization out of the pain of bad conscience and named it "sin."

We thus find that bad conscience, like *ressentiment*, can easily be applied in a culturally essentialist and reductive manner. At best, Deleuze's analysis of bad conscience brings out a series of psychoanalytic insights into the ways that repression and the internalization of reactive forces leads to a passivity and weakness of will. But Deleuze furthers a cultural essentializing of *ressentiment* as endemic to certain cultures, going so far as to write, "*ressentiment* and bad conscience are constitutive of the humanity of man, nihilism is the a priori concept of universal history."[47] Deleuze even divides humanity into the men of *ressentiment* and the free men.

In *Logic of Sense*, a highly experimental text written at the height of the 1960s counterculture, Deleuze inverts the liberal Nietzschean sadomasochistic idea of the social world as being split between men of *ressentiment* and the free men. He writes that "the revolutionary alone is free from *ressentiment*, by means of which one always participates in, and profits by, an oppressive order."[48] Deleuze made this observation at the height of the Vietnam War, at a moment when the world was on fire with revolutionary upheaval.

As a left-Nietzschean, Deleuze describes how one can harness a revolutionary exit from *ressentiment* through an ethics of moderate and prudential liberatory aesthetics. *Logic of Sense* is perhaps Deleuze's most interesting work, precisely for the fact that it offers such a moderate form of libertinism. But as it pertains to his treatment of *ressentiment*, it bears noting that he construes it as a general condition of liberal capitalist life. Such an essential framework means that we lose specificity and a more precise determination of what constitutes a mode of living that is not of *ressentiment* in Deleuze's analysis. The downside to this analysis of *ressentiment* at the level of metaphysical forces is that, inevitably, everything becomes fascist, and everything becomes reactionary. Only the rare Nietzschean *Übermensch* can find an exit.

But while Deleuze's view on *ressentiment* is problematic in its vagueness, the liberal sadomasochist vision of a society based on winners and losers is the more common form of *ressentiment* in general. Since there is no real standard of success in the achievement society, the very meaning of "winner" is relative. As such, even highly successful people internalize their success as inadequate and fraudulent, even if they have achieved success beyond their original expectations.

The "winner takes all" mentality of our society leads to a relativism of success such that even the middle and upper-middle class can experience feelings of individual resentment that often go unaddressed. The phenomenon of imposter syndrome among younger generations in academia is one such symptom of this generalized myth. More and more people who have made it in modern life feel their success and the legitimacy of their station or rank in their given institution are unearned. The impostor is faced with the fact that the entire basis of the winner-loser myth is just that, a myth, and that their success was afforded by a wide swath of social capital and connections, not exclusively by the grit of the lone individual. But the point is that the ideology of the winner-loser society is one in which everyone must look at their own success as if they are totally independent, for without this perspective, the massive structural disadvantages of the system would have to be processed.

So ubiquitous is this individualist myth that society is composed of winners and losers that some have argued this framework is now connected to a much wider racial and class coding system. Alenka Zupančič has pointed out in a quite convincing way that

> if traditional racism tended to socialize biological features — that is, directly translate them into cultural and symbolic points of a given social order — contemporary racism works in the opposite direction. It tends to "naturalize" the differences and features produced by the sociosymbolic order.[49]

In neoliberal society, the losers are treated like a racialized underclass, a deplorable stock who have only themselves to blame for their wretched condition.

Zupančič's insights into contemporary racism link us back to what Losurdo pinpoints as the core idea of Nietzsche's racism, that in the future racism will move away from the vulgar Darwinist or even Wagnerian conception of racial stratification based on skin color. In our time, racial difference tends to be construed at the level of the strong and the weak, or the well-formed/ill-formed dichotomy. Like the hammer of *ressentiment* that Brown and other liberal Nietzscheans wield, the embrace of a Nietzschean perspective on society as composed of winners and losers only works to retrench a false understanding of class conflict as driven by liberal and capitalist imperatives.

We have isolated two types *ressentiment*: the first is what we are calling transversal *ressentiment*, which is thought to infect an entire community, from the Black Lives Matter movement and the Make America Great Again movement to the Silicon Valley tech-startup community. Transversal *ressentiment* confers a definitive judgment on a group, and as we saw with Brown's critique of white, male Americans, this accusation runs the risk of shutting down any possible transformation of the group in question. In a sense, to declare a group to be riven with *ressentiment* is to relegate them to the status of a secular evil for which no solidarity or cooperation is possible, let alone any change among the members themselves. The second form of *ressentiment* is what we are calling "*ressentiment* in general*," which names a structural form of *ressentiment* that is produced as an outgrowth of the capitalist machine itself. This is market-driven *ressentiment* and importantly tends to affect the middle class and the petit-bourgeoisie rather than the working class.

The idea of *ressentiment* has left a mythology imprinted on our culture which is enshrined in the false idea that society is made up of winners and losers. There is a profound psychic turmoil that this myth drives in us, a turmoil that can form entire communities based around the idea that this myth is in fact true. The "incel" or "involuntary celibate" community of disgruntled men who have embraced their fate as losers and refuse any romantic connection entirely is one such example. The incel has internalized the fiction of the sadomasochist myth and punishes themselves in a classic case of bad conscience. But if we declare the incel to be of *ressentiment*, are we not just adding more fuel to the mythical fire that caused them to appear as such? What is needed is a total break from the myth that our society, in all its class domination and inequality, is at all reflective of a winner-loser dichotomy.

The sadomasochistic myth of a society of winners and losers has driven Nietzscheanism ever since Nietzsche died. The myth has had serious political consequences. As Sloterdijk remarks,

> The free spirit brand ran a greater risk of being imitated by a success-hungry movement of losers. Fascisms, past and future, are politically nothing other than insurrections of energy-charged losers, who, for a time of exception, change the rules in order to appear as victors.[50]

The "winner takes all" mantra of capitalism is only accelerated in the Nietzschean community of readers, which, as Sloterdijk notes, can lead to catastrophic and indeed fascist political ends. We are thus left with two toxic brews that come about when a community of *Übermenschen* sees themselves as resentful winners and when the liberal Nietzschean philosopher insists on throwing the hammer of *ressentiment* only to ensure that nothing ever changes in political life.

Lacan, Nietzsche, and the Neo-Feudal Thesis

The famous argument of Francis Fukuyama in *The End of History and the Last Man* offers up a liberal Nietzschean vision of social life. Fukuyama is a philosopher of international relations who was trained by Leo Strauss, which may be why, unlike left-Nietzscheans, he recognizes that Nietzsche's views on democracy and equality are problematic, even to a liberal worldview. What Nietzsche got right, in Fukuyama's view, is the idea that what moves history is a dissatisfaction with liberty and equality itself. Thus, in a Nietzschean revision of Hegel's master-slave dialectic, Fukuyama argues that recognition is not self-sustaining — it relies on pre-modern, non-universal forms of recognition to function properly. Fukuyama's famous essay aimed to understand the roots of economic behavior, which he argues lay in the realm of consciousness and culture and not in the material domain. By this he means to say that economic behavior is driven by the desire for recognition by others, and this drive exists as an autonomous state, prior even to consciousness.

Taking his cue from a reading of Nietzsche's "Last Man," Fukuyama argues that liberal democratic, capitalist social life weakens what he calls the "thymotic" drives, a concept inspired by the Greek idea of *thymos*. But there are two thymotic urges that rival one another in contemporary society: The first is *megalothymia*, which can be explained as an all-out embrace of the society of winners and losers, the drive to accept the status quo and to pursue individual greatness. The other drive that mediates *megalothymia* is *isothymia*, or "the desire to be recognized as the equal of other people."[51] Written at the time of the collapse of the Soviet Union, Fukuyama declared liberal capitalism to have triumphed in its capacity to satiate this deeper thymotic urge.

These two thymotic tendencies are split between a passive isothymotic urge toward equality and a more strength-oriented and thus more active drive of megalothymia. But the problem with this dichotomy is that it limits the very basis of a fuller thymotic expression — the best society can offer — to a vision of liberal meritocratic ends. When liberal meritocratic social promises fall apart — as they did after 2008 — this leads to a ruthless capitalist will to power; and yet Fukuyama argues that the boredom and malaise of the Last Man are the driving engines of left-wing rebellions, especially those of the 1960s and 1970s New Left. The cadres of socialist militants protesting unjust labor conditions, for example, don't rise to a fuller form of thymotic enactment in Fukuyama's vision because their objectives are bound up with the nihilism of demands for equality. But it is ironic that Fukuyama maintained this Nietzschean view of rebellions from below as bottoming out over equality, because more recently he has switched his viewpoint and argued for a renewed form of socialist politics to curb the excesses of neoliberal inequality.[52]

For Fukuyama, by strengthening the recognitive mechanisms of liberal capitalism — the right to property ownership, the battle for prestige on the market, the meritocratic struggle for achievement — these outlets are made to seem adequate domains for the expression of irrational drives to occur in. Fukuyama argues that the megalothymotic drive to irrational mastery over others is best sublimated through the entrepreneurial market. The end of history is thus another name for the persistence of the market and entrepreneurial, liberal capitalism as the most resilient system for the management of man's irrational drives. Instead of a great war to satiate this thymotic urge for mastery, liberal meritocratic capitalism offers up the market for these unruly drives and urges to find satiation and recognition in.

But Fukuyama fails to theorize what happens when such conditions fall into total disenchantment with liberal capitalism as a system itself. Fukuyama may have a vague desire for socialism in the future, but he fails to understand the crisis of capitalism since 2008. To suggest that the cycle of protests that 2008 gave rise to in Occupy Wall Street, the Tea Party, Bernie Sanders, and Jeremy Corbyn were propelled by boredom is nothing less than an insult to those who have fought the system. In fact, the post-2008 social order has shown how the thymotic urge to rebel against the status quo possesses more signs of strength and vitality than the entrepreneurial paths that Fukuyama champions. This is why Fukuyama's theory of the end of history has been met with such contempt; any time capitalism undergoes a profound shockwave from an economic crash, popular rebellions typically follow.

Most people only read Fukuyama's shorter article on "The End of History and the Last Man" and neglect his more elaborate argument in the book with the same title. In the book, Fukuyama reads Hegel's master-slave dialectic through the lens of the great Russian émigré statesman and philosopher Alexandre Kojève. In Kojève's reading of Hegel, it is the "battle for prestige" that determines the dialectic in history. Recognition is not self-sustaining, nor is economic or material well-being the determining basis of struggles for recognition. Fukuyama reveals his allegiance to Nietzsche on this point as he furthermore argues that recognition "relies on pre-modern forms of non-universal forms of recognition to function properly."[53] Although Kojève warns that the end of history is a grim prospect whereby "man no longer changes" because "there is no longer any use in changing the true principles that undergird his existence,"[54] Fukuyama seems to welcome the end of history and the triumph of liberal capitalism as a particular solution to the battle for prestige.[55]

But Fukuyama's premise, that liberal capitalism provides the best social form for the expression of the great thymotic struggles for prestige, totally falls apart in a post-2008 economic scenario. As Will Davies writes of post-2008 capitalism, the social order entered a punitive stage in which the vast majority are governed by austerity at the workplace, diminishing access to healthcare, and debt bondage through student loan and medical debt.[56] Post-2008 capitalism has shut down the prospect of meritocratic entrepreneurialism that Fukuyama champions, and has given rise to the sense that capitalism is both in crisis but experiencing a profound stagnation that resembles a feudal social arrangement.

The neo-feudal thesis is marked by the collapse of social mobility, especially for the working class. The neo-feudal trend is witnessed in the rigidification of class experience that we find in several domains of social life, such as the rise of non-assortative marriages (people no longer tend to marry outside of their class) — if you are born into a class, you tend to stay in that class. This is a trend that intensified dramatically with the rise of neoliberalism in the late 1970s and has only accelerated since. In one 2022 study, only 8 percent of creative-industry professionals in the United Kingdom —artists, writers, filmmakers, and so forth — were from working-class backgrounds.[57] The working class is now subject to an exorbitant rise in premature deaths and drug overdoses.[58] As McKenzie Wark and some of the neo-feudal theorists such as Jodi Dean argue, these dynamics and social trends do not point to a post-capitalist version of capitalism, but rather to the re-emergence of feudal contradictions and modes of domination, forms that have always been part and parcel of capitalist social life.[59] They point to the re-emergence of feudal contradictions and modes of domination, forms that have always been part and parcel of capitalist social life.

Although it is a controversial proposal, it is worth examining the basic idea of the neo-feudal thesis, especially in regard to the changes to capitalism following the 2008 crash. If capitalism's crises produce a return to feudalism, this stands as a convincing argument against capitalism *as such*. Or so the argument goes. But the flip side of the neo-feudal thesis is found in the argument that capitalism must be returned so that it might better live up to its anti-feudal promises of social mobility and individual freedom. Marx understood that crisis is what defines capitalism, and that in such moments of crisis and breakdown there emerge important cultural effects. It is these cultural effects that link the neo-feudal thesis back to Nietzsche and Nietzscheanism. Nietzsche was an open advocate for the crises of capitalism and the decadence they kick up, which offer up a chance to accelerate the brutality and misery that they reveal.

Let's examine the neo-feudal thesis in more detail. Its advocates argue that capitalism, following the 2008 crash, tends to no longer generate profit from the surplus value created by waged workers through the production of commodities. Profit is now primarily coming from giant, quasi-feudal tech oligopolies like Twitter, Facebook, and Google, and from financial instruments that prop up a much wider asset-owning class. Thus, the very strategy of quantitative easing of middle-class and mostly baby-boomer stock portfolios has allowed capitalism to persist without its same edge of market dynamism. This dynamic is combined with the new "platform capitalism" led by Silicon Valley oligarchic companies, whose power and capital exceeds most independent nation-states. These mini-fiefdom companies extract profit and value through monopoly, coercion, and rent.

The neo-feudal order of society can be observed in the changing idea of what it means to "get rich." Many popular TV shows, like *Breaking Bad* and Netflix's *Ozark*, portray families struggling to survive in a rigged economy and having to rely on the black market to stay ahead — the drama of these shows revolves around the characters making millions of dollars... but importantly, no one changes class position. The class dynamics in these popular television shows are better described as *caste struggles* in the neo-feudal era. Class is now more *visibly* fixed, and the ideology of American bootstrap grit and social mobility is more and more acknowledged as a sham.

The prospect that contemporary class struggle is more feudal than it is capitalist will aggravate any reader of Marx's *Capital*, given that both Marx and Engels insist time and again that capitalism constitutes a clean break from feudal dependencies. But many Marxists, such as Arno Mayer in his important work *The Persistence of the Old Regime*, have pointed to the persistence of feudal residues within capitalism. Thus, it is not that the social order has entered a neo-feudal arrangement as such, it is rather that the contradictions of contemporary capitalism reveal the persistence and the re-emergence of feudal relations of domination. How could capitalism improve itself if it has sunk to such a level that even its core tenets and promises, such as social mobility, seem fundamentally strained and ineffective?

What the neo-feudal thesis tells us is that capitalism has already become something worse. Importantly, the neo-feudal thesis arose at the precise moment at which the world underwent fully globalized capitalism. The truth is that capitalism has never shrugged off its feudal and caste residues since the French Revolution, even when it entered a stage of full globalization. The transition from feudalism to capitalism is so decisive for Marx because capitalism opens an entirely new mode of the class struggle; that is, capitalism gives birth to a proletarian class of unpropertied laborers, as well as of those barred from wage labor, who form the nucleus of both the persistence of capitalism and its potential demise. Marx theorized the proletariat both as a class which is vital to the reproduction of capitalism and as having the revolutionary agency to usher the capitalist order into communism.

Although Marx theorized the transition from feudal to capitalist relations in stark and dramatic terms, this does not mean that more regressive feudal social forms did not — and do not continue to — persist in capitalist social life. As Yanis Varoufakis has noted regarding the post-2020 COVID crisis of capitalism:

It is not, of course, that traditional capitalist sectors have disappeared. In the early nineteenth century, many feudal relations remained intact, but capitalist relations had begun to dominate. Today, capitalist relations remain intact, but techno-feudalist relations have begun to overtake them.[60]

The neo-feudal thesis threatens to disrupt our understanding of the very basis of class struggle in the sense that, if it is true, then Marx's proletariat, understood through the labor theory of value, loses its revolutionary power as a great antagonist to capital. If capital no longer requires labor to reproduce value in the way it traditionally did in the industrially dominated capitalism of Marx's time, what happens to proletarian struggle?

Before we address the question of working-class emancipation, we must further examine the persistence of feudal residues within capitalism, this time with the help of Nietzsche. The persistence of a feudal residue in today's hyper-capitalism links us directly to the proposal that Nietzsche gave birth to the society of singularities. At an intuitive level, the very idea of singularity — at least at face value — seems to be a highly capitalist notion; an ideal only realizable in a society where each person can compete to achieve the distinction that comes with self-realization and individualist singularity. But in fact, the idea of singularity is far more elusive than it seems. As the French psychoanalyst Jacques Lacan has argued, singularity is fundamentally bound up with the persistence of an aristocratic idea of social distinction. In what follows, we propose to stage a *rapprochement* between Lacan and Nietzsche on the question of the neo-feudal thesis by looking at how both thinkers offer concepts and insights that explain the logic of the persistence of a feudal structure in the culture of modern capitalism.

In Seminar 17 of his *The Other Side of Psychoanalysis*, which was delivered at the height of one of the most sustained anti-capitalist rebellions in the twentieth century — the May '68 uprising across France — Lacan faced a horde of unruly students. They were eager to understand the meaning of their revolt, and Lacan used the seminar to raise questions of particular concern to the left. Is revolution possible? What are the psychic impediments to achieving revolution in today's age?

Lacan told the students gathered for his seminar that they were plagued by the disappearance of the affect of shame in modern capitalist life, and he drew a comparison to the feudal period as a time in which subjective singularity was more guaranteed and stable. In the terms of Lacan's structuralist theory of psychoanalysis, this means that singularity was situated as a "master signifier" in the feudal era, and that the capitalist era witnesses the steadily increasing instability of this order. Capitalism is defined by the absence of this guarantee, and in the time of the aristocracy it was the affect of shame that ensured that this fixed order appeared as a contingency, as luck. Capitalism makes visible a new crisis of singularity precisely in the sense that its guarantee of singularity is unclear; it is so radically contingent that it foments a hyper-*shamelessness*.

Lacan hits on an insight that Nietzsche aimed to directly enact in his philosophy, the paradoxical notion that a social order of feudal dependencies, where rank order is situated and fixed, is one where luck and contingency are not a source of despair but of joyful affirmation. Although Nietzsche preached to the "philosophers of the future" that they be "full of malice against the lures of dependence,"[61] the achievement of such radical subjective freedom is not possible for the large swath of workers under capitalism. This is a fact that Nietzsche knew full well, which is why he insisted that "my philosophy aims at an ordering of rank: not at an 'individualistic morality.'"[62]

Lacan and Nietzsche help us to see the paradox at the heart of capitalist social relations and that the residue of aristocratic feudal relations of dependency is reproduced by virtue of the class struggle and its embedded layers of inequality. This fact means that for Lacan, capitalism unleashes a "profound shame at being alive," and he argued — with a somewhat reactionary agenda — that whenever there is a protest or a challenge to the social order, this shame is revealed head on. Thus, the May '68 protestors could be psychoanalyzed as desiring their shame to be revealed to them. And Lacan was willing to make it plain that they "desired a master," and moreover, that capitalism will grant them one.[63] What the revolt of May '68 showed to Lacan is that the students' desire was in fact directed toward a wish for the restoration of a master who might put this loosened shame back in its place. This means that even revolutionary desire is bound up with what Jacques-Alain Miller calls the "secret of nobility."[64] Capitalism deprives the subject of a master, and this is a prospect that marks modernity; but at the same time, a specter haunts modern life that calls out for the reinstating of a master to fill in the missing harmony of the otherwise anarchic social order. For all its presumptions of total subjective freedom and liberty, capitalism longs for a return, and it reproduces a return to feudal relations of dependency time and again.

Just a couple of years after this seminar, in 1974, in a widely viewed performance called *Television*, Lacan remarked that as capitalism intensifies, more and more people will insist on segregation. The logic of segregation is reproduced in conditions of full capitalism because capitalism erodes social bonds and, through a logic of "surplus," makes a scandal out of enjoyment itself. Indeed, for Lacan enjoyment becomes a political problem that is particularly acute where the commodity logic determines what is most singular for the subject. Lacan thus saw that in conditions of the society of singularities, where everyone is forced to be their best brand, this leads to a profound subjective emptiness and a reactionary tendency to segregate off into communities where enjoyment can be sheltered from those who might threaten one's own accumulation of enjoyment.

Nietzsche aimed to limit and curtail the possibility of

extending greater leisure time for experiments in subjective freedom and singularity among the working masses. Indeed, he saw that the age of singularities was on the horizon: "We live a prelude or postlude, according to our tastes and talents, and the best we can do in this interregnum is to be as much as possible our own reges and to establish small experimental states. We are experiments: if we want to be!"[65] Under capitalism, there is no guarantee of what Lacan would call the "S1," or the guarantee of social life as guided by a sense of the "luck of the aristocracy."[66]

Capitalism transforms the very stability of the master signifier into units of value that function as a stand-in for a master. The problem is that this stand-in figure does not satisfy, but leaves the subject in a condition of unsatisfied desire.[67] Capitalism never guarantees a master signifier, and instead exposes the reality of this absence, which leads shame to run amok. It is this running amok of shame that links the problem back to *ressentiment*. For what Lacan draws out here is that capitalism foments shame because it provides no stable source of meaning other than a consumptive mode of seeking satisfaction in which attaining commodities leave the subject unsatisfied. In this way, Fukuyama's megalothymotic man, eager to exert himself will inevitably run into deadlocks because capitalism guarantees no assured source for either their recognition or the attainment of satisfaction.

Any pursuit of recognition under capitalism, precisely because it is tethered to the instrumentalized logic of commodity exchange, will likely underwhelm the deeper thymotic drives. Capitalism is a system that produces resentments and a profound shame at being alive, because there is no master signifier — for example, the mentor, teacher, or philosopher — to stabilize our achievements and guarantee recognition of them. In other words, Lacan develops an idea of alienation in his idea of the "discourse of the capitalist" by showing that capitalist social life does not provide more lasting forms of enjoyment to the subject.[68] Writing in the era of Fordist, mass-consumer-capitalist social life, Lacan saw the drive to consume as instrumentalizing our enjoyment and paradoxically destabilizing us subjectively. Capitalism distorts the boundaries of shame and thus fosters resentments and exclusions across groups. In such conditions, Lacan says that the honest person is the one who "enrobes and veils the real of which this shame is the affect."[69] For Lacan, it would be the method of the psychoanalytic cure through analysis that would offer a more prudential treatment of the crisis of shame that capitalism brings about.

Lacan points to the way that as the commodity logic of capitalism envelops more and more of social life, from the intimate spheres of everyday romance to the very source of meaning — the society of singularities — this creates a process akin to Nietzsche's notion of the pathos of distance. To return to the suggestion that Lacan makes in *Television*, that capitalism intensifies relations of segregation, we can see that not only does a longing for the symbolic stability of the aristocracy return, but the tendency of social relations also moves toward a segregationist logic. In the society of singularities, communities are organized around their unique enjoyments, and these enjoyments function to situate the community in relation to other communities.

The return to tradition, from the rise of fundamentalist religious expression to the ubiquitous spread of identity politics, is proof of Lacan's notion that segregation is the order of the day in today's capitalism. Nietzsche's important concept of the pathos of distance strikes a similar tone to Lacan in this regard, with the exception that the pathos of distance was construed by Nietzsche as an explicit aim for the *Übermensch*. Lacan expressed a profound skepticism about the prospect of segregation, and he especially worried over its implications for new forms of racism in the future. Nietzsche aimed to sediment the pathos of distance into a new conception of racialized difference-making.

That capitalism structurally produces logics of segregation would have undoubtedly been welcomed by Nietzsche. Nietzsche's philosophy, in its Janus-faced radicalism, sought to maintain two seemingly contradictory things at the same time: the first is a hardening of the pathos of distance, and the second is segregation. "The superior classes possess a monopoly not merely of property and pleasure but of the higher virtues as well: they embody all the learning, all the taste, all the fortitude, all the intelligence, all the sense of personal honor and all the sense of social obligation."[70]

Secondly, Nietzsche pinpointed how the capitalism of his time was undergoing a profound reshuffling and that nothing was guaranteed at all. This instability of the social order, of course, is a sunk feature of capitalism; this is to say, Marx already identified that crisis is the most constant feature of capitalism. The Nietzschean philosopher must retain one foot in the old order and one foot in the flexible anarchic sea of decadent, bourgeois capitalism as it weathers crisis after crisis. The brutalism that these crises impose on the working class must be furthermore perceived by the strongest among the working class as natural. Socialism stands as the great antagonist to this Janus-faced agenda because, as one of Nietzsche's heroes, Ralph Waldo Emerson wrote, if socialism is achieved, "man would be too feeble to produce genius any longer."[71]

To recapitulate, we have aimed to locate two forms of *ressentiment* polemics: first, the accusation of *ressentiment* leveled at communities, which are said to be wracked by it, and second, the more general *ressentiment* of the one who has played the game and lost out. But what do the so-called losers think of their betters, of the ones who possess the outward traits of a winner? Reckwitz identifies the so-called winners as the middle and upper-middle class who are defined by their values of openness, empathy, cosmopolitanism, and entrepreneurialism.[72] The losers are associated with the values of the underclass, but there are no coherent or consistent values that mark this so-called underclass. The entire framework of a Manichean division of winners and losers is severely flawed and must be rejected *tout court*. The more important question remains how to transcend the fictional framework of the winner-loser idea of society in the first place. Such a transcendence is one that must refuse to even enter the arena of liberal polemics of *ressentiment*, which ultimately divide legitimate from illegitimate resentments.

To address the problem of resentment in politics today, we must cultivate political organizations capable of channeling resentments into opportunities for working-class solidarities. What is missing in liberal polemics of *ressentiment* is a rigorous analysis of how the working class experiences and processes its resentments that is not coded by bourgeois projections onto those resentments. At issue here is the absence of working-class expression and literacy about working-class experience, which is too often suppressed and repressed. These repressions do not lead to working-class *ressentiment*, but they shape a left which is not capable of channeling the rage and the disappointment of working-class life into sublimating outlets that lead to political mobilization.

Political organization must aim to harness a working-class collective perspective on social suffering so that the affects of envy, shame, and jealousy can be sublimated through political practice and organizing. This will also involve making the very idea of resentment into an affect that is not treated as taboo or as a transgression of the norms of the community. Typically, we vent our resentments only in the private domain of our very close friends; after all, how many friendships do you have in which you feel you cannot speak to *all* your resentments? For all his reactionary commitments, Scheler is right that resentment only festers when it is not given an outlet, and without an adequate channel through which the common resentments we experience can find new targets that are not the same culture-war targets of liberal *ressentiment*, working-class discontent risks remaining passive.

CHAPTER EIGHT
After Elective Affinity, or How to Read Like a Parasite

Every time one comes upon some admirer of Nietzsche, it is worth asking himself and trying to find out if his "superman" ideas, opposed to conventional morality, are of genuine Nietzschean origin. In other words, are they the result of a mental elaboration located in the sphere of "high culture" or do they have much more modest origins?

Antonio Gramsci, *Cultural Writings*[1]

Nietzsche emerged as a problem for the left even before his death in 1900. Popular lore about him steadily set in across Europe, and "Nietzsche fever" circled the globe, shaping the politics and culture of intellectual life in countries from Japan to the Americas and beyond. Nietzsche's philosophy was an inescapable presence on the left during the fin de siècle period running up to World War II. While German soldiers were sent into the trenches with a copy of *The New Testament* and *Thus Spoke Zarathustra*, the Great War did not spell the end of Nietzsche's place at the center of political life. As a testament to his staying power, just over a decade later the English philosopher Bertrand Russell remarked that World War II was "Nietzsche's war." Despite his tainted association with Nazism and the history of polemics against Nietzsche on the left, he re-emerged practically unscathed after World

War II. A new academic industry of Nietzschean studies and a new translation and interpretive method, a "hermeneutics of innocence," became enshrined as the new mediators of Nietzschean thought. It seemed that Nietzsche's prophetic claim that his philosophy will only truly be realized "after great socialistic wars" was finally proven right.

But the curious fact is that the rise of this *defanged* Nietzsche after 1945 still produced a certain type of politics, even though the treatment of Nietzsche was apolitical or even anti-political. As we showed in our analysis of Huey Newton, Gilles Deleuze, and other post-war Nietzscheans, Nietzsche was brought into the left based on an elective affinity with leftist and Marxist thought. Elective affinity refers to the chemical mixing of two properties with vastly different compositions, and the post-war hermeneutics of innocence has continuously misportrayed the chemical makeup of the Nietzsche sample. This has led to a mixing of Nietzsche with Marx in an all too perfunctory fashion, and the left's thinking that these two substances — oil and water — might naturally gel together. Nietzsche was given a completely ahistorical treatment as a philosopher, and none of the political core of his thought was truly emphasized. But as we have argued, understanding Nietzsche without an understanding of his core political agenda forces the reader, especially on the left, to miss out on his perspicacious insights into politics. The irony is that Marx is always treated with the weight of history on his shoulders, but Nietzsche is treated as a free-floating, dehistoricized philosopher. And this is part of the reason why French Nietzscheans such as Deleuze and Bataille could so confidently place him in the light of Marxism — only Marx suffered the guilt of history; Nietzsche was a free-floating rebel.

We have aimed to reverse this placement and mixing of the two philosophers. Our plea to the left is that Nietzsche be read *in light of* a new Marxist critique. We must read Nietzsche as an enemy to the left, even though such a reading may very well upend all of the passionate attachments Nietzsche brings out in his readers. Despite the highly seductive and extraordinarily individualist obsessions that he invokes in us, a new Marxist critique of Nietzsche encourages us to abandon our adolescent attachments. Class struggle has returned to the limelight in our time following the 2008 crash. Our times now resemble the pre-1848 period and the period of the Second International, when Nietzsche was read as an enemy to the rationalist, socialist tradition.

The time of the May '68, rebel-counterculture Nietzsche has come and gone. We are in a moment in which full capitalism appears to be returning to its feudal roots, and the class struggle of our time now tells us that we must work through Nietzsche. Not only must we historically situate our understanding of Nietzsche, we must also learn from socialists and Marxists who have seen Nietzsche as a parasite on the left and who have worked through his presence and benefited from the theoretical surplus he offers. This parasitical reading is not a reading of full abolition or cancellation, it is a method of working through, of dialectically retaining and preserving what he offers as we approach him head on, with clear eyes, and without illusions.

The first parasitical critique of Nietzsche from a socialist perspective came as early as 1892, from the German political figure Kurt Eisner. Eisner's *Psychopathia Spiritualis: Friedrich Nietzsche und die Apostel der Zukunft* ("Spiritual Psychopathy: Friedrich Nietzsche and the Apostle of the Future") is a remarkable text, written by someone who had undergone a conversion to Nietzsche's spiritual doctrines but who recognized his Janus-faced philosophy in all its esoteric subtlety and reactionary danger.

Eisner's work treats Nietzsche as a parasite both to socialism and to the wider objective of working-class emancipation. For Eisner, it is only by entering the Nietzschean labyrinth and seeking an exit that the "monster" might be rerouted. Eisner reads Nietzsche as a clear enemy that must be defeated. And he is right. We must situate Nietzsche as an enemy to the left, not as a free-floating apolitical or anti-political philosopher, because doing so both makes one's engagement with Nietzsche truer to his Janus-faced philosophy and strengthens the left, especially the working class. We will call this method of engagement the *parasitical reading* of Nietzsche.

Only after the stakes of Nietzsche's reactionary politics were assessed would Eisner argue for a democratization of Nietzsche's aristocratic principle. The parasitical reading thus led to a reversal of Nietzsche in Eisner, akin to Jack London's hardscrabble attempt to reverse Nietzschean insights for working-class and proletarian liberation. Huey Newton also offers a parasitical reading of Nietzsche, which takes elements of Nietzsche's doctrines of perspectivism and applies them to the task of radicalizing black Americans. In the case of Eisner and London, their attempts to reverse Nietzsche's reactionary agenda came at a time when revolutionizing capitalism required a confrontation with the presence of aristocratic rule within the bourgeoisie. The fall of the Austro-Hungarian empire, World War I, and the Russian Revolution of 1917 were events that tore down the aristocratic elements of bourgeois society. This is why Eisner's reversal of Nietzsche's reactionary philosophy was still intended to preserve aristocratic rank order amid a socialist transfer of power to the working class.

How else might the working class negate the ruling class than by mixing and imbuing itself with an aristocratism from below? But Eisner revealed his naïvety at the same time. He argued that democracy would become a "pan-aristocracy" in which the very meaning of aristocracy would reveal itself as "altruism rather than ruthlessness and selfishness."[2] Eisner argued Nietzsche's thought should be seen as "a transitional stage on the way to socialism," and he was flatly wrong when he declared that "the future is not Nietzsche's!"[3]

It is worth pointing out that Eisner went on to lead a successful socialist revolution that toppled the Bavarian monarchy in 1918. The sociologist Max Weber wrote of Eisner as an example of "charismatic leadership," and he expressed reservations that the "literati" leaders that grew around Eisner would be competent administrators in a new socialist government. As Jan Rehmann has pointed out in his invaluable critique of Weber from a Marxist point of view, although Weber pointed to Eisner as a charismatic leader, the actual ruling bloc that he brought into power after 1918 in Bavaria was far from Weber's preferred form of political management.[4] Weber polemicized against the "utter inability of the radical literati to direct the economy," and he preferred a "bourgeois-socialist administration convened on the basis of equal representation."[5] Eisner's successful toppling of the aristocracy led Weber to prefer a form of government in which the bourgeoisie emerges as the primary organizing bloc."[6]

Despite his naïve optimism that Nietzsche would be overcome through the victory of the socialist bloc in the class struggle, Eisner's contribution to the Marxist and socialist study of Nietzsche is found in the way that he opened up the parasitical method of critique. A parasite must be sweated out once it seizes the body of the host, and Eisner points to a method of working through Nietzsche — of letting him take his course and sweating him out — that influenced subsequent leftist thinkers like the German socialist Franz Mehring and also Leon Trotsky in his first published work, 1900's "On the Philosophy of the Superman." This approach to reading Nietzsche on the left reached its crescendo in György Lukács's *The Destruction of Reason*, which represents a concerted appraisal of Nietzsche following World War II that was so thorough in its analysis of Nietzsche's Janus-faced philosophy that it would contribute to Lukács's effective cancellation by Theodor Adorno and other Frankfurt School philosophers.[7]

It would take the dust of the Cold War to settle and the gradual emergence of fully globalized neoliberal capitalism to set in before any return of the Marxist critique of Nietzsche could take place. Geoff Waite's *Nietzsche's Corps/e* was published in 1996 as a shot in the dark, a courageous effort written at the peak of Derridean deconstruction and the triumph of the hermeneutics of innocence, the hegemonic mode of reading Nietzsche at the time. Derrida's deconstructionist Nietzschean thought made no room for a Marxist critique of Nietzsche. Such critiques, as Stanley Aronowitz noted in his review of *The Destruction of Reason*, were seen as too vulgar by academic post-structuralists and semiologists.[8]

Since Waite's intervention, the Marxist critique of Nietzsche has only grown, from Ishay Landa's reading of Nietzsche and popular culture and Malcolm Bull's *Anti-Nietzsche*, to Jan Rehmann's *Deconstructing Postmodernist Nietzscheanism* and Domenico Losurdo's *Nietzsche, Aristocratic Rebel*, published in 2002. These works provide invaluable context to Nietzsche's political thought, and they open a new direction for the interpretation and application of it. Losurdo has provided the most convincing case that the unity of Nietzsche's thought revolves more around history, genealogy, morality, and a fundamental political radicalism than it does around language, art, and aesthetics, which is the predominant philosophical view on Nietzsche. These works reveal that when we fail to read Nietzsche as a productive enemy of the left, we risk a too easy synthesis — an elective affinity — between Nietzsche and Marx, or between Nietzsche and the left more generally. Nietzsche must be read as an enemy of the left — but an important one who offers us a wealth of insights for understanding social suffering, art, history, and politics.

From a historical materialist perspective, Nietzsche's theoretical surplus has two intersecting layers. Firstly his ideas offer a paradoxical support for elite structures and a celebration of the brutality of the system of capitalism as natural and par for the course. Viewing Nietzsche as a parasite on the left means that we are not content to discard him in some perfunctory way. Why would a thinker who has so fundamentally shaped our culture be discarded? The heart of the new Marxist critique of Nietzsche is a new method of reading his concepts, not a full-stop cancellation. The parasitical approach must proceed with a reading of Nietzsche that is grounded in a historical-materialist perspective on his concepts, which means that they must be traced back to the political context that informed them.

The second layer of the theoretical surplus is found in the way Nietzsche helps us unravel deeply embedded bourgeois forms of life that often seem intractable from a proletarian and working-class perspective. Why are we prone to resentment and envy? And how do resentment and envy present barriers to fuller self-realization? As we aimed to demonstrate in our chapter on *ressentiment*, the Nietzschean application of *ressentiment* preserves liberal political polemics that harden and retrench existing divisions. Indeed, as Sjoerd van Tuinen so aptly notes, the deployment of *ressentiment* effectively changes nothing in the political situation.

The truth is that we benefit from Nietzsche's insights into race when we read them as driven by a reactionary political agenda. How do racism and racialization function in capitalist society? And what is the ideological function of racial capitalism? These are vital questions that the left must process, and Nietzsche's thought opens a way of thinking about race which provides a profoundly negative lesson. Although Nietzsche was a proponent of eugenics, and could even be seen as a spiritual godfather of later eugenicist movements,[9] his thought does not lend itself to the same racial ideas or logics as eugenics. As with most concepts in Nietzsche, it is created for a society to come, and Nietzsche sought to "transversalize" race. More precisely, Nietzsche sought to concoct a vision of society in which racial exclusions and segregations are made immanent to the capitalist division of labor.

As Losurdo demonstrates by unpacking the concept of transversal racialization, Nietzsche believed that if capitalism created conditions in which clear distinctions between winners and losers were enacted, the social order would be healthier. This means that hardwired deep into Nietzschean thought — on the right and the left — is a sadomasochistic vision of the world. Nietzsche must be read from the position of a victor, a thinker whose concepts already possess hegemony; this is to say, Nietzscheanism is one of the most important ideologies that our society needs. It justifies a society of rank order, it naturalizes the brutality of the market, and it generates a method for the ruling class to distance themselves from capitalism with a romantic and mythical justification for the persistence of capitalism.

The Italian left-Nietzschean Gianni Vattimo has pointed to one of the main reasons the hermeneutics of innocence came about. Vattimo observed of Nietzsche's dissociation from politics that

> the shift that Heidegger effected on interpretations of Nietzsche, especially with his ample studies published in 1961, consisted in the proposal to read Nietzsche in relation to Aristotle — that is, as a thinker whose central theme was being, a metaphysical thinker and not simply a moralist, "psychologist," or "critic of culture."[10]

Heidegger's reading of Nietzsche contributed to the defanging of Nietzsche's politics in a way that was arguably more influential than Kaufmann's whitewashing translations.

His reading of Nietzsche brought the thinker into the realm of purely speculative metaphysics and opened the door for subsequent generations of writers, from Derrida to countless American academics, to incorporate Nietzsche into their work on a purely philosophical terrain. Future studies of Nietzsche must open up a deeper engagement with the metaphysical and purely philosophical Nietzsche that takes on the parasitical method of reading him. The parasitical method aims to trace what Waite calls "the properly Nietzschean intent to exert proleptic, esoteric, subliminal effect, traces of his *actio in distans*" on the left.[11] The success or failure of Nietzsche on the left depends on both the left's capacity to detect Nietzschean *trasformismo* (that is, his ability to deploy his opponents to the benefit of his own community-building enterprise) and on the insistence on reading Nietzsche as a parasitical force that must be worked-through.

In contrast to the parasitical reading, the left has tended to opt for an elective-affinity method in reading Nietzsche. In this approach, Nietzsche's politics is taken as a side feature and is considered marginal to his thought overall. When the fact that Nietzsche held reactionary views is acknowledged — and not covered up and sidelined, as we saw in Kaufmann's unethical translations — it is taken to pose no determinative judgment on his project or concepts. Nietzsche's strengths are found in what Adorno called his "ironist" relativism; there is no center to Nietzsche according to the elective-affinity approach. But such an approach is dangerous precisely in the way that Nietzsche's politics enter in through the back door when they are not acknowledged as central to his work.

The elective affinity model has prevailed in post-war French Nietzschean thought, and its influence on the left has been immense. Let us examine Georges Bataille as a case study in elective affinity. Bataille once wrote a strange statement that reads like a Zen *kōan*: "Nietzsche is the only philosopher outside of communism."[12] It is difficult to discern precisely how Bataille figures that Nietzsche is outside of communism. Is the statement to be read as an admission that Nietzsche is the arch-reactionary to communism? Must it be read with the caveat that the left must encounter Nietzsche's reactionary agenda and work through his thought accordingly? Perhaps Bataille recognized Nietzsche's anti-communist and anti-socialist agenda. Unfortunately, none of these assumptions are borne out in Bataille's interpretation.

For Bataille, Nietzsche is a thinker *for* communism because he offers an esoteric doctrine of liberation that communist theory has not adequately captured. No one can read

Nietzsche authentically without "being" Nietzsche, according to Bataille. He writes, "I mean by that, without being, fully and irrevocably, in the same situation in which he [Nietzsche] found himself."[13] Nietzsche thus emerges as a timeless philosopher for us moderns — indeed, he remains the most important contemporary. Bataille writes:

> Communism, in struggling to liberate man, reduces man to the means of his liberation. It never speaks, it seems to it to be premature (or unintelligible) to speak of the man, who, in the instant of his sovereignty, has no sovereign useful value beyond that instant itself (who is in order to be and not in order to be useful, in order to serve, who, in a word, is not a tool, is not a thing, but a sovereign being).[14]

Nietzsche is placed at the center of the communist project as the philosopher who provides a realization of man's excessive singularity, which both capitalism and state socialism have failed to adequately discover. Nietzsche provides a spiritual realization of singularity that Bataille develops in *The Accursed Share*. Ishay Landa performs a very productive critique of Bataille's Nietzschean commitments by linking Bataille's project back to the problem of "romantic anticapitalism." Nietzsche's emphasis on a form of individualism that is only reached beyond the stultifying Last Man of consumer capitalist society is a position that Bataille adopts in his thought. This results in a fundamentally hostile conception of the masses. Landa convincingly argues that

> Bataille ends up projecting capitalism, particularly its specific failings — its irrationality, its wastefulness, its crises — onto nature. Here again capitalism is provided with an indirect

apologetic outlet, inasmuch as attention is diverted from society and history to natural, and hence insurmountable, "deeper" causes which humanity can hardly expect to control.[15]

Bataille opposes the general economy in hyper-accelerationist, Nietzschean terms. Bataille aims for a solar acceleration beyond the general economy of capitalism, and in so doing he warns against any egalitarian raising of living standards. Bataille takes issue with the demand to raise the standard of living across the board. Egalitarian approaches do not pose a "dangerous breaking loose" but "a guarantee against the risk of servitude, not a will to assume those risks without which there is no freedom."[16] In Bataille's left-Nietzschean vision, we are served up a militantly radical politics in which a new spiritualism emerges as the primary objective to communist politics. Although much can be said regarding Bataille's Nietzschean communism, the central point we wish to convey is the way it reproduces a critique of capitalism that remains effectively an indirect apologetics for capitalism.

Class Emancipation and Equality

We have argued that Nietzscheanism functions as a cultural form of power and an ideology of contemporary capitalism, and we recognize that this is a deeply upsetting prospect to any left-Nietzschean. But the argument we have staked out goes further than this, by showing how the *indirect* apologetics of capitalism in Nietzscheanism function within left-Nietzschean thought itself. Such a prospect, that Nietzsche is a compromised figure of thought for the left, that his concepts possess a function for maintaining class power especially, will no doubt sting the left-Nietzschean reader. But the sting of a crestfallen hero should be welcome news to any *true* Nietzschean, given that Nietzsche teaches his readers to *risk* losing him before truly finding him again. In this way, the new Marxist critique of Nietzsche aims to read Nietzsche as a parasitical presence on the left, a figure who opens problems that we otherwise take for granted.

We have focused on Nietzsche's presence *within* the left, not within the right. This is because Nietzsche is only capable of appearing as a symptom on the left, whereas on the right he does not disturb the ideological harmony. The left swims upstream with Nietzsche, the right floats downstream with him. Nietzsche is like a pair of jeans being pulled in opposite directions at the same time, either side pulling with all their might to retain something of value for their ideological community. The effect of this tug of war is that Nietzsche enters politics to *neutralize* political antagonisms born from class antagonism. This is the heart of what we have named Nietzsche's nominalism: the invention of political concepts that are meant to eradicate the egalitarian basis of liberation and to mute proletarian consciousness. Nietzschean concepts shore up a community that is eager to militantly struggle for liberation toward ends that are radically individualist. On offer with Nietzsche is an alluring, flexible, but ultimately parasitical individualism.

Nietzsche's *Übermensch* ethics is open enough to welcome liberal cosmopolitanism in a neoconservative variety (Fukuyama), and it is capable of fitting into militant, anti-colonial, racial emancipatory movements such as the Black Panthers (Newton) as well as liberatory counterculture anarchism (Deleuze). What these variants of Nietzscheanism share is a skepticism toward equality and a refusal of the question of emancipation as centered on class. However Newton and Jack London stand out as exceptions to this tendency in some regard, given that both thinkers acknowledge Nietzsche's aristocratic elitism and look to overturn it toward more radical ends for proletarian liberation. Bataille's wager that Nietzsche teaches the left something that Marx — or any socialist form of emancipation — did not capture revolves around the mythical and the esoteric doctrines that Nietzsche developed. One must enter Nietzsche's laboratory with a historical perspective, and any project that seeks to place Nietzsche as a timeless philosopher must be seriously questioned, especially in matters of politics. Nietzsche returns us to the problem of the individual, and in this return to the subject, we must understand that Nietzsche aimed to eradicate class itself as an element of conflict and antagonism.

For many leftists, the Nietzschean community is alluring as it promises to effectuate a great opposition to the ruling class or the bourgeoisie. It is this hyper-destructive ethics that emerges in the Nietzschean theory of rebellion. But the end point of this drama is the staging of a struggle in vain. Nietzscheanism on the left tends to name a bourgeois type of militancy, a pseudoradicalism which appeals to the entire spectrum of the bourgeoisie, from the ultra-liberal leftist to the far-right fascist. Nietzsche's aristocratic baggage, his anti-egalitarianism, his support for Bonapartist political regimes and for maintaining the perpetuation of slavery even in a modern, cosmopolitan, liberal social order cannot be discarded in any treatment of him.

We have placed Nietzsche's thought in relation to the social being that he analyzed in the concrete political and social situation in which he lived. What has emerged is a thinker who is a perverse educator of the left; a thinker who teaches the left about social suffering in capitalist social life, and who invented a philosophy of masks, deceptions, and lures — a nominalist political thought *par excellence* — in which class suffering is permanently rerouted away from class struggle. Nietzschean concepts aim to pacify the class struggle entirely. It is not an exaggeration to say that Nietzsche remains one of the greatest threats to the possible activation of working-class struggle It is only by working through Nietzsche that a true understanding of his parasitical force on the left can be brought to the fore and a process can begin by which the left *de-Nietzscheanizes* itself. One of the most important places to start in any such effort is to re-interrogate the centrality of the working class in social and political struggle.

The elective affinity between Nietzsche and Marx has resulted in a left that has lost its way in many respects. One of the main symptoms that leftist philosophers working in the tradition of Nietzschean Marxism have shown as a result is that the left has tended, by and large, to abandon the centrality of the working class as the agent of emancipation, a prospect that Ellen Meiksins Wood has detailed in her important polemic *The Retreat from Class: The New True Socialism*, published in 1986, which we will revisit shortly. Inspired by Nietzsche, Marxist philosophers have gone so far as to deny the prospect of any improvement in living standards for the working class (Bataille), or have rejected egalitarianism outright (Tamás), whereas others seek out substitutes for the working class in theorizing the proletariat (Badiou). These are signs of a left that has formed an elective affinity with Nietzsche.

Let us now turn to an analysis of how Nietzsche, once infused with Marx, affects the question of class. How is the prospect of the abolition of class, a goal that Marx and Engels set out in *The Communist Manifesto*, addressed by the left today? There is no better example of the Nietzschean influence on Marxist class theory than the essay "Telling the Truth About Class" by Hungarian philosopher G.M. Tamás. Tamás begins his essay with the claim that the Nietzschean notion of *ressentiment* "alludes to the possible influence of such an incommensurability upon our ability to discover truth."[17]

It is appropriate that Tamás concedes to a Nietzschean perspectivist orientation in his analysis at the very beginning of his essay. The fact that Nietzschean perspectivism, as we demonstrated in Chapter Three, was forged with an explicit critique of the burgeoning movements of the working class in Nietzsche's time is no small irony. Tamás sees in the post-1970s "full capitalism" period, the decline in the labor movement, and the liquidation of the working class a surprising opportunity to reconnect with Marx's original insight into the working class. For Tamás, the precarious situation of the working class today means that we are freed from the illusion that class can or should ever be thought of as a cultural site of hegemony in the wider class struggle.

To ground this pessimistic claim, Tamás says that Marxism has been driven by two fundamental tendencies toward working-class liberation: the first is inaugurated by Rousseau and the other by Marx. In the long history of Marxism, only a Rousseauist conception of class has been experimented with, and the truer Marxist effort of emancipation of the working class has not been attempted. "It may be said that many, perhaps most socialists who have sincerely believed they were Marxists, have in fact been Rousseauists."[18] But the sort of Marxism that Tamás declares Rousseauist is the sort that is completely absent in the neoliberal age. If a Marxism that aims to cultivate working-class culture, that aims to remediate the suffering of the working class through reform parties and revolutionary socialist parties, is Rousseauist and must be abandoned, then we have effectively shut down any possible revitalization of socialism in our time. The apparent culprits behind this supposedly "soft" Marxism are thinkers such as Engels and E.P. Thompson, for whom the objective is not the abolishment of the proletariat but the apotheosis and triumphant survival of the working class. Thompson and Engels err in the way that they move Marxism away from class and toward "the people," thus giving Marxism a populist bent.

For Tamás, Marxism is not based on the proletariat's realizing any great potential or merit but rather on its misery. The proletariat is "limited by the permanent re-evaluation by the market and the transient historicity of everything"[19] What this means is that Engels, E.P. Thompson, and other so-called Rousseauist Marxists mistake the abolition of class for the abolition of caste; that is, they think they are fighting the ruling class in a capitalist society, but the practical effect of advocating for working-class survival and power results in a contestation with the bourgeoisie understood more as a caste than as a class. The irony of this argument stings us even further after we consider that full capitalism (this is to say, neoliberalism) now is regressing to a neo-feudal arrangement. Tamás says that the persistence of the aristocracy was only combated historically by the appearance of a revolutionary workers' movement. Given this historical fact, he draws attention to the question of how such a regression of social life as we currently face, namely the return to neo-feudalism, might ever be combated without a revitalized working-class movement. The downside to the neo-feudal thesis is that it strips away any understanding of class based in conflictual relations to other classes and points to an inert basis of class conflict. But the upside to the neo-feudal thesis can be discovered in the potential politicization that it implies for the working class, who experience the weight of class stagnation and significant decline in their quality of life.

There are two core issues at play here. The first is the question of the cultivation of class literacy and the politicization of a working-class perspective and its connection to the idea of equality. As we explored in our discussion of social suffering in the last chapter, today's working class is depoliticized and has in most cases internalized a conception of liberal equality as the norm; specifically, the working class does not see itself in terms of class oppression or exploitation. A shift toward a radically alternative conception of equality is an urgent requirement of socialist political education in our time. But in Tamás's vision, Marxist socialism retreats from the class struggle when it emphasizes equality, and he argues that Marx's mature theory in *Capital* is opposed to the prospect of any project that would harness or build working-class culture. At issue is the strategy of how class is to be abolished. In Tamás's bleak vision, the strengthening of the working class leads to greater equality but not to the abolition of class as such. We thus find an argument that is somewhat reminiscent of Bataille's refusal of any raising of living standards, but now argued from the perspective of a theory of class abolition that is so total and so abstract that it is impossible to imagine. Tamás's exhortations against Rousseauist Marxism end up bringing his entire analysis into the most rarefied clouds of philosophical abstraction. Although Tamás invokes Ellen Meiksins Wood and *The Retreat from Class* to make his argument, it is hard to see how Wood would ever agree with his framing of the problem.

Writing in the late 1980s, Wood argued that Marxism has regressed to the status of what Marx and Engels named the "true theory of socialism," or a movement that seeks the truth of socialism through philosophical speculation but not in the lived experience and struggles of the working class as they exist. For Marx, "true" socialism is summed up thus: since socialism

> ceased to express the struggle of one class against another... [the "true" socialist] felt conscious of... representing, not true requirements, but the requirements of Truth; not the interests of the proletariat, but the interests of Human Nature, of Man in general, who belongs to no class, has no reality, who exists only in the misty realm of philosophical fantasy.[20]

Tamás advocates a cold and bleak Marxism in which the working class is meant to dissolve itself without building its own resolve or cultural or political strength. Tamás, in a very similar fashion to the value-form of Marxist Michael Heinrich, argues that whenever you begin to stress cultural hegemony and egalitarianism for the working class, you miss the insight of class abolition from a Marxist point of view. The working class should not confront capitalism by any effort that would strengthen its might as a revolutionary force, as to do so would be to wage a feudal struggle against capitalism. Such a struggle would entail the working class having to confront its own humiliation and *ressentiment*, but not its alienation. For Tamás, alienation is so ubiquitous under capitalism that to even attempt to differentiate alienation by way of class would be to revert to a cultural and not an economic assault on capitalism. This hits on the paradox of class as Tamás sees it, namely that the exploited must become a revolutionary agency bent on their own abolition as a class.

It is true that bourgeois equality is taken to be equality before the law, when in reality this equality is a partial form of equality materially rooted in perpetuating the interests of the capitalist class in tandem with the state; this is to say, equality in capitalism is based on relations of exploitation that are taken to be natural and justified before the law. This raises a crucial question for proletarian action and praxis: How can an alternative conception of equality to bourgeois equality be cultivated in the consciousness of the proletariat? Such a cultivation is not only a precondition for any proletarian action, but also a desire that must be furthered among the working class. Lenin referred to it as consciousness of full equality that might exist beyond the law after a revolutionary moment:

> [Equality is] man's consciousness of himself in the element of practice, i.e., therefore, man's consciousness of other men as his equals and man's relation to other men as his equals. Equality is the French expression for the unity of human essence, for man's consciousness of his species and his attitude toward his species, for the practical identity of man with man, i.e., for the social or human relation of man to man.[21]

Viewed in the context of an elective-affinity reading of Nietzsche, the very concept of class abolition lacks any concern with the question of equality whatsoever. But Marxism requires that the proletariat develop a consciousness of what equality will consist of in a society that is post-revolutionary. The maxim that is to guide the communist society — "From each according to their ability, to each according to their need" — requires the cultivation of new ideas of full equality that are distinct from bourgeois ideas of equality. The project of the abolition of class, therefore, must entail a re-interrogation and a re-invention of equality to come.

In our age of neoliberal capitalism, the ruling ideology has already trained us to despise equality, and thus any political Marxism today must place a major onus on redefining and insisting on a commitment to it as an idea. The significance of the proletariat's struggle for equality, and especially of equality to come, will be made evident if we correctly interpret equality as referring to the abolition of classes and the dictatorship of the proletariat that is necessary to achieve it. As Lenin once remarked,

> As soon as equality is achieved for all members of society in relation to ownership of the means of production, that is, equality of labor and wages, humanity will inevitably be confronted with the question of advancing further from formal equality to actual equality.[22]

Tamás's Nietzschean Marxism is revealed in his distrust of the masses as a revolutionary agency. He refers to the masses despairingly as "the people" — a populism — and he argues that any conception of the people only leads down a Rousseauist-Marxist trap that reproduces a conception of a feudal revolt against capitalism. Tamás interprets Marx's emphasis on the abolition of class as if the class struggle today possessed a revolutionary impetus or drive, when the truth is that it does not.

In Marx's time, communists were defined by their steadfast commitments to revolution. As Balibar notes, "The few non-revolutionary communist bourgeois who made their appearance since the time of Babeuf were a rare occurrence;

the vast majority of the communists in all countries are revolutionary."[23] But as we examined in the previous chapter, we are far from the level of intensified revolutionary class consciousness among the working class as Marx experienced in his time. This fact suggests that a working-class praxis must be cultivated, and that the process of building the cultural resolve of working-class counterpower remains at the center of Marxist practice.

But Tamás claims that we can circumvent the task of building working-class culture, that we can somehow magically move from alienation to class abolition by getting around the thorny problem of resentment. He argues that working-class culture-building only leads to *ressentiment*, but this only perpetuates the continued depoliticization of the working class by preventing the problem of social suffering truly coming to the surface. The proletarian working class is not distinguished by its suffering, but it must discover the means to collectively express and to vent the suffering born from exploitation, otherwise collective solidarity will be impossible. What we aimed to demonstrate in our discussion of resentment and social suffering is that embracing Nietzsche's concept of *ressentiment* only continues to further mute the experience of the working class and thus further pacifies its agency.

We have argued that Nietzsche's concepts have political effects when they are deployed: *ressentiment* freezes liberal polemics that effectively prevent working-class solidarity as they rigidify irrational conceptions of friend/enemy and insider/outsider divisions. Nietzsche's concept of *ressentiment* prevents us from getting to the real core of political antagonisms as it shuts down forms of suffering as incommunicable, and this specifically disguises types of suffering born from capitalist exploitation. Against the predominant reading of

Nietzschean *ressentiment*, we have shown that it furthers liberal political polemics that work to intensify existing bourgeois and liberal moralisms by nominally relegating enemies as non-communicative.

The class struggle needs a healthy dose of Rousseauist and Jacobin equality in order to fight the persistence of the feudal residues in capitalism. Such a struggle requires that Nietzsche be pinpointed as a deleterious presence in the class struggle, a presence that paradoxically regresses its adherents and followers to an all-out embrace of the status quo in the name of an acceleration beyond its limits. The class struggle is still playing out under the shadow of the unmet demands of the Jacobins. We must face the revolutionary prospect that Marx opens in his *Theses on Feuerbach* — "Philosophers have only interpreted the world, the point is to change it."[24] Nietzscheanism may very well represent the most comprehensive effort in philosophy to push back on "Thesis XI." Lenin once remarked that revolutionary activity is such that "the changing of oneself coincides with the changing of conditions (of existence)."[25] This proposition stands as the true threat to any elective affinity between Nietzsche and Marx.

How to Read Like a Parasite

The soul that has the longest ladder and reaches down deepest — how should the most parasites not sit on that?

Nietzsche, *Thus Spoke Zarathustra*[26]

In the final section of Nietzsche's *Thus Spoke Zarathustra*, we learn that the men who accompany Zarathustra into his cave are merely precursors to the higher men, they are not the higher men themselves. They are frauds. These supposed higher men had "become like little children" to Zarathustra after they had refused to renounce their piety, having prayed to the ass.[27] After he is let down by the higher men, Zarathustra gathers them together for a final test and leads them to wander in the dark eternity of midnight. In this moment of sublime darkness, he asks who among them will be "master of the world?" The men all retire for a night's sleep in Zarathustra's cave. When the morning comes, Zarathustra rises while the higher men all sleep. As he soaks in the morning sun, the slow and steady roar of a lion can be heard in the distance. Upon hearing this, the higher men flee the cave and disappear in an instant. Zarathustra calls forth for his "fellow-sufferers," but to no avail, the men are nowhere to be found. The soothsayer's warning had come true, and Zarathustra is left alone to face the noontide.

It is striking that Nietzsche ends *Zarathustra* with a section entitled "The Sign." The sign, we learn, is the lion's roar that reveals the higher men as frauds. It was already predicted by the soothsayer that this would happen, that the higher men would not live out their calling. The Nietzschean community ends in failure and fraudulence, that is, Zarathustra still waits for his *true* higher men to come; all of this was predicted. The effect this has on the reader is obvious: it goes to fortify the community-building appeal that Nietzsche is after. Who will seek to rival the higher men?

The message is clear: you, the reader, must aim higher than the *supposed* higher men. This ending reveals an important strategy of Nietzsche's community-building praxis; namely, it leaves the reader with a constant question about the very status of the supposed higher men. Are they frauds and losers after all? Are we frauds and losers? It doesn't matter if the higher men think they are higher men or not, what matters is whether they *have* read Nietzsche. The ending of *Zarathustra* poses a question back to us, as readers: Will we flee in cowardice when the sign comes, or will we face it with Zarathustra? The sign is esoterically made into a question that is buried in the very notion of how to be a member of the Nietzschean community. Let us further imagine that we are left-Nietzscheans and understand the sign as the preparation for the revolution.

We ask ourselves, at this late hour, after all we've unearthed regarding the function and the design of the Nietzschean arsenal of concepts, how do we work with Nietzsche? We have sought to offer a self-defense manual for any reader, a glimpse into the darker side of his thought so that we can know where it appears and how it is reproduced in Nietzscheanism. But there is more work to do. The host can be parasitized, but he should never be canceled.

Nietzsche spoke of the parasite throughout his writings, and he said that the greatest among us are host to many parasites: "Where the strong are weak, and the noble all too mild — there it builds its disgusting nest: the parasite lives where the great have small wounded recesses."[28] As the Nietzsche scholar Matthew Dill points out, a parasite "takes power away from one's environment," and "with parasitic pursuits of power, we attain an increase in our feeling of power at the expense of (the power of) one or more hosts."[29] The metaphor of the parasite is so central to Nietzsche that he analyzes society and the individual according to how many parasites it can endure.

Nietzsche warned against bad parasites, or what he called the "anti-artist" parasite who, like Spinoza or the figure of the priest, suffers from a lack of a feeling of power. The better sort of parasite is the one who has overcome *ressentiment* and who enters into a "suffering from superabundance itself."[30] It is this second, superabundant form of suffering that is so central to Nietzsche's entire community-building strategy because it gets us closest to a form of becoming which has successfully overcome resistances. There are two kinds of sufferers: first, those who suffer from the over-fullness of life, they want a Dionysian art and likewise a tragic view of life, a tragic insight; and then those who suffer from the impoverishment of life and seek rest, stillness, calm seas, redemption from themselves through art and knowledge, or intoxication, convulsions, anesthesia, and madness.

There are two ways of relating to the will to power, according to Dill. The first is the "instrumentalist thesis" of the will to power, which is bent on the bad form of parasitism, that only seeks an increase in the feeling of power; the second is the "structural thesis," which refers to the power that emerges after we have encountered and overcome resistances.[31] This latter form of power is one that has harnessed not merely power but force (*Kraft*). If "all *ressentiment*s [are] absent where there is a great abundance of force," the *Übermensch* now suffers from the "overfullness of life."[32] The parasite who has not overcome their resistances suffers from a lack of the feeling of power and thus deals with what Dill calls an "overflow of power," not a "superabundance of power."[33] This distinction is crucial for understanding the way Nietzsche wants us to parasitize him, to overcome him: "*Now I bid you lose me and find yourselves; and only when you have all denied me will I return to you.*"[34]

Even when the higher men have gained a superabundance of force, they still let the master down, they still refuse the sign out of fear. The implicit message is that even among the fellow sufferers of the higher level, there is never proper uniformity or obedience, and everyone flees out of fear. If the will to power manifests itself in all human action, and if some human actions are higher manifestations of the will to power and others are lower, Nietzsche offers a means by which to analyze human action as the encountering and overcoming of resistance, supplemented with a ranking system of these actions based on the amount of resistance each action encounters and overcomes.[35]

But a problem arises that Nietzsche's understanding of the means to overcome resistance requires conformity with the existing social order. This is the point at which the doctrine of the eternal return meets the will to power and forces us to confront — as parasites — whether we have truly overcome Nietzsche's community. What sort of revolutionary change to the social order does Nietzsche's community permit? The problem of conformity is implicit in Nietzsche, which is why Sloterdijk has pointed out that Nietzsche must be supplemented with Emerson. In Sloterdijk's view, Emerson's message of self-reliance is a more powerful means of individual liberation than Nietzsche's, and while both thinkers preach a form of self-becoming in distinction to the ambivalent (or weak and power-deprived) masses, Emerson teaches the reader to embrace non-conformity, whereas Nietzsche maintains a notion of community based on *imitation*.

Nietzsche's liberation doctrines are meant to facilitate and safeguard rare geniuses and higher men, as are Emerson's, but Nietzsche's free spirits are driven by a sadomasochist higher man. A psychoanalytic reading of *Zarathustra*'s conclusion would construe the position of Zarathustra as that of the uncastratable father; an unsurpassable barrier stands as the pre-condition to the development of Nietzschean becoming. To embrace an uncastrated father and accept him as the guarantor of the social order is to embrace a sadomasochist conception of social life, to insist that the world is divided immanently on a plane of forces where some ascend and others descend. In this perverted world, the free spirits cultivate their masks, and Nietzsche recognizes that the cultivation of the mask functions differently according to one's class origin. The idea of the mask is meant to enact a distance from the "weaker ones," or those who do not see the mask as a disguise.[36] As he writes in *The Wanderer and His Shadow*, those of humbler origin, "who at bottom always envy culture and see no mask in the mask" are made excited by envy of the mask.[37] The problem brings us back to Nietzsche's immanent commentary on the class character of the intellectual in his community-building project, a prospect that Gramsci was deeply concerned with in Nietzsche, namely, Nietzscheanism has the propensity to cultivate a political community that aims to maintain elite hierarchies of the social order. The parasites, on Nietzsche's own terms, are thus encouraged to conform to the existing order, not to fundamentally alter it.

The motif of the mask is thus far from a non-conformist aesthetic, especially when we historically situate what Nietzsche thought about the forces of socialism and egalitarian movements. These movements of the left were a problem, as they forced the mask to come out into the open, they forced people to think about their personal motivations and to focus on their own sensual pleasures. Nietzsche saw movements of the left as bent on self-preservation, and "the wish to preserve oneself is a symptom of a condition of distress, of a limitation of the really fundamental instinct of life which aims at the expansion of power, and in so doing frequently risks and even sacrifices self-preservation."[38]

What is a parasite to do? The parasite rejects the model of elective affinity, it rejects the ranking obsession of

Nietzsche, it rejects any insistence on the eradication or the pacification of all that is supposedly weak and lower. We know these distinctions are derived from the standpoint of the private bourgeois citizen; they know nothing of the lived experience of other positions, nor do they care to. At best, the Nietzschean philosophy can offer the working class and the proletariat, or those discarded from the private bourgeois position, the chance to enter the community-building cave and prove themselves.

Marx once borrowed the motif of "old mole" from Shakespeare's *Hamlet*, where it refers to the dead father who cannot be surpassed. In *The Eighteenth Brumaire of Louis Bonaparte*, Marx refers to the proletariat as in a state of "purgatory," buried under the ground like a mole. After the rise of Bonaparte III, a figure that Nietzsche championed for his retrenchment of rank order, Marx argued that Bonaparte made the law of the ruling class into the general will of all society. While Marx's "old mole" is an active agent for the abolition of bourgeois society, the destruction of bourgeois society cannot be led by an elite cadre of intellectual higher men alone. Rather, the working class must be organized independent of bourgeois politics, and its liberatory power must come from below. When we make an elective affinity out of Nietzsche and Marx, the reality of the independent organization of the working class and the central importance Marx placed on it will most often get thrown out the window.

There are times when Nietzsche appears to the left as an inescapable figure, and at no point was this truer than in Russia leading up to and following the Bolshevik Revolution. As the historian Isaac Deutscher once put it, the Bolshevik Revolution aimed, "from the depths of its misery" to "embrace the idea of a republic of philosophers, not its Platonic version in which an oligarchy of pundits rule, but a republic wealthy enough to make every citizen a philosopher and a worker."[39] The signs are everywhere today, Nietzsche has again returned as an inescapable figure. How will we exit Zarathustra's cave on the morning that the sign appears? The signs appear everywhere in the wake of the great crash of 2008, and they have led us to read Nietzsche in a completely new light. Class relations have once again receded into a quasi-feudal social order. It just so happens that Nietzsche himself lived in similarly turbulent times as ours, when socialism was rising and falling in popularity among the masses, and we saw how he calibrated his political thought accordingly.

Our proposal is as follows: If Nietzsche is again inescapable, we do not aim for his cancelation, as that would only strengthen his cause. Our aim is to enter the community as fugitives, unwelcome, at a lower rank that we are, with the intention to completely work through him. As parasites, this is our mantra: *Not out but through*. There is a double parasitical exchange at work here: we ingest the parasite Nietzsche just as he ingests us as we work through and sweat him out. We aim to burrow into Nietzsche as parasites and use his insights against him. That's the only way we can escape. When he tells us that "the production of great individual specimens" requires "enormous work and restlessness of the human being. It requires overcoming even more than it does insight,"[40] we have to take him at his word.

What do we know? While Nietzsche placed great importance on forgetting, we seek to remember, we aim to bring what we know to the tribe, to the cave. We know that, in reflecting on the movements of socialism and democracy that were empowering the working class in his time, Nietzsche preferred to foster the social conditions of austerity and brutalism.

These conditions were conducive to the cultivation of genius and the preservation of elite, bourgeois, artistic intellectuals subtracted from wage labor. This led to the formulation of a highly sophisticated "romantic anti-capitalism," which treated the violent whims of capitalist private property and class struggle as natural aspects of human social life.

In a private notebook entry from 1875, Nietzsche invokes Schopenhauer as an exemplary genius who was only possible in the long sweep of history due to long "moments of sublime isolation." But, he adds, these moments of isolation (we remember how central *otium* is to Nietzsche's entire political thought) have become inaccessible to everyday life and to everyday minds. He continues:

> It should be a universal law: every person has the right to speak about his inner experiences if and only if he is able to find his own words with which to describe them. It goes against all propriety, and in principle even against all honesty, to treat the language of great minds as though it were not someone's property and were simply found lying around on the street somewhere.[41]

The call to the Nietzschean community is premised on reproducing an elect of rare geniuses who formulate their genius based on the extension of the private bourgeois subject. It is this subject that we parasitize and seek to overcome, knowing full well that their leisure time has been denied to us. We fight Nietzsche like fugitives. We are ready to run away at a moment's notice, but we are not afraid of the lion's roar. We run because we have experience of being gaslighted, not by him, but by the conditions we have faced in the world.

We are moles before we are parasites. We refuse the

sadomasochistic idea that humanity could ever be construed as ascending and descending. We reject Nietzsche's very idea of rank order for we know the point from where it emerges; namely, the private bourgeois citizen. We know full well that this subject wants to exist and reign supreme for the next two thousand years. We choose to parasitize Nietzsche because we know we have much to learn from him, we know his views on *otium* reveal a truth about the importance of leisure. But this truth must be steered in a fundamentally different direction than he wishes. *Otium* must be radically democratized and turned into a socialist demand. Where Nietzsche aims only to maintain a system in which the masses are content in austerity and suffer at a lower level than the rare geniuses exempt from wage labor, we aim to radically open up *otium*. Any vision of political life that is concerned with collective freedom must center *otium*, especially in our age, which has lost touch with its own desire for *otium* and leisure.

We do not approach Nietzsche with a shallow enmity. Our enmity is cultivated by an eye toward the preservation of humanity, with an eye toward the laboring masses who, in all their suffering, long for freedom. The socialist intellectuals that agitate for working-class consciousness, the ones that Nietzsche deems resentful spiders and moral tarantulas,[42] these are our comrades. Any critique Nietzsche may offer of the utopian socialists or the liberal utilitarian socialists only heightens the obscurity of the Marxist position, and once we deploy Nietzsche to critique liberal socialists, we submit to an uncritical elective affinity with Nietzsche.

We have different enemies than Nietzsche. This is one of the unfortunate outcomes of the model of elective affinity between Marx and Nietzsche: it had us thinking that Nietzsche and Marx somehow shared the same critique of

Dühring's anti-Semitic thought or even of utopian socialism. These are superficial lines of commonality between the two thinkers. When we push Nietzsche's political thought in line with Marx's, as we have done in terms of religion and revolution, we find radical divergence. We see two paths diverge over the most important questions: Can revolution for equality succeed in emancipating or even in enacting a cathartic moment for the working class? Is there anything salvageable within Christianity? For Nietzsche, Christianity's capacity to enforce rank order and caste rule are what must be preserved, whereas for Marx it is the unrealizable appeal to egalitarian universalism that bourgeois society cannot fully achieve. When it comes to Christianity, Nietzsche's accelerationism stands in strong contrast to Marx's dialectical approach. As it pertains to the prospect of a revolution in the name of increasing equality, this idea only spells disaster and the compounding of *ressentiment* for Nietzsche. Whereas for Marx, revolutions from below are not driven by intractable forces of envy and resentment that pervert their fundamental coherence.

With all that said, we should never be ashamed to learn from Nietzsche. Nietzsche's enmity toward egalitarian and socialistic thought informs our own enmity toward his agenda. We heed Jung's advice in approaching Nietzsche: we proceed with caution. We reject any vision of society in which the suffering of the masses under capitalism takes place at a level that is qualitatively at a distance (the pathos of distance) from any so-called higher men. It helps that we know the so-called higher men tend to see themselves as losers and frauds at the door of an uncastratable father. We are not opposed to great and exceptional geniuses; we are opposed to a society — such as the one we currently live in — that defines rare and exceptional geniuses based on the suppression of the collective welfare of the international working class. We refuse any solution to the production of genius that is conditioned by Nietzsche's pathos of distance, a philosophy that insists that the masses remain in squalor and misery.

After Elective Affinity

Zarathustra ends with an unfinished appeal to the continual re-initiation of the reader into the Nietzschean community. This unfinished basis is also reflective of Nietzsche's wider method, what the French philosopher Paul Ricœur famously called the "hermeneutics of suspicion." Marx never completed *Capital*, and thus we lack a manual for communist society, just as we lack a clear elaboration of the class dynamics that might assist us in organizing the proletarian revolution. The Nietzschean community is also left unfinished and unfulfilled. But as such, it is left open to reproduce over and over.

Ricœur says that Nietzsche along with Freud and Marx constructed the three great hermeneutics of suspicion, by which he means that each thinker "tears off masks" and "reduces disguises." This is a method which tends to look upon the whole of consciousness primarily as "false" consciousness, and each thinker offers a cipher for interpreting the modern condition.[43] Nietzsche's will to power, Marx's theory of social being, and Freud's unconscious are the "cipher" concepts Ricœur identifies as most central. Each thinker thus deciphers the hidden depths of modern life. The selection of the will to power as Nietzsche's most central concept is a curious choice given that many scholars have pointed out that it is incomplete.[44] For Ricœur, Nietzsche looks to value and identifies the key to lying and masks as being on the side of the "force" and "weakness" of the will to power. He argues that *The Genealogy of Morals*, Marx's concept of ideology, and Freud's theory of ideals and illusions "represent three convergent procedures of demystification."[45]

As the queer theorist Eve Sedgwick has argued, the hermeneutics of suspicion has become nearly inescapable in contemporary critical thought, philosophy, comparative literature, and critical theory — indeed, it has become a "mandatory injunction rather than a possibility among other possibilities."[46] What the hermeneutics of suspicion boils down to, in Sedgwick's eyes, is a method of "paranoid reading," a method of interpretation that puts its faith in exposure and demystification.[47] The method is meant to bring to the surface a logic of the world, to *expose* the hidden function of dissatisfied desire and the workings of the unconscious as with Freud, or to reveal the hidden abode of production that resides in the wage labor relation, which is the source of capitalist value in capitalism.

The question that we want to drive home is not whether Nietzsche's thought offers up a hermeneutic of suspicion — it does. The question we wish to ask is: What sort of paranoia does Nietzsche's critique run on? It is here that we benefit from reading Nietzsche's suspicion as driven, fundamentally, by the long arc of revolutionary history. Nietzsche is paranoid over the very prospect of the revolutionary tradition, especially its egalitarian and working-class emancipatory direction. This suspicion is qualitatively different to that of Freud and Marx, who were both committed to a rationalist orientation and to the most radical ends of the Enlightenment tradition. While Nietzsche's relationship to the Enlightenment is complex and indeed a feature of his middle period, his reactionary political agenda is not separable from his concepts and is not immune to any Enlightenment commitments he may have had.

We have sought to show how *ressentiment* is a highly problematic concept because its function is to ontologize a condition as applying inherently to an individual or group in a way that effectively bars them from transformation. This makes it a concept that does not forge class solidarities, and which maintains orders of existing rank. We have sought to show how Nietzsche's concepts possess a surplus dynamic and function when they are deployed which aims to enact his wider social and political vision. This vision is highly sophisticated and inseparable from his concepts.

Sedgwick has presented an influential critique of the hermeneutics of suspicion by asking what the method of exposure has achieved in a society where, more and more, the "evidence of systemic oppression" no longer requires exposing in order to be known.[48] Our assumption that one must be paranoid in order to unearth the truth about one's enemy may not necessarily aid us in getting rid of our enemies. Moreover, Sedgwick says, just because you have enemies doesn't mean you have to be paranoid. And this is a valid point: the brutality of our system is now completely out in the open. It is no small irony that Nietzsche's political thought also envisioned a social order such as the one that Sedgwick describes. As we saw in our discussion of Nietzsche's support for suppressing egalitarianism and socialism, he championed a society in which brutality is elevated to a natural principle.

Sedgwick has offered an alternative to the paranoid method of the hermeneutics of suspicion in what she names the reparative mode of reading. To read from a reparative position is to surrender the knowing, anxious, paranoid determination that no horror, however apparently unthinkable, shall ever come to the reader as new; to a reparatively positioned reader, it can seem realistic and necessary to experience surprise. Because there can be terrible surprises, however, there can also be good ones.[49] Turning to the psychoanalyst Melanie Klein, Sedgwick says the paranoid position is anxious, raging against part-objects, while the depressive position seeks to "'repair' the murderous part-objects into something like a whole — *though I would emphasize not necessarily like any preexisting whole.*"[50]

A path for further study into Nietzsche can be driven by the question of how a more reparative analysis and method might assess the function of Nietzschean concepts, both his and those of his followers and acolytes. However, any reparative reading of Nietzsche would also have to maintain a healthy dose of paranoia in order to continually keep his esoteric and aristocratic agenda at the top of one's assessment and analysis.

Our critique has focused on the undeniable *political* function of Nietzsche's concepts at a time when his influence has become embedded in the left. In the early 1960s, Lukács looked back on the rise of the Nazis in Germany, and he saw the Marxist intellectuals, many of whom were his close friends — Ernst Bloch, Theodor Adorno, Walter Benjamin — embrace what he called "right-wing epistemology and left-wing ethics."[51] Left-wing ethics maintains a utopian and even revolutionary commitment, while right-wing epistemology views social reality and matters of truth from an aristocratic position. A left-wing ethics was used to mobilize socialist forces against fascist reaction, and Nietzsche's was, unsurprisingly, the right-wing epistemology through which the left sought to combat fascism. We have not focused on Nietzsche within the right, as ample studies have done so already; we have aimed for a clearer understanding of Nietzsche within the left so that we don't continue to repeat the same mistake. Parasitizing Nietzsche is not the same thing as deploying him for the left. It is only by working through Nietzsche in his full political depth and sadistic brilliance that we can understand his thought and begin to learn from him.

References

1   Nietzsche, Friedrich *Unpublished Fragments from the period of Unfashionable Observations*, translated by Richard T. Gray. Stanford University Press, 2009. p. 277.

2   Bataille, Georges "Nietzsche in the Light of Marxism" from *Nietzsche's Return*, Vol. I, Semiotexte, 1977. p. 116.

3   Bloom, Allan "Leftist Nietzscheanism or Vice Versa." from *The Closing of the American Mind*, Simon and Schuster, 1989. p. 224.

4   Nietzsche, Friedrich *Thus Spoke Zarathustra, A Book for All and None*, translated by Adrian Del Caro, Cambridge University Press, 2006. p. 34.

5   Ibid, p. 59

CHAPTER ONE
We Live in Nietzsche's World. So What?

1   Isaacson, Walter *Steve Jobs*, Simon & Schuster, 2011.

2   Nietzsche, Friedrich *Human, All Too Human: A Book for Free Spirits* translated by R.J. Hollingdale, Cambridge University Press, 1996. pp. 168 – 169

3   Draper, Hal *Karl Marx's Theory of Revolution: State and Bureaucracy*, Vol I, Monthly Review Press, New York, NY. 1977. pp. 257 – 259

4   Nietzsche, Friedrich *Thus Spoke Zarathustra: A Book for All and None*, translated by Adrian de Caro, Cambridge University Press, 2006. p. 59

5   Nietzsche, Friedrich *Beyond Good and Evil*, Random House, 1996. p. 6.

6   Kagg, John *Hiking with Nietzsche: On Becoming Who You Are*, Farrar, Straus and Giroux, 2018.

7   Sloterdijk, Peter *Nietzsche, Apostle*, Semiotexte, 2005. p. 9.

8   Ibid, p. 78.

9   Nietzsche, Friedrich *Ecce Homo*, translated by Anthony M. Ludovici and Paul Cohn, Create Space Independent Publishing Platform, 2018. p. 33

10 H.Con.Res.9 – "Denouncing the horrors of socialism." 118th United States Congress (2023–2024), available online from: https://www.congress.gov/bill/118th-congress/house-concurrent-resolution/9

11 Lukács, Georg "The Destruction of Humanism in German Ideology" translated by Anton P. Available online from: https://www.marxists.org/archive/lukacs/works/nietzsche/ch03.htm. First published as *Die Zerstörung des Humanismus in der deutschen Ideologie*, in: *Wie ist Deutschland zum Zentrum der reaktionären Ideologie geworden?* Veröffentlichungen des Lukács-Archivs, 1982. pp. 299–311

12 In 2022, only 27 percent of Americans surveyed by the Gallup polling group expressed trust in institutions. See Jones, Jeffery "Confidence in U.S. Institutions Down; Average at New Low," Gallup Organization, July 5, 2022, available online from: https://news.gallup.com/poll/394283/confidence-institutions-down-average-new-low.aspx.

13 Landa, Ishay *The Overman in the Marketplace: Nietzschean Heroism in Popular Culture*, Lexington Books, 2009. p. 6.

14 Ibid, p. 2.

15 Ibid, p. 5.

16 Jung, Carl *Nietzsche's Zarathustra: Notes on the Seminar Given in 1934–1939*, edited and translated by James L. Jarrett. Princeton University Press, 1988. p. 475.

17 Nietzsche, Friedrich *Unpublished Fragments Spring 1885–1886,* translated by Adrian Del Caro, Stanford University Press, 2020. p. 14

18 Brennan, Timothy *Borrowed Light: Vico, Hegel and the Colonies.* Stanford University Press, 2014. p. 146.

19 Losurdo, Domenico *Nietzsche, Aristocratic Rebel: Intellectual Biography and Critical Balance Sheet,* Historical Materialism, 2020. p. 449.

20 Adorno, Theodor "Reconciliation Under Duress" from *Aesthetics and Politics,* Verso, 2007. p. 160.

21 Nietzsche, Friedrich *Thus Spoke Zarathustra,* translated by Thomas Common, Logos Publishing, 2017. pp. 475–476.

22 Jung, Karl *Nietzsche's Zarathustra,* Vol. II, edited and translated by James L Jarrett, Princeton University Press, 1988. pp. 909–910.

23 See Kurt Rudolf Fischer's comments in the discussion of Robert E. McGinn's "Verwandlungen von Nietzsches Ubermenschen in der Literatur des Mittelmeerraumes: d'Annunzio, Marinetti, und Kazantzakis," Nietzsche-Studien 10/11 1981–1982. p. 611.

24 Eisner, Kurt *Psychopathia spiritualis. Friedrich Nietzsche und die Apostel der Zukunft.* Verlag von Wilhelm Friedrich, 1892. p. iv.

25 Dickler, Jessica "Share of Americans living paycheck to paycheck rises to 63%," CNBC News, December 15, 2022, available online from: https://www.cnbc.com/2022/12/15/amid-high-inflation-63percent-of-americans-are-living-paycheck-to-paycheck.html

26 There are several studies that have examined Nietzsche and the far right, including *Dangerous Minds: Nietzsche, Heidegger, and the Return of the Far Right* by Ronald Beiner, as well as *Nietzsche and the Nazis* by Steven R.C. Hicks. Another important study, *The Birth of Fascist Ideology* by Zeev Sternhell, places Nietzsche's vitalist irrationalism at the very center of the rise of Italian fascism. And a work which we discuss frequently in this book, *The Destruction of Reason* by György Lukács, also makes the case that Nietzsche had a direct influence on the far right and German fascism.

27 Nietzsche, Friedrich *Thus Spoke Zarathustra*. p. 28.

28 Although we touch on the politics of translation in Nietzsche in this book, the agenda of translators such as Walter Kaufmann are very important to historically situate as a trend that emerged after the Second World War across Anglo-American academic departments. Kaufmann stands out as a highly important translator and arguably the most emblematic of an effort to de-emphasize Nietzsche's more reactionary political agenda. Given how widely read Kaufmann's translations of Nietzsche's work have been in the Anglo-American context, we argue that this agenda has significantly shaped popular appraisals of Nietzsche as defanged and apolitical. Importantly, this does not mean that the entirety of Kaufmann's translations must be discarded, but it does mean that in specific instances in which political themes are addressed, there is a tendency for Kaufmann to attempt to render Nietzsche's intentions more obscure and less direct than they often truly are.

29 Waite, Geoff "The Politics of Reading Formations: Nietzsche in Imperial Germany (1870 — 1919),". *Enclitic* Vol. 7, §1. p. 192.

CHAPTER TWO
Understanding Nietzsche's Style

1 Nietzsche, Friedrich *The Gay Science*, translated by Walter Kaufmann, Vintage, 1974. p. 381.

2 Ibid, p. 37

3 Nietzsche, Friedrich *Unpublished Fragments, Spring 1888*, Stanford University Press, 2020. p. xiii.

4 Nietzsche, Friedrich *Unpublished Fragments, 1884*, Stanford University Press, 2020. p. 263.

5 Nietzsche, Friedrich *The Gay Science*. p. 149.

6 Nietzsche, Friedrich *Thus Spoke Zarathustra*. p. 237.

7 Nietzsche, Friedrich *Thus Spoke Zarathustra*. p. 255 and see aphorism "IV, Retired from Service."

8   Nietzsche, Friedrich *The Gay Science*. p. 221.

9   Nietzsche, Friedrich *Complete Correspondence*, edited by Giorgi Colli and Mazzino Montinari, De Gruyter, 1975. p. 588.

10 Nietzsche, Friedrich *The Gay Science*. p. 220 (italics mine).

11 Ibid, p. 220 (italics mine, chosen for emphasis).

12 Nietzsche, Friedrich "Sämtliche Werke: Kritische Studienausgabe," from *15 Bänden*, Vol. 10, translated by Leo Strauss. Berlin: de Gruyter, 1967– 77. p. 244.

13 Nietzsche, Friedrich *Thus Spoke Zarathustra*. p. 38

14 Waite, Geoff *Nietzsche's Corps/e: Aesthetics, Politics, Prophecy, or, the Spectacular Technoculture of Everyday Life*, Duke University Press, 1996. p. 25.

15 Ibid. p. 214

16 Zupančič, Alenka *The Shortest Shadow: Nietzsche's Philosophy of the Two*, MIT Press, 2003. p. 12.

17 Ibid. p. 12

18 Nietzsche, Friedrich *Nietzsche's Anti-Philosophy Seminar from 1992-1993*, translated by Kim, Wanyoung, Atropos Press, 2023 (forthcoming).

19 In his lectures on Zarathustra, Strauss asks, "in situations of extreme scarcity", where all men cannot preserve themselves, what is the meaning of the unqualified prohibition against robbing and killing? Nietzsche would say such prohibitions would lead to a lowering of man. All the warlike qualities in man would disappear" (Strauss, p. 203).

20 Aschheim, Stephen *Nietzsche in Germany*, University of California Press, 1992. p. 4.

21 Strauss, Leo *Lectures on Nietzsche's Zarathustra*, University of Chicago Press, 2016. p. 3 (italics mine).

22 Heidegger, Martin *Nietzsche*, translated by David Farrell Krell, Harper & Row, 1979, p. 82; Derrida, Jacques *Spurs: Nietzsche's Styles*, translated by Barbara Harlow, University of Chicago Press, 1979.

23 Derrida, Jacques *Otobiographies: The Teaching of Nietzsche and the Politics of the Proper Name*, translated by Avital Ronnell, Shocken Books, 1987. p. 7.

24 Nietzsche, Friedrich *Ecce Homo*, p. 31.

25 Roudinesco, Elisabeth *Lacan and Co. A History of Psychoanalysis in France, 1925-1985*, University of Chicago Press, 1990. p. 6.

26 Ibid, p. 24.

27 Losurdo writes, quoting Nietzsche in a letter to a friend, "The lectures were 'decisively exhortative and, in comparison with *The Birth [of Tragedy]*, should be regarded as popular or exoteric'" (B, II, 1, 296) see Losurdo, Domenico *Aristocratic Rebel.* p. 80.

28 Losurdo, Domenico *Aristocratic Rebel.* p. 81.

29 Nietzsche, Friedrich *On the Future of Our Educational Institutions*, p. 112.

30 Losurdo, Domenico *Aristocratic Rebel.* pp. 928–929.

31 Ibid, p. 38.

32 Nietzsche, Friedrich *Ecce Homo: How To Become What Your Are*, translated by Duncan Large. Oxford University Press, 2007. p. 88.

33 Ibid, p. 48.

34 Nietzsche, Friedrich *On the Future of Our Educational Institutions: Six Public Lectures*, translated by Damion Searls. New York Review of Books, 2016. p. 13.

35 See Nietzsche's letter to his fraternity friend, Gersdorff, *Complete Correspondence*, edited by Giorgi Colli and Mazzino Montinari, De Gruyter, 1975. pp. 224 – 229.

36 Ibid. pp. 224 – 229.

CHAPTER THREE
The Political Context of Perspectivism

1 Caygill, Howard "The Return of Nietzsche and Marx" from *Force and Understanding*, Bloomsbury Academic, 2021. p. 29.

2   Nietzsche, Friedrich *Thus Spoke Zarathustra*. pp. 224–249.

3   Deleuze, Gilles *Nietzsche and Philosophy*, translated by Hugh
     Tomlinson, Columbia University Press, 2006. pp. 164–165.

4   To get a better idea of the way that analytic philosophers write
     about Nietzsche's idea of perspectivism, see Clark, Maudemaire
     Nietzsche on Truth and Philosophy Cambridge University Press,
     2009 and Reginster, Bernard "The Paradox of Perspectivism"
     Philosophy and Phenomenological Research Vol. 62, No. 1 (Jan.,
     2001), pp. 217-233.

         In this book, our aim is to read the concept in a far more
     political context before understanding its purely epistemological
     contributions whereas these authors tend to read the concept as
     decontextualized from Nietzsche's political and social context.
     The same decontextualization is also present in Gilles Deleuze's
     treatment of the concept in his work *Nietzsche and Philosophy*
     Columbia University Press, 2006 which we discuss in chapter four.

5   Balibar, Ètienne *Masses, Classes, Ideas: Studies on Politics and
     Philosophy Before and After Marx*, translated by James Swenson,
     Verso, 1994. p. 94.

6   Nietzsche, Friedrich *The Birth of Tragedy and Other Writings*, edited
     by Raymond Geuss and Ronald Speirs, translated by Ronald
     Speirs, Cambridge University Press, Cambridge, 1999. pp.
     86 - 87.

7   Losurdo, Domenico *Aristocratic Rebel.* p. 684.

8   Dombowsky, Don *Nietzsche and Napoleon: The Dionysian Conspiracy*,
     University of Wales Press, 2014. p. 35.

9   James, C.L.R. "C.L.R. James in Conversation with Stuart Hall,"
     produced and directed by Mike Dibb, 1986, available online
     from: https://www.youtube.com/watch?v=_Gf0KUxgZfI&ab_
     channel=susie2010ism

10   Dombowsky, Don *Dionysian Conspiracy: Nietzsche and Napoleon*,
     University of Wales Press, 2014. p. 39.

11   Karatani, Kojin *History and Repetition*, edited by Seiji M. Lippit, Columbia University Press, 2011. p. 34.

12   Gramsci, Antonio *Prison Notebooks*, translated by Antonio Callari and Joseph A. Buttigieg, Columbia University Press, 2011. p. 222.

13   Clover, Joshua *Riot. Strike. Riot*, Verso Books, 2016. (See Chapter Eight).

14   Dombowsky, Don *Nietzsche and Napoleon*. pp. 110–115.

15   Losurdo, Domenico *Aristocratic Rebel*. p. 30.

16   Nietzsche, Friedrich *The Birth of Tragedy and Other Writings* translated by Ronald Speirs Cambridge University Press, 1999. p. 74.

17   Ibid, p. 31.

18   Losurdo, Domenico *Aristocratic Rebel* p. 31.

19   Nietzsche, Friedrich *Samtliche Were. Kritische Studienausgabe*, Critical Studies Edition, edited by Giorgio Colli and Mazzino Montinari, De Gruyter, 1980. VII, p. 504.

20   Nietzsche, Friedrich *The Anti-Christ*, translated by Oscar Levy and with an Introduction by H.L. Mencken, Alfred A Knopf, 2006. p. 57.

21   Losurdo, Domenico *Aristocratic Rebel*. p. 636.

22   Losurdo provides a useful overview of the ways Nietzsche treats the "freethinker" (Freidenker), showing how Nietzsche moved from a positive embrace of the freethinker to a position that saw them as of a lower rank: plebeian. One aphorism states, "But there are few that have the right to 'pure air': those that would not be ruined by the pure air. That in order to refute the suspicion that I would want to invite 'freethinkers' into my gardens." (Nietzsche, Friedrich *Samtliche Were. Kritische Studienausgabe*. XIV, p. 352).

23   Losurdo, Domenico *Aristocratic Rebel*. p. 106.

24   Nietzsche, Friedrich *Complete Correspondence*. p. 515.

25   Nietzsche, Friedrich *Complete Correspondence*. p. 471.

26 Losurdo, Domenico "Realism and Nominalism as Political Categories," *Presses Universitaires de France, Revue de Métaphysique et de Morale*, April-June, 1996, Vol. 101, § 2. pp. 211–223.

27 It is this more ambiguous category of the social being of the philosopher in relation to the capitalist order, which Lukács periodizes in his analysis of irrationalism within philosophy, that will be expanded in Lukács's incomplete later work *Ontology of Social Being* — a three-volume work published in 1978 by Merlin Press.

28 Korsch, Karl *Marxism and Philosophy*, Verso Books, 2013. p. 105.

29 Hegel, G.W.F. *Lectures on the Philosophy of Religion*, Vol. III, Oxford University Press, 2008. p. 98.

30 Nietzsche, Friedrich *Anti-Christ*. p. 57.

31 Losurdo, Domenico *Aristocratic Rebel*. p. 650.

32 Nietzsche, Friedrich *Samtliche Were. Kritische Studienausgabe*. p. 515.

CHAPTER FOUR
The Center of Nietzsche's Political Thought: A Continuous Polemic against Marxism and Socialism

1 To take one pertinent example, Leo Strauss, in his lectures on *Thus Spoke Zarathustra*, notes that Nietzsche's aristocratic politics and critique of socialism are marginal to the profound philosophical insights that Nietzsche brings to bear. We propose a reversal of this claim, that it is only through a centering of Nietzsche's politics that we can understand the profundity of his thought.

2 See the entry "Nietzsche" in the Stanford Encyclopedia of Philosophy, available online from: https://plato.stanford.edu/entries/nietzsche

3 Brobjer, Thomas *Nietzsche's Philosophical Context: An Intellectual Biography*, University of Illinois Press, 2008. pp. 11–12.

4   Losurdo, Domenico *Aristocratic Rebel*. p. 439.

5   Nietzsche, Friedrich *Samtliche Were. Kritische Studienausgabe*. p. 432.

6   Bourdieu, Pierre *Pascalian Meditations*, translated by Richard Nice, University of Stanford Press, 2000. p. 30.

7   For a full treatment of Pierre Bourdieu's ideas on academic philosophers, see Bourdieu, Pierre *Pascalian Meditations* translated by Richard Nice, Stanford University Press, 2000.

8   Nietzsche, Friedrich *Human All Too Human*. P. 10

9   Nietzsche, Friedrich *The Gay Science*. I, p. 18.

10 It is important to note that one of Kaufmann's apologetic and revisionist moves in his translation of *The Gay Science* is to add a footnote regarding Nietzsche's use of the term "slavish" to refer to the "autonomous" and "liberated" as opposed to submissive qualities of a slave.

11 Nietzsche, Friedrich *The Gay Science*. p. 188.

12 Waite, Geoff *Nietzsche's Corps/e*. p. 501

13 Nietzsche, Friedrich *Unfashionable Observations*. p. 63.

14 Nietzsche, Friedrich *Complete Correspondence* XI edited by Giorgi Colli and Mazzino Montinari, Berlin-New York: De Gruyter, 1975. p. 440

15 Laruelle, François *Intellectuals and Power* trans. Anthony Paul Smith Polity Press, 2015, p. 19

16 For a description and summary of the four key stages of Nietzsche's thought see Losurdo, *Aristocratic Rebel*, pp. 348 — 349.

17 Waite, Geoff *Nietzsche's Corps/e*. pp. 20, 308.

18 Nietzsche, Friedrich *Human, All Too Human*. p. 439.

19 Lukács, György *Destruction of Reason*, Verso Books, 2021. p. 313.

20 Ibid. p. 313.

21 Dombowsky, Don *Nietzsche's Political Writings*, Palgrave Macmillan, 2008. p. 292.

22 Ibid, p. 136.

23 Ibid, p. 117.

24 Nietzsche, Friedrich *Thus Spoke Zarathustra.* p. 56.

25 Nietzsche, Friedrich *Daybreak: Thoughts on the Prejudices of Morality* translated by R.J. Hollingdale. Cambridge University Press, 1997 P. 125 – 126.

26 Dombowsky, Don *Nietzsche's Political Writings.* p. 12.

27 Nietzsche, Friedrich *Thus Spoke Zarathustra* translated by Thomas Common. Random House, 2006. p. 123 – 124

28 Losurdo, *Aristocratic Rebel.* p. 447.

29 Nietzsche, Friedrich *The Gay Science.* p. 99.

30 Nietzsche, Friedrich "The Free Spirit, 1878–1880," from Dombrowski, Don *Nietzsche's Political Writings.* p. 113.

31 Ibid, p. 101.

32 Nietzsche, Friedrich *Human, All Too Human.* pp. 165 – 166.

33 Nietzsche, Friedrich *Human, All Too Human* pp. 383 – 384.

34 Nietzsche, Friedrich *Miscellaneous Maxims and Opinions, 1879*, §304, from Dombrowski, Don *Nietzsche's Political Writings.* p. 101.

35 One point that is important to spotlight in our reading of Nietzsche is the fact that there were many aspects of Christianity that he favored, such as Christianity's influence on bourgeois revolutions in China. In other words, true to his reactionary and aristocratic point of view, Nietzsche favored aspects of non-egalitarian Christianity. See Losurdo, Domenico *Aristocratic Rebel.* p. 339. And see our discussion of Nietzsche's admiration for Pascal, a philosopher who followed Jansenism, one of the most conservative theological strains in the Catholic Church.

36 Nietzsche, Friedrich *Miscellaneous Maxims and Opinions*, 1879, §304, from Dombrowski, Don *Nietzsche's Political Writings.* p. 101.

37 Ibid, p. 282.

38 Ibid, p. 177.

39 Ibid, p. 112.

40 Bergman, Peter *Nietzsche "The Last Antipolitical German,"* Indiana University Press, 1987. pp. 108–110.

41 Nietzsche, Friedrich *Human, All Too Human.* p. 166.

42   Ibid, p. 165.

43   Nietzsche, Friedrich *The Will to Power*, translated by R.J.
     Hollingdale and Walter Kaufmann. Winsfield and Nicholson,
     1967. p. 399.

44   Nietzsche, Friedrich *Human, All Too Human*. p. 166.

45   Nietzsche, Friedrich *Ecce Homo*. p. 10.

46   Nietzsche, Friedrich *The Will to Power*. p. 162.

47   Nietzsche, Friedrich *The Will to Power*. p. 476.

48   Nietzsche, Friedrich *The Will to Power*, p. 477.

49   Nietzsche, Friedrich *Twilight of the Idols and the Anti-Christ*,
     translated by R.J. Hollingdale. Penguin Books, 1998. p. 5.

50   Lukács, György *The Destruction of Reason*, Verso Books,
     2021. p. 316.

51   Lukács, György *Die Zerstörung des Humanismus in der deutschen
     Ideologie*, from *Wie ist Deutschland zum Zentrum der reaktionären Ideologie
     geworden?*, translated by Anton P. Veröffentlichungen des Lukács-
     Archives, 1982. pp. 299–311, available online from: https://www.
     marxists.org/archive/lukacs/works/nietzsche/ch03.htm

52   Lukács, György *The Destruction of Reason*. p. 380.

53   Nietzsche, Friedrich *Twilight of the Idols*. p. 108

54   Nietzsche, Friedrich *The Gay Science*. p. 259.

55   Frim, Landon and Fluss, Harrison "Back to the Future" from
     Anti-Science and the Assault on Democracy, Prometheus Books,
     2018. p. 178.

56   Ibid, p. 179.

57   Deleuze, Gilles and Guattari, Felix *Anti-Oedipus: Capitalism and
     Schizophrenia*, translated by Robert Hurley, Penguin Books,
     2009. p. 55.

58   Bastani, Aaron *Fully Automated Luxury Communism*, Verso
     Books, 2019.

59 Topinka, Robert "Back to a Past that Was Futuristic: The Alt-Right and the Uncanny Form of Racism," *b2o: an online journal*, October 14, 2019, available online from: https://www.boundary2.org/2019/10/robert-topinka-back-to-a-past-that-was-futuristic-the-alt-right-and-the-uncanny-form-of-racism/

60 Frim, Landon and Fluss, Harrison "Behemoth and Leviathan: The Fascist Bestiary of the Alt-Right," *Salvage Magazine*. December 21, 2017.

61 Wood, Ellen Meiksins *The Retreat from Class: The New True Socialism*, Verso Books. p. 449.

62 Frim, Landon and Fluss, Harrison *Anti-Science and the Assault on Democracy*. p. 181.

63 Nietzsche, Friedrich *Human, All Too Human: A Book for Free Spirits*, translated by Gary Handwerk. Stanford University Press, 1995. p. 249

64 Ibid, p. 260.

CHAPTER FIVE
Nietzsche within the Left

1 Nietzsche, Friedrich *Ecce Homo*. p. 7.

2 Nietzsche, Friedrich *Ecce Homo*. p. 193.

3 Losurdo, Domenico *Aristocratic Rebel*. pp. 75–76

4 Nietzsche, Friedrich *Unpublished Fragments (Spring 1885 – Spring 1886)*, translated by Adrian del Caro Stanford University Press, 2020. p. 150

5 Plekhanov, Georgi *Unaddressed Letters. Art and Social Life*, translated by Eugene Hirschfeld, Foreign Languages Publishing House, 1957. pp. 46–47.

6 Aschheim, Stephen *Nietzsche in Germany*, p. 36.

7 Rehmann, Jan *Deconstructing Postmodern Nietzscheanism*, Historical Materialism, 2022. p. 43.

8   Waite, Geoff "The Politics of Reading Formations: The Case of
    Nietzsche in Imperial Germany (1870-1919)" *New German Critique*,
    Vol. 29, spring–summer, 1983. p. 31.

9   Letter from Friedrich Nietzsche to J. F. Overbeck, 24 March,
    1887, quoted in Löwith, Karl *From Hegel to Nietzsche: The Revolution
    in Nineteenth-Century Thought*, Rinehart and Winston, 1965. p. 423.

10 Aschheim, Stephen *Nietzsche in Germany*. p. 102.

11 Ibid, p. 44.

12 Eisner, Kurt *Psychopathia Spiritualis: Friedrich Nietzsche und die Apostel
    der Zukunft*, Wilhelm Friedrich, 1892. p. 9.

13 Brenner, Timothy *Borrowed Light: Vico, Hegel, and the Colonies*,
    Stanford University Press, 2014. p. 140.

14 Levi, Oscar *The Complete Works Friedrich Nietzsche*, Vol XIV,
    translated by Anthony M. Ludovici, T.N. Foulis, 2019. pp.
    102–103.

15 Nietzsche, Friedrich *The Anti-Christ*. p. 25.

16 Mencken, H.L. *The Philosophy of Friedrich Nietzsche*, Bottom of the
    Hill Publishing, 2012. p. 4.

17 Nietzsche, Friedrich *The Anti-Christ*. p. 29.

18 Ibid, p. 81.

19 Ibid, p. 87.

20 Wilson, Edmund *Shores of Light: A Literary Chronicle of the Twenties
    and Thirties*, Northeastern Press, 2019. p. 293.

21 Nietzsche, Friedrich *The Anti-Christ* trans. p. x.

22 Darrow, Clarence "Closing Argument, The State of Illinois v.
    Nathan Leopold & Richard Loeb," August 22, 1924, available
    online from: http://law2.umkc.edu/faculty/projects/ftrials/
    leoploeb/darrowclosing.html

23 Ibid.

24 Ibid.

25 Wilson, Edmund *Shores of Light*. p. 478.

26 London, Jack "How I Became a Socialist," from *The Portable Jack London*, edited by Earle Labor, Penguin, 1994. pp. 458–459.

27 Foner, Philip S. *The Social Writings of Jack London*, Citadel Press, 1964. p. 35.

28 Ibid, p. 35.

29 London, Jack "What Life Means to Me" from *Revolution and Other Essays*, Macmillan, 1910, available online from: https://monadnock.net/london/life.html

30 Landa, Ishay *The Overman in the Marketplace: Nietzschean Heroism in Popular Culture*, Lexington Books, 2017. p. 5.

31 Losurdo, Domenico *Aristocratic Rebel*. p. 742.

32 Nietzsche, Friedrich *Human, All Too Human*. p. 257.

33 Nietzsche, Friedrich *Unpublished Fragments 1885–1886*. p. 17.

34 Nietzsche, Friedrich *Thus Spoke Zarathustra*. p. 82.

35 Waite, Geoff *Nietzsche's Corps/e*. p. 169.

36 Trotsky, Leon "On the Philosophy of the Superman," from *Vostochnoye Obozriene*, Vols. 284, 286, 287, 289, available online from: https://www.marxists.org/archive/trotsky/1900/12/nietzsche.htm

37 Badiou, Alain *Alain Badiou on the Russian Revolution of 1917*, Verso Books, 2017, available online from: https://www.versobooks.com/blogs/3325-alain-badiou-on-the-russian-revolution-of-october-1917

38 Gramsci, Antonio "The Great Revolution Against 'Capital,'" translated by Natalie Campbell, available online from: https://www.marxists.org/archive/gramsci/1917/12/revolution-against-capital.htm

39 Ibid.

40 Glatzer, Bernice Rosenthal *New Myth, New World: From Nietzsche to Stalinism*, Pennsylvania State University, 2002. p. 149.

41 Waite, Geoff *Nietzsche's Corps/e*. p. 342.

42 Waite, Geoff "The Politics of Reading Formations: The Case of Nietzsche in Imperial Germany (1870-1919)" *New German Critique*, Vol. 29. pp. 185–209.

43 Glatzer, Bernice Rosenthal *New Myth, New Man*. p. 129.

44 Bukharin, Nikolai "Mad Prophet (Friedrich Nietzsche)," available online from: http://www.autodidactproject.org/other/nietzsche_bukharin.html

45 Bataille, Georges "Nietzsche in the Light of Marxism," from *Nietzsche's Return*, Vol. I, Semiotexte, 1977. p. 116.

46 Deleuze, Gilles "Pensée nomade" from *Nietzsche Aujourd hui*, translated by Jacqueline Wallace U.G.E, 1973. p. 11.

47 Ibid, p. 13.

48 Ibid. p. 14.

49 Deleuze, Gilles *Nietzsche and Philosophy.* p. 136.

50 Ibid, p. 137.

51 Ibid. p. 137.

52 Ibid. p. 221.

53 Ibid, p. 197.

54 Nietzsche, Friedrich *Ecce Homo*. p. 89

55 Nietzsche, Friedrich *Zarathustra*. p. 30.

56 Deleuze, Gilles *Nietzsche and Philosophy*. p. 78.

57 Deleuze, Gilles *Nomad Thought*. p. 139.

58 Rehmann, Jan *Deconstructing Postmodern Nietzscheanism*, Historical Materialism, 2022. p. 146.

59 Newton, Huey and Blake, Herman *Revolutionary Suicide*, Penguin, 2009. p. 157.

60 Newton, Huey *To Die for the People: The Writings of Huey P. Newton*. Random House, 1972. p. 178

61 Nicos Poulantzas *State, Power, Socialism*, translated by Patrick Camiller, Verso Books, 1978. p. 149.

62 Nietzsche, Friedrich "On Truth and Lie in an Extra-Moral Sense Fragment," from *The Nachlass*, translated by Walter Kaufmann. p. 3

63   Brennan, Timothy *Borrowed Light: Vico, Hegel, and the Colonies*, Stanford University Press, 2014. pp. 52, 140.

64   Jeffries, Judson *Huey Newton: Radical Theorist*, University Press of Mississippi, 2002. p. 135.

65   Ibid, pp. 45–46.

66   Ibid, p. 45.

67   Newton, Huey and Erikson, Erik *In Search of Common Ground*, W.W. Norton & Company, 1973. p. 50.

68   Jefferies, Judson, *Huey Newton: Revolutionary Theorist*. p. 45–46.

69   Newton, Huey and Blake, Herman *Revolutionary Suicide*, p. 13.

70   Nietzsche, Friedrich *The Anti-Christ*. p. 57

71   Losurdo, Domenico *Aristocratic Rebel*. p. 475.

72   Brennan, Timothy *Borrowed Light*. pp. 43, 140.

73   Deleuze, Gilles *Nietzsche and Philosophy*. p. 30.

CHAPTER SIX
Elective Enmities: Marx and Nietzsche

1   Nietzsche, Friedrich *The Gay Science*. p. 47.

2   Marx, Karl *A Contribution to the Critique of Hegel's Philosophy of Right*, translated by A. Jolin and J. O'Malley, edited by J. O'Malley, Cambridge University Press, 1970.

3   Marx, Karl and Engels, Friedrich *Collected Works of Karl Marx and Friedrich Engels, 1844-45 Vol 4*, International Publishers, 1975. p. 39.

4   Warren, Mark *Nietzsche and Political Thought*, MIT Press, 1988. p. 64.

5   Losurdo, Domenico *Aristocratic Rebel*. p. 438.

6   Ibid, p. 438.

7   Marx, Karl *Capital: Critique of Political Economy*, Vol. I. translated by Samuel Moore and Edward Aveling, Aristeus Books, 2012. p. 176.

8   Losurdo, Domenico *Aristocratic Rebel*. p. 439.

9   Stepelevich, Lawrence S. "Engels letter to Arnold Ruge" from
     The Young Hegelians: An Anthology, Humanities Press, 1983. p. 554.

10   Nietzsche, Friedrich *Kritische Studienausgabe*, Vol. 13, edited by
     Giorgio Colli and Mazino Montinari, de Gruyter, 1999. p. 193.

11   Nietzsche, Friedrich *Zarathustra* p. 83.

12   Marx, Karl "Introduction," from *Contribution to the Critique of
     Hegel's Philosophy of Law*, Vol. 3, 2005. p. 182.

13   Nietzsche, Friedrich *The Gay Science*. p. 354.

14   Balibar, Ètienne *Masses, Classes, Ideas: Studies on Politics and
     Philosophy Before and After Marx*, translated by James Swenson.
     Routledge, 1994. p. 95.

15   Landa, Ishay "Aroma or Shadow Marx vs. Nietzsche on
     Religion" *Nature, Society, and Thought*, Vol. 18, no. 4, 2005. p. 472.

16   Rehmann, Jan *Deconstructing Postmodernist Nietzscheanism.* pp.
     156–157.

17   It is striking that the French Nietzscheans after World War II
     stand out as perhaps the lone exception to the predominant
     thinking that the eternal return is not to be understood as a
     religious doctrine, especially Deleuze and Foucault.

18   Benjamin, Walter *Walter Benjamin: Selected Writings 1913–1926*,
     Vol.1, translated by Rodney Livingstone. Belknap Harvard Press,
     1996. p. 288–291.

19   Losurdo, Domenico *Aristocratic Rebel*. p. 476.

20   Ibid. p. 476.

21   Ratner-Rosenhagen, Jennifer *American Nietzsche: A History of an Icon
     and His Ideas*, University of Chicago Press, 2012.

22   Lukács, György *The Destruction of Reason*, p. 378.

23   Nietzsche, Friedrich *The Gay Science*, p. 341.

24   Hallward, Peter "Blanqui's Bifurcations" *Radical Philosophy*,
     Vol. 185, May/Jun 2014, available online from: https://www.
     radicalphilosophy.com/article/blanquis-bifurcations

25 Löwith, Karl *From Hegel to Nietzsche: The Revolution in Nineteenth-Century Thought*, translated by David E. Green, Columbia University Press, 1991. pp. 86–87.

26 Strauss, Leo *Leo Strauss on Nietzsche's Thus Spoke Zarathustra*, University of Chicago Press, 2017. pp. 9–10.

27 "What I relate," Nietzsche wrote in the preface to *The Will to Power*, "is the history of the next two centuries [written] as a spirit of daring and experiment that has already lost its way once in every labyrinth of the future; as a soothsayer bird-spirit who looks back when relating what will come; as the first perfect nihilist of Europe who, however, has even now lived through the whole of nihilism, to the end, leaving it behind, outside himself." Nietzsche, Friedrich *The Will to Power*. p. 3.

28 Strauss, Leo *Lectures on Thus Spoke Zarathustra*. p. 187.

29 Ibid, p. 188.

30 Nietzsche, Friedrich *Human, All Too Human*. p. 480.

31 Sloterdijk, Peter *You Must Change Your Life*, Polity, 2014. p. 401.

32 Ibid, p. 45.

33 Goldmann, Lucien *A Study of Tragic Vision in the Pensées of Pascal and the Tragedies of Racine*, translated by Michael Lowy, Verso Books, 2016. p. 53.

34 Goldmann, Lucien *The Hidden God*. p. 54.

35 Forster-Nietzsche, Elisabeth *Oas Leben Friedrich Nietzsche*, Vol. II, Naumann, 2011. pp. 883–884.

36 Nietzsche, Friedrich *Unpublished Fragment (Spring 1885-Spring)*, translated by Adrian Del Caro, Stanford University Press, 2020. pp. 25, 34.

37 Ibid. p. 34.

38 Ibid, p. 34.

39 Nietzsche, Friedrich *Dawn: Thoughts on the Presumptions of Morality* translated by Adrian del Caro, Standford University Press, 2020. p. 136.

40 Ibid, p. 378

41 Goldmann, Lucien *The Hidden God*. p. 167.

42 Lukács, György *The Destruction of Reason*. p. 107.

43 Nietzsche, Friedrich *Unpublished Writings from the period of Unfashionable Observations* translated by Richard T. Gray. Stanford University Press, 1995. p. 277

44 Nietzsche, Friedrich *The Birth of Tragedy*. p. 64.

45 Balibar, Ètienne *Masses*. p. 94.

46 Caygill, Howard *Force and Understanding: Writings on Philosophy and Resistance*, Bloomsbury Academic, 2021. p. 39.

47 Ibid, p. 40.

48 Bull, Malcolm *Anti-Nietzsche*, Verso Books, 2014. p. 167.

49 Ibid, p. 170.

50 Ibid, p. 166.

51 Wilson, Edmund *Shores of Light*. p. 292.

52 Ibid. p. 292.

53 Nietzsche, Friedrich *Beyond Good and Evil*. p. 214.

54 Losurdo, Domenico *Aristocratic Rebel*. p. 910.

55 Nietzsche, Friedrich *Will to Power* p. 399

CHAPTER SEVEN
Ressentiment **and the Politics of Social Suffering**

1 It is important to remember that the subtitle to *The Genealogy of Morals*, "A Polemic," implies that Nietzsche aimed for a redefinition of the very category of polemic.

2 Nietzsche, Friedrich *Thus Spoke Zarathustra*. p. 51.

3 Nietzsche, Friedrich *Beyond Good and Evil*. p. 54.

4 Ibid. p. 41.

5 Nietzsche, Friedrich *Thus Spoke Zarathustra*. p. 56.

6 Nietzsche, Friedrich *Unpublished Fragments 1884*. p. 255.

7 Nietzsche, Friedrich *Thus Spoke Zarathustra*. p. 35.

8 Nietzsche, Friedrich *Human, All Too Human* p. 248

9   Nietzsche, Friedrich *The Dionysian Vision of the World* translated by
     Ira Allen. Univocal, 2013. p. 37.

10   Nietzsche, Friedrich *Beyond Good and Evil*. p. 214.

11   Ibid. p. 162.

12   Ibid, p. 220.

13   Nietzsche, Friedrich *Prefaces to Unwritten Works* translated by
     Michael Grenke. St. Augustine Press, 2004. p. 36

14   Nietzsche, Friedrich *Grossoktav-Ausgabe vol. XIII*. edited by Mazzino
     Montinari and Giorgio Colli. Walter de Gruyter, 1999. p. 43.

15   Nietzsche, Friedrich *The Gay Science*. p. 32

16   Dickinson, Emily Life *The Poems of Emily Dickinson: Series One*
     Lit2Go Edition, 2023. Poem 19: The Mystery of Pain. Available
     online from https://etc.usf.edu/lit2go/114/the-poems-of-emily-
     dickinson-series-one/2346/life-poem-19-the-mystery-of-pain

17   A signature move of the hermeneutics of innocence is to over-
     emphasize Christianity's place as Nietzsche's primary antagonist.
     As we have sought to show, and as Lukács, Losurdo, Dombowsky,
     Waite, and Landa have demonstrated, such a reading is only
     partial at best, and completely ahistorical at worst.

18   Scheler, Max *Ressentiment*, translated Lewis B. Coser and William
     W. Holdheim, Marquette University Press, 1994. p. 29.

19   Ibid, p. 31.

20   Ibid. p. 31.

21   Ibid, p. 80.

22   Ibid, p. 85.

23   Ibid, p. 102.

24   Ibid. p. 69.

25   Ibid, p. 103.

26   Ibid, p. 37.

27   Ibid, p. 41.

28   Nietzsche, Friedrich *Thus Spoke Zarathustra*. p. 57.

29   Van Tuinen, Sjoerd *The Irenics of Ressentiment: From Good Sense to
     Common Sense*, Bloomsbury Academic, 2018. p. 240.

30   Van Tuinen, Sjoerd "The resentment-*ressentiment* complex: a critique of liberal discourse" Global Discourse, Special Issue: The Politics of Negative Emotions, Vol 10, No, 2. pp. 237–253 Bristol University Press, 2020. p 240.

31   Ibid, p. 238.

32   Brown, Wendy *In the Ruins of Neoliberalism: The Rise of Antidemocratic Politics in the West*, Columbia University Press, 2019. p. 28.

33   Ibid, p. 42.

34   Ibid, p. 163.

35   Scheler, Max *Ressentiment*. p. 6.

36   Silva, Jennifer *Coming Up Short: Working-Class Adulthood in an Age of Uncertainty*, Oxford University Press, 2015. pp. 255–256.

37   Scheler, Max *Ressentiment*. p. 6.

38   Silva, Jennifer *Coming Up Short*. p. 155.

39   Ibid, pp. 151–152.

40   Berlant, Lauren *Cruel Optimism*, Duke University Press, 2011.

41   Han, Byung-Chul *Burnout Society*, Stanford University Press, 2010. p. 19.

42   Ibid, p. 9.

43   Reckwitz, Andreas *Society of Singularities*, translated by Valentine A. Pakis, Polity Press, 2020. p. 250.

44   Ibid, p. 251.

45   Ibid, p. 206.

46   Deleuze, Gilles *Nietzsche and Philosophy*. p. 128.

47   Deleuze, Gilles *Logic of Sense*, translated Mark Lester and Charles Stivale, Columbia University Press, 1993. p. 166.

48   Ibid, p. 166.

49   Alenka Zupančič *The Odd One In*, MIT Press, 2008. p. 6.

50   Sloterdijk, Peter *Nietzsche Apostle*. p. 77.

51   Fukuyama, Francis *The End of History and the Last Man*, The Free Press, 1992. p. 182.

52 Eaton, George "Francis Fukuyama interview: 'Socialism ought to come back,' *New Statesman*, 17 October, 2018, available online from: https://www.newstatesman.com/politics/2018/10/francis-fukuyama-interview-socialism-ought-come-back

53 Fukuyama, Francis *The End of History*, p. 89.

54 Ibid, pp. 229–230.

55 Ibid, pp. 148–149.

56 Davies, William "The New Neoliberalism" *New Left Review*, Vol.121 p. 132.

57 Brook, Orian, Miles, Andrews. and Taylor, Mark "Social Mobility and 'Openness' in Creative Occupations since the 1970s," *British Sociological Association*, 2022. available online from: https://journals.sagepub.com/doi/full/10.1177/00380385221129953

58 "The term "deaths of despair" comes from Princeton economists Anne Case and Angus Deaton, who set out to understand what accounted for falling US life expectancy. They learned that the fastest-rising death rates among Americans were from drug overdoses, suicide, and alcoholic liver disease. Deaths from these causes have increased between 56 percent and 387 percent, depending on the age cohort, over the past two decades, averaging 70,000 per year." See Introcaso, David "Deaths of despair: the unrecognized tragedy of working class immiseration," *Stat News*, 29 December, 2021, available online from: https://www.statnews.com/2021/12/29/deaths-of-despair-unrecognized-tragedy-working-class-immiseration

59 To get a better sense of the neo-feudal thesis from a Marxist perspective, see Wark, Mckensie *Capital is Dead: Is This Something Worse?* Verso Books, 2019 and Dean, Jodi "Neofeudalism: The End of Capitalism?" Los Angeles Review of Books, May 12, 2020, available online from: https://lareviewofbooks.org/article/neofeudalism-the-end-of-capitalism

60 Varoufakis, Yanis "Techno-Feudalism Is Taking Over," *Project Syndicate*, 28 June, 2021, available online from: https://www.project-syndicate.org/commentary/techno-feudalism-replacing-market-capitalism-by-yanis-varoufakis-2021-06

61 Nietzsche, Friedrich *Beyond Good and Evil*. p. 251.

62 Nietzsche Friedrich *The Will to Power* p. 162.

63 Miller, Jacques-Alain "On Shame," from *Reflections on Seminar XVII Jacques Lacan and the Other Side of Psychoanalysis*, edited by Justin Clements and Russell Grigg, Duke University Press, 2006. pp. 20–28.

64 Ibid, p. 21.

65 Nietzsche, Friedrich *Dawn*, p. 232.

66 Miller Jacques-Alain "On Shame." p. 20.

67 For an excellent breakdown of Lacan's discourse of the capitalist, see Van Huele, Stijn "Capitalist Discourse, Subjectivity and Lacanian Psychoanalysis." *Frontiers of Psychology* Volume 7, 2016, avaialbe online from https://www.frontiersin.org/articles/10.3389/fpsyg.2016.01948/full

68 Ibid.

69 Miller, Jacques-Alain "On Shame." p. 25.

70 Wilson, Edmund *Shores of Light*. p. 292.

71 Newfield, Christopher *The Emerson Effect: Individualism and Submission in America*, University of Chicago Press. 1996. p. 235.

72 Reckwitz, Andreas *Society of Singularities*. p. 205.

CHAPTER EIGHT
After Elective Affinity, or How to Read Like a Parasite

1 Gramsci, Antonio *Selections from Cultural Writings*, translated by William Boelhower, Haymarket Books, 2012. p. 355.

2 Aschheim, Stephen *Nietzsche in Germany*. pp. 95–99.

3 Eisner, Kurt *Psychopathia Spiritualis*. p. 13.

4   Rehmann, Jan *Max Weber: Modernization as Passive Revolution A Gramscian Analysis*, translated by Max Henninger, *Historical Materialism*, Vol. 78, 2014. p. 110.

5   Ibid, p. 147.

6   Ibid, p. 147.

7   Adorno, Theodor *Reconciliation Under Duress.* p. 160.

8   Aronowitz, Stanley *Georg Lukacs Reconsidered: Critical Essays in Politics, Philosophy and Aesthetics*, edited by Michael J. Thompson, Bloomsbury Publishing, 2013. p. 64.

9   Stone, Dan "Nietzsche and Eugenics," from *Nietzsche, Race and Eugenics in Edwardian and Interwar Britain*, Liverpool University Press, 2002. pp. 62–65.

10 Vattimo, Gianni "Nietzsche and Heidegger," from *Nietzsche in Italy*, edited by Thomas Harrison, Anma Libri, 1988. pp. 22–23.

11 Waite, Geoff *Nietzsche's Corps/e.* p. 373.

12 Bataille, Georges *"Nietzsche in the Light of Marxism,"* from *Nietzsche's Return*, Vol. I, Semiotexte 1977. p. 116.

13 Ibid, p. 116.

14 Ibid, p. 118.

15 Landa, Ishay "Bataille's Libidinal Economics: Capitalism as an Open Wound" *Critical Sociology*, Vol. 41, Issue 4–5, 2014. p. 5.

16 Bataille, Georges *The Accursed Share*, Vol. I, Zone Books, 1991. p. 38.

17 Tamás, Gáspár Miklós "Telling the Truth About Class," *Socialist Register*, Vol. 42, 2006. p. 1.

18 Ibid, p. 3.

19 Ibid, p. 3.

20 Wood, Ellen-Meiksins *The Retreat from Class: On The New True Socialism*, Verso Books, 1996. p. 179.

21 Marx, Karl and Engels, Friedrich *The Holy Family*, translated by Richard Dixon, Foreign Languages Publishing House, 1956. p. 56

22 Lenin, Vladimir *The State and Revolution*, translated by Brian Baggins. Progress Publishers, 1977. pp. 94–95.

23 Marx, Karl *Collected Works*, Vol. V, Lawrence & Wishart, 2010. p. 226.

24 Marx, Karl and Engels, Friedrich *Collected Works*, Vol. I. pp. 13–15.

25 Marx, Karl and Engels, Friedrich *Collected Works*, Vol. V. p. 214.

26 Nietzsche, Friedrich *Thus Spoke Zarathustra* Cambridge University Press, 2006. p. 233.

27 Ibid, p. 355.

28 Ibid, p. 167.

29 Ibid, p. 207.

30 Nietzsche, Friedrich *The Birth of Tragedy* p. 5.

31 Dill, Matt "Parasitism and Overflow in Nietzsche's Doctrine of Will to Power" *Journal of Nietzsche Studies*, Vol. 48, Issue 2, 2017. p. 200

32 Ibid, p. 202.

33 Ibid. p. 202.

34 Nietzsche, Friedrich *Thus Spoke Zarathustra* p. 3.

35 Dill, Matt "Parasitism and Overflow in Nietzsche's Doctrine of Will to Power" p. 192.

36 Nietzsche, Friedrich *Human, All Too Human* pp. 283 – 284.

37 Ibid, p. 284.

38 Nietzsche, Friedrich *The Gay Science.* p. 291.

39 Deutscher, Isaac *The Prophet Armed*, Verso Books, 2004. p. 231.

40 Ansell-Pearson, Keith and Large, Duncan "On the Utility and Liability of History for Life," from *The Nietzsche Reader*, Blackwell. 2006. p. 136.

41 Nietzsche, Friedrich *Unpublished Fragments from the Period of Unfashionable Observations* translated by Richard T. Gray Stanford University Press, 1995. p. 352.

42 Nietzsche, Friedrich *Dawn* p. 4.

43 Ricœur, Paul *Freud and Philosophy: An Essay on Interpretation*, translated by Dennis Savage, Yale University Press, 1977. p. 34.

44 It must be stated that Nietzsche's work *The Will to Power* is an incomplete and fragmentary project and much of what Nietzsche developed of the concept was posthumously compiled by his sister from his notes and fragments.

45 Ibid, p. 34.

46 Sedgwick, Eve Kosofsky, Barale, Michèle Aina, Goldberg, Jonathan, Moon, Michael *Touching Feeling* Duke University Press, 2002. p. 125.

47 Ibid, p. 134.

48 Ibid. p. 134.

49 Ibid, p. 146.

50 Ibid, p. 128.

51 Lukács, György "Preface," from *Theory of the Novel*, Merlin Press, 1961, available online from: https://www.marxists.org/archive/lukacs/works/theory-novel/preface.htm

Acknowledgements

It is an exhilarating experience to write a book about Nietzsche. Although the actual writing of this book began in 2020, I have been preparing to write this book ever since Nietzsche first seized me some twenty years ago. My favorite parts of this book were written in fits of inspiration, typically very early in the morning. The chapter on *ressentiment* was written in a cabin deep in West Virginia. Most of my ideas emerged on long walks or after conversations with other philosophers and readers of Marx and Nietzsche.

There are several people that helped to strengthen the arguments of this book. Specifically, I would like to thank the philosopher Tijana Okić and the Nietzsche specialist Don Dombowsky for their constructive feedback on early drafts. I would like to offer a special thanks to the philosopher Harrison Fluss for our many exchanges and conversations on Nietzsche and Marx. A big thanks is owed to Brandon Miller for his critical feedback on the Huey Newton section. Josh Turner of Repeater Books provided tireless editing and managed the process of bringing this book to life. Tariq Goddard of Repeater Books offered early input which proved immensely helpful. And finally, I would like to thank my wife Beth for her unwavering trust and love.

REPEATER BOOKS

is dedicated to the creation of a new reality. The landscape of twenty-first-century arts and letters is faded and inert, riven by fashionable cynicism, egotistical self-reference and a nostalgia for the recent past. Repeater intends to add its voice to those movements that wish to enter history and assert control over its currents, gathering together scattered and isolated voices with those who have already called for an escape from Capitalist Realism. Our desire is to publish in every sphere and genre, combining vigorous dissent and a pragmatic willingness to succeed where messianic abstraction and quiescent co-option have stalled: abstention is not an option: we are alive and we don't agree.